A Combat Artist in World War II

A Combat Artist

THE UNIVERSITY PRESS OF KENTUCKY

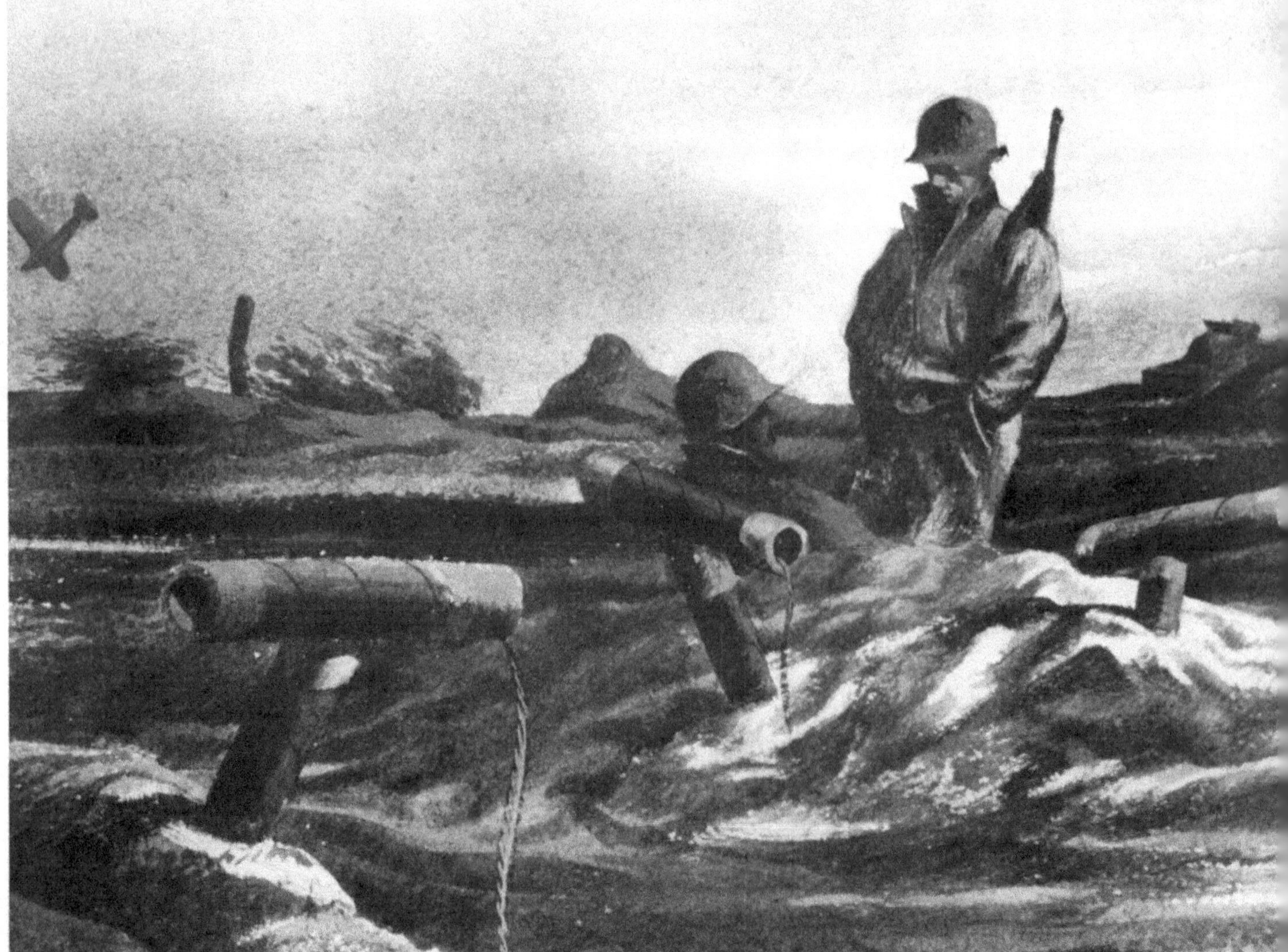

in World War II

EDWARD REEP

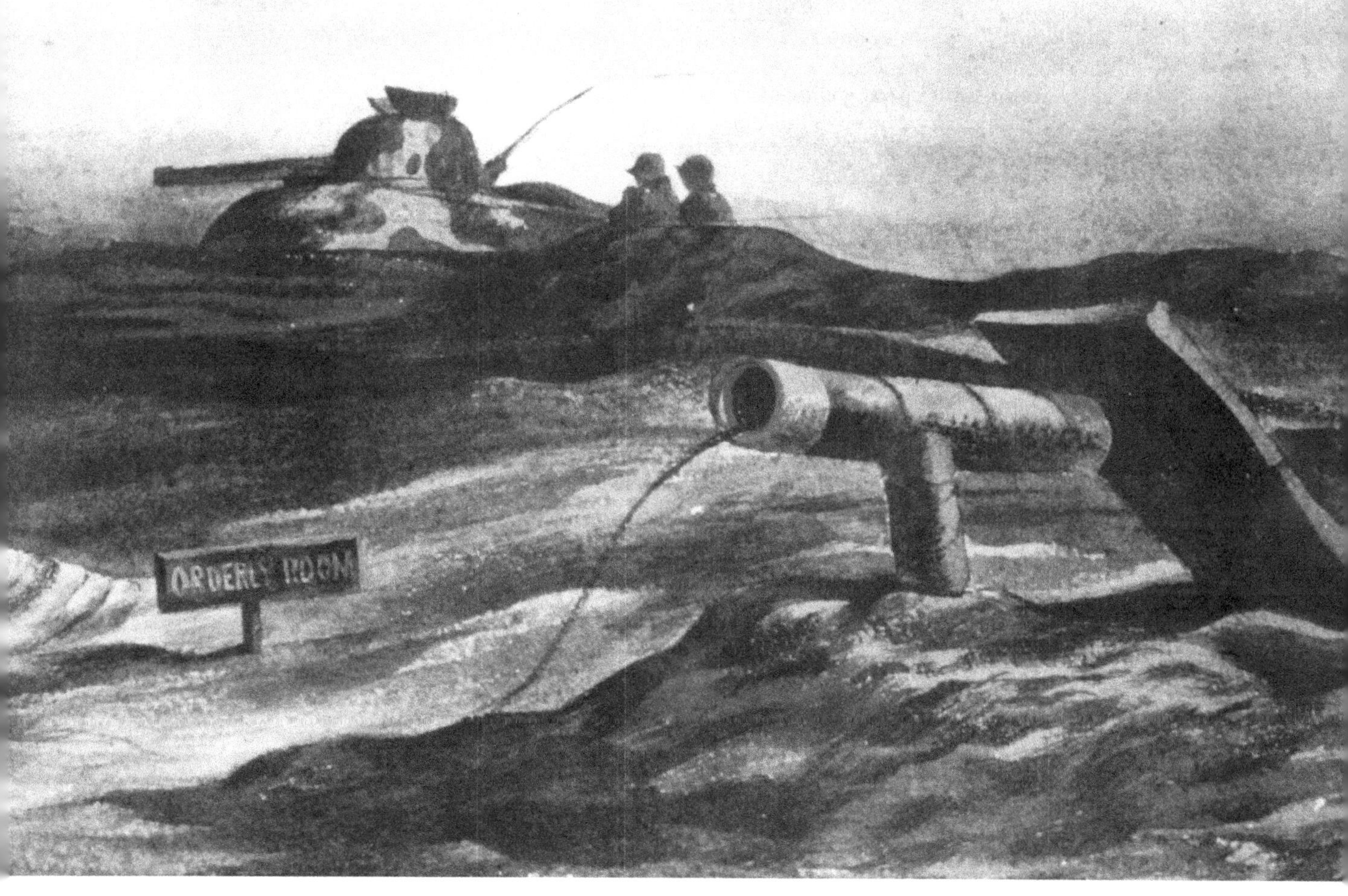

Publication of this book has been assisted by a grant from East Carolina University.

Title page spread: "Orderly Room at Anzio," Edward Reep, 1944.

Scholarly publisher for the Commonwealth, serving Bellarmine College, Berea College, Centre College of Kentucky, Eastern Kentucky University, The Filson Club, Georgetown College, Kentucky Historical Society, Kentucky State University, Morehead State University, Murray State University, Northern Kentucky University, Transylvania University, University of Kentucky, University of Louisville, and Western Kentucky University.

Editorial and Sales Offices: Lexington, Kentucky 40506-0024

Library of Congress Cataloging-in-Publication Data

Reep, Edward, 1918–
A combat artist in World War II.

Includes index.
1. Reep, Edward, 1918– . 2. Artists—United States—Biography. 3. World War, 1939–1945—Personal narratives, American. 4. World War, 1939–1945—Art and the war. 5. World War, 1939–1945—Campaigns—Italy—Pictorial works. I. Title.
N6537.R33A2 1987 759.13 [B] 86-22380

ISBN 978-0-8131-5453-4

Contents

Illustrations

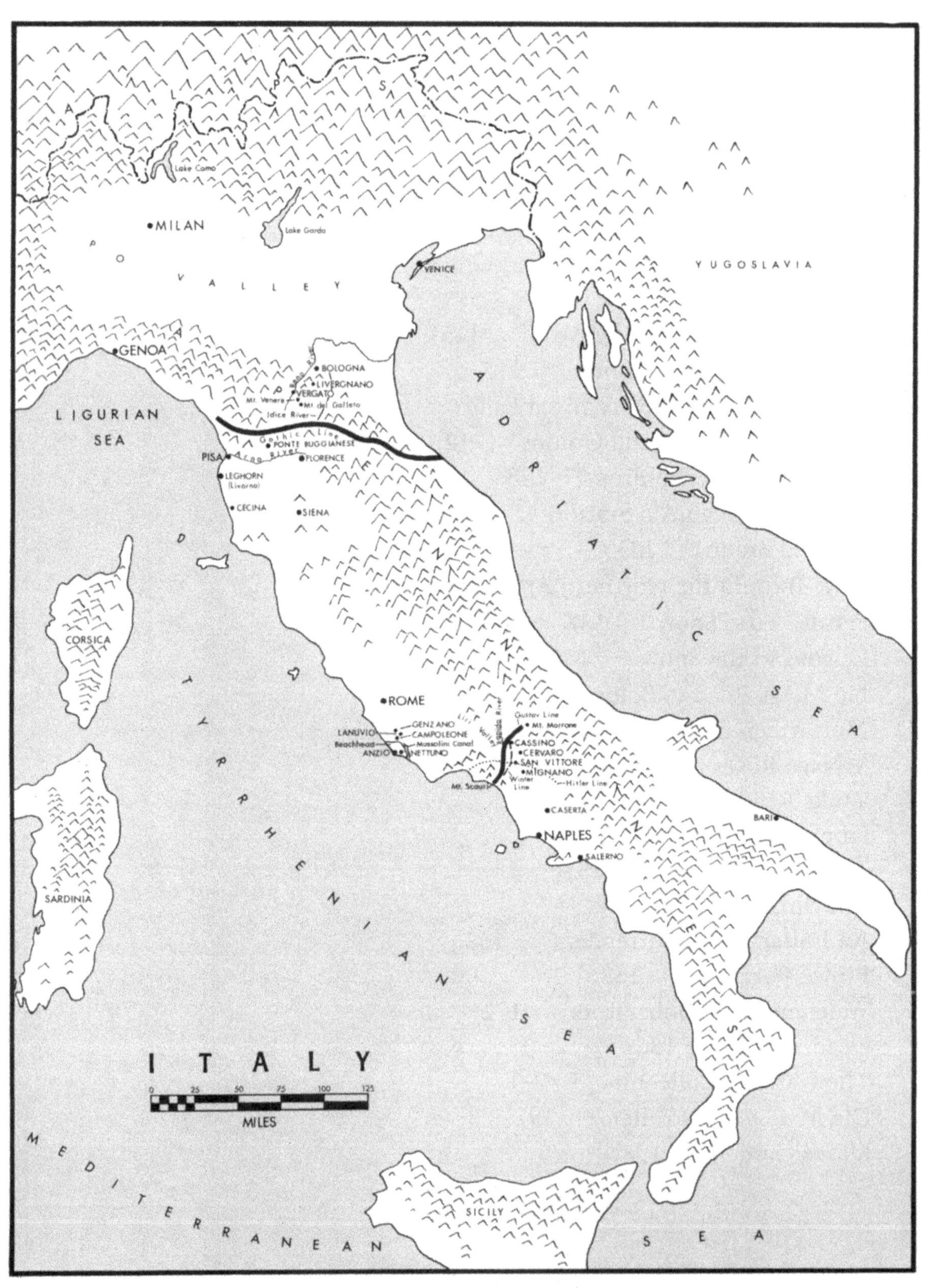
ITALY
MILES
0 25 50 75 100 125
YUGOSLAVIA
Lake Como
Lake Garda
MILAN
PO VALLEY
VENICE
GENOA
LIGURIAN SEA
BOLOGNA
LIVERGNANO
VERGATO
Mt. Venere
Mt del Galleto
Idice River
Reno River
Gothic Line
PONTE BUGGIANESE
PISA
Arno River
FLORENCE
LEGHORN (Livorno)
CECINA
SIENA
CORSICA
SARDINIA
ROME
GENZANO
LANUVIO
CAMPOLEONE
Beachhead
Mussolini Canal
ANZIO
NETTUNO
Gustav Line
Mt. Morrone
Rapido River
CASSINO
CERVARO
SAN VITTORE
MIGNANO
Winter Line
Hitler Line
Mt. Scauri
CASERTA
NAPLES
SALERNO
BARI
SICILY
ADRIATIC SEA
TYRRHENIAN SEA
MEDITERRANEAN SEA

Foreword

During World War II in Italy, the Historical Section of the Fifth Army was an amazing group of about thirty men. Some were historians who had already earned their Ph.D.'s; others were former graduate students in history who had been caught up in the draft. Their historical studies in the field were supported by typists and excellent mapmakers (one had been an animator for Walt Disney). Still others kept in order the records turned in every month by each unit in the Fifth Army, from chemical mortar battalions to divisions and corps; when we moved, we usually needed two trucks just for the wooden boxes of documents.

There was also a section of artists, sent out to the Mediterranean theater to be painters but soon administratively marooned by the fulminations of a Mississippi congressman at this "waste" of military personnel. Eventually, they wound up with us and continued to be artists. One liked to sketch engineers at work; another, the sad Italians in the wake of our advance; a third preferred to draw soldiers in rest areas. As chief of the Historical Section I gave each full rein, and the result was a very diversified portrayal of an army in an alien land. Their work was used to illustrate the first three of the nine volumes of the Fifth Army's history (the only army, incidentally, to publish a complete account of its operations); then, after General Mark Clark's ban on such decoration was removed by his translation to a higher command, paintings and sketches appeared again in the final volumes.

The artist whose wartime activity is handsomely illustrated in this volume was then a captain who, as he has described vividly in the following pages, preferred to get forward to the scene of action. When back at base, Ed Reep was an invaluable support in soothing artistic temperaments and always a witty jester. His work will speak for itself here, but I would assure the reader that he was then and has continued to be a distinguished artist and a remarkably thoughtful and vigorous man.

Chester G. Starr

Preface

I'm not certain that the story of a war artist, or an artist-soldier at war, has ever been told. Renowned artists have painted heroic scenes of great battles commemorating one thing or another, but they were mostly commissioned long after the battles were waged. Other artists have been commissioned to visit war-torn areas briefly and make notes of the devastation and horror. To my knowledge, however, very few artists who were members of the armed services drew and painted daily and then fought alongside their comrades when necessary.

Battles are cloaked in a different wardrobe under the latter circumstances. The grim realities of daily boredom, anxiety, and frustration are omnipresent. That rare mixture of grief and comedy—so exquisite, so subtle, and so private—is difficult to detect even as it unfolds before your eyes. Ernie Pyle would live in the foxholes for a few days and then repair to the relative comfort and safety of a rear command post where, in a drunken stupor, he would write compassionately of what he had seen. I knew Ernie. He was a brave man. He introduced me to my obligations, and from then on I vowed to remain on the front lines as often as possible and for longer periods.

Many times I painted and sketched while a battle raged. I was shelled, mortared, and strafed—the last a terrifying experience. At Monte Cassino the earth trembled (and so did my hand) as I attempted to paint the historic bombing of the magnificent abbey. At Anzio I innocently waited for the monstrous German cannon "Anzio Annie" to lob its shells into the harbor so that I could study and record the gigantic geysers of water shooting skyward. (At that point it didn't occur to me that one might do me in.) I joined reconnaissance patrols to seek out the enemy. More willing than knowledgeable, I almost destroyed myself on two occasions through my own stupidity. By war's end I was fairly well trained.

It is possible that in every major conflict involving mankind, an artist, official or otherwise, was present to record the event. Museums throughout the world brim with artifacts, sketches, and magnificent paintings attesting to the role of the artist engaged in documenting war; still more evidence may be found among the architectural remains of earliest civilizations, notably in tombs and sarcophagi. More often than not, the artist was commissioned to document a historic battle, understandably in commemoration of some sweeping victory won by a vainglorious warlord. Other artists, having been witness to or participants in the struggle, took notes, made sketches, and returned to recreate their impressions on a more elaborate scale at war's end.

In 1975 the U.S. Army Center of Military History in Washington, D.C., published a series of full-color reproductions of paintings executed by American artists and exclusively pertaining to American wars. This colorful series is entitled *Army Art: The Revolution to Vietnam*. Included are the works of Robert Goodes (Revolutionary War, 1775), James Walker (Mexican War, 1847, and Civil War, 1864), Charles Johnson Post (Cuba, 1898), Frederick Remington (Indian Wars, c. 1891), W.A. Aylward (World War I, 1918), Aaron Bohrod and myself (World War II, 1943), Howard Brodie (Korea, 1951), and Hereward Lester Cooke (Vietnam, 1967). Of this small group of artists, most seem to have worked at the scene of battle or at least to have witnessed the conflict. Curiously, Robert Goodes's painting is clearly dated 1856, almost eight decades after the Revolutionary War; hence, it is obviously a recreated statement.

My mission was to document the war as it happened. Early in 1943, the War Department, with the blessing of Secretary Henry Stimson, formed an Art Advisory Committee that was charged with selecting and assigning artists to various theaters of operation. Originally, several units were planned, each comprising two to six artists, both military and civilian. Once the earliest of these official war artists were at work in their theaters, glowing reports flowed back stateside. In all, 42 artists were selected, 19 civilians and 23 soldiers. I was one of the soldiers.

Perhaps our role can be explained best by quoting from the memorandum that George Biddle, original chairman of the War Department Art Advisory Committee, sent to the overseas art units in April 1943.

> In this war there will be a greater amount than ever before of factual reporting, of photographs and moving pictures. You are not sent out merely as news-gatherers. You have been selected as outstanding American artists, who will record the war in all its phases, and its impact on you as artists and as human beings. The War Department Art Advisory Committee is giving you as much latitude as possible in your method of work, whether by sketches done on the spot, sketches made from memory, or from notes taken on the spot, for it is recognized that an artist does his best work when he is not tied down by narrow technical limitations. What we insist on is the best work you are individually capable of; and the *most integrated picture of war in all its phases* that your group is capable of. This will require team play on your part as well as individual effort. It is suggested that you will freely discuss each other's work and assignments, always in the hope of new suggestions and new enthusiasm. Any subject is in order, if as artists you feel it is part of War; battle scenes and the front line; battle landscapes; the wounded, the dying and the dead; prisoners of war; field hospitals and base hospitals; wrecked habitations and bombing scenes; character sketches of our own troops, of prisoners, of the natives of the country you visit . . . the tactical implements of war; embarkation and debarkation scenes; the nobility, courage, cowardice, cruelty, boredom of war. . . . Try to omit nothing; duplicate to your heart's content. Express if you can—realistically or symbolically—the essence and spirit of War. You may be guided by Blake's mysticism, by Goya's cynicism and savagery, by Delacroix's romanticism, by Daumier's humanity and tenderness; or better still follow your own inevitable star.

This memo, plus other comments Biddle was purported to have made regarding a *necessary freedom* for the artist, got the art group in hot water with certain members of Congress, who saw to it that our funding was canceled. Senator Theodore Bilbo and Representative Joe Starnes in particular, if memory serves, referred to money spent for artists on the field of combat as "boondoggling."

But the program did not disappear completely. In our theater—North Africa and then Italy—after our funds were eliminated and all the civilian artists had been sent home, General Eisenhower placed me in "command" of a unit of five artists. (Military logic bore out Professor Gumperson's Laws of Probability: since I was the youngest and least experienced artist of the lot, it was only proper and fitting that I should become the leader.) With the army attempting partially to restore the project that Congress had emasculated, we gathered in Naples to begin our work.

Throughout my life I have speculated upon why I did one thing or another, why I was asked to participate in some appetizing project or what would have happened had I not been in that place at that time. Almost every thoughtful person I've known ponders the balance of fate and luck. In grammar school my fourth grade teacher, Mrs. Auten, presented fascinating art lessons far beyond the realm of ordinary instruction. From that time forward I painted and worked as an artist, and am still at it. But Mr. Biddle's term "outstanding American artist" did not really apply to me; my career had hardly begun. I produced a couple of paintings during basic training that picked up prizes and were reproduced in *Life* magazine; apparently from that slim exposure, my name was selected as a potential war artist.

I was even more inexperienced as a soldier. I volunteered without a shred of knowledge about how the army functioned, who outranked whom, or what would be expected of me. I had never hunted and only briefly owned a 22-caliber rifle. One day I shot a bird and agonized over that incident for months.

Yet as an artist in wartime, on the battlefield in particular, I found a certain enigmatic, almost freakish peace and contentment. I could lose myself in the act of painting to the extent that all other concerns were crowded out of my mind. On several occasions I became so engrossed in my work that the enemy came close to doing me in. I used to speculate as to why those trigger-happy Jerries wanted to eliminate an artist. How would that benefit them?

I never wore my officer's insignia while at the front. I first removed my lieutenant's bars when I read that the shiny metal might reflect light and reveal one's position to the enemy; later I discovered that it was much better for me in my particular assignment not to wear them. I was able to move with more freedom; the barriers so rigidly adhered to between officers and enlisted men vanished, and I found that as an individual I threatened nary a soul. Most of the time I was on my own, precisely as I had hoped.

I honestly believe that, to a great extent, no one gives a damn about rank *on the battlefield*. Each person has a duty to perform, and it is attended to and done efficiently or you are found out and you are finished. I didn't encounter any cowards on the field of battle—maybe frightened men unable to cope or hurt and exhausted. For many, endless days and months on the line led to a sort of punch-drunk weariness; others could handle it. Being an artist with my personal goals before me constantly must have kept me going.

Of course, when I arrived in Italy, I hadn't the vaguest idea of what a battlefield looked like. I harbored some kind of naive notion that you could *see* the "front lines," almost as if there were a sign posted there proclaiming them; this forced me to drive directly toward the sound of gunfire at my first opportunity. The other artists seemed less eager than I was to go up front, most confining themselves to recording the ravages of war's wake, but eventually two or three acquitted themselves with honor by venturing into combat areas and even participating in battle. Each of us had to get his bearings in his own way.

It became mandatory for me to recognize the separate, distinctive contributions that the artists could make and not force my will upon any of them (if, indeed, that had been possible). As a result, the North African-Italian unit of artists probably produced the most comprehensive or catholic documentation of the war in general: the fighting, civilians in foreign lands, and Allied soldiers from England, India, Australia, France, Brazil, and elsewhere functioning in battle or engaged in recreation. The completed work executed by all of the art units currently resides in the archives of the Center of Military History, Department of the Army, in Washington.

I have attempted to tell this story in words. My recollections are made more vivid by the paintings and drawings accompanying the text. The visual document never lets me forget even the most trivial events. I was a young man and knew little of international politics and military strategy. In retrospect, I now appreciate how our leaders struggled and agonized. Nothing was known for certain—mistakes, misjudgments, and personality conflicts among my superiors were commonplace. Strategies backfired, and lives were needlessly lost. Yet we all persisted and pulled together. The boys who went to war and were fortunate enough to return became men overnight.

I have refrained from writing about the other artists' efforts; I already stand in admiration of their work. This narrative and its illustrations pertain to a single artist's vision, his responses, his prejudices and frailties, and his compassion.

I wish to thank the United States Army Center of Military History for their able assistance in providing photographs of my paintings and sketches from their collection, and Mr. Mark Smith for his cartographical contribution. I am indebted to Dr. Henry Ferrell of East Carolina University and Dr. Chester Starr of the University of Michigan for their counsel and guidance. A special note of thanks goes to the two anonymous readers for the University Press of Kentucky, whose sagacious observations I chose to view as priceless encouragement. Finally, I am grateful to East Carolina University for a grant that assisted in publication of this book.

To my wife, Patsy, whose image was before me throughout the long war and whose ear I virtually demanded while suffering through the exhumation of buried passions, I wish to express my gratitude, sympathy, and enduring love.

CHAPTER ONE

Before the War

The Armistice signaling the end of World War I was declared when I was six months of age. It was November 11, 1918, and I'm told that I was separated from my mother for an agonizing period of time as she joined a frenzied, joyous throng on the Brooklyn Bridge to celebrate the great victory. On July 11, 1941, five months before the infamous Japanese attack on Pearl Harbor, I entered military service as an army private. In the years intervening, I had no inkling of who did what in the military or who outranked whom, in war or at peace.

Five arduous years of art school training lay behind me, and though war had not yet been declared, the smell of it was everywhere. Hitler had been ravaging Europe for some time and was then at Britain's throat; America might well be his next goal. I rushed to volunteer my services. If the United States did enter the war, at least I would be trained; if not, I could begin my professional art career without fear of the draft.

On my first day in the army I became acquainted with its perverse ways. When we lined up at Fort MacArthur—an induction center in San Pedro, not too distant from Los Angeles—a show of hands by non-smokers was called for, and as a consequence I spent the next hour "policing up" the parade grounds. I had innocently believed that the army would be overjoyed to inherit a real artist and would assign me at once to a camouflage or other art-related unit—but that proved to be wishful thinking. I was a buck-ass private; nobody ranked lower on the army totem pole, and despite doing exceptionally well on the intelligence test given that first day, I was herded off with all the other recruits for basic training at Camp Roberts in dusty, sweltering, isolated central California, a member of the 83rd Infantry Training Battalion.

I can't explain my excessive innocence, especially when my art school experiences had cautioned me time after time to be wary. Earning my way through school at the peak of the Great Depression had forced me to pick up freelance assignments, which meant that I was at the mercy of some pretty artful hustlers. Entrepreneurs skulk about schools of art in search of greenhorns willing to sell their services for the promise of big money—the *promise* often all that's forthcoming. I did careful hand-lettering, sign-painting, complex medical drawings for a local brain surgeon, and an abortive comic strip for John Coleman Burroughs, the son of Edgar Rice Burroughs, who created *Tarzan*. But the most remarkable freelance assignment of all was one I refused to do for Orson Welles, the boy wonder of the day.

Mr. Welles's agent had contacted our school in search of a student artist who could draw the human figure reasonably well, and I was recommended for the assignment. Brimming with excitement, I visited him at the RKO Studios in Hollywood. After considerable haggling, he finally prepared a contract agreeable to all. Orson casually announced that when my drawings were complete he would trace them on onionskin paper and sign them as his own (he was revising or reediting Shakespeare), so that the title page could read "illustrated by Orson Welles." He informed me of this without the faintest trace of ego or embarrassment; it was simply his method. Such minor concerns as plagiarism and ethics seemed never to have entered his mind. I told the great man to get someone else—and departed. I'm not altogether certain he planned to allow Shakespeare a credit line.

The Art Center School in Los Angeles was run by Edward A. "Tink" Adams, a hard-boiled and sometimes ruthless man who worked the hell out of everyone. He made certain that we were thoroughly trained as technicians, though not as draughtsmen or innovators. Adams was an intolerant man in many ways: he opposed having a library at the school, detested the world of academe with its sororities and fraternities, and for all I know may have resented fine artists or painters. His students faced long working hours, often around the clock; anyone who did not comply could be tossed out of school without notice.

On my first day in drawing class I was confronted with a naked lady posing on the model stand right before my eyes, in broad daylight. Then a male model, who was supposed to wear a jockstrap, appeared on the stand unadorned, and I nearly died again. I attended classes night and day, six days a week, and eventually won the working scholarship that kept me in school. My part of the bargain was to clean nine johns, three times a day. All scholarship students swept, cleaned, painted, and repaired facilities at the school year round—and were grateful for the opportunity.

There was little time for frivolity, but we managed to snatch a few minutes of horseplay. At lunch in the nearby park we played touch football and sparred a bit after classes, but being without shower facilities, we returned to our studios a bit gamey. Lunch consisted of a quart of milk, a fresh roll, and a slice of ham or cheese—all this for nine or ten cents. A full-course dinner, which none of us could afford, cost 35 cents; instead, we ate at the local Chili Bowl, where for a nickel we could feast on a huge bowl of chili and all the soda crackers we could tolerate.

As grueling as the art school regime had been, memories of it vanished quickly upon my enlistment into the army. Basic training consumed our time to the extent that we lost all contact with the outside world, but at least I was eating regularly, getting good sleep, and exercising daily. After the rigors of art school, this segment of army life was a snap.

I had rushed to join up with the prospect of serving alongside a classmate of mine, Tony Miller, who had been drafted. That plan misfired, but I wound up with another character from art school by the name of Gordon Mellor, a real nut in almost every sense of the word, yet a magnificent draughtsman in spite of Tink Adams. Gordon had envisioned a career as a boxer prior to his entrance into art school, but in his first bout he was decked immediately and gave up the notion. Serving with Gordon was a break for me, because his drawings were a great inspiration and I learned much from them.

One day in basic training at Camp Roberts, Gordon and I were assigned to KP duty together, and that was a mistake from the outset. We were ordered to peel what appeared to be a million potatoes stored in huge galvanized trash cans. About half an hour into the task Gordy started chuckling to himself, and I glanced over to discover that he was not *peeling* the spuds but *carving* them into imposing penises. Naturally I thought that was a great idea and immediately tried to outperform him; the competition made our work much more enjoyable. Unfortunately, the mess sergeant, a humorless man, didn't share our enthusiasm for the "happening," artistic as it was. He first put us to work slicing up our pretty sculptures with strict orders to be sure they were disguised, and as a further reward he placed us on KP for a solid week of cleaning all the grease traps under the sinks, the rottenest, smelliest job in the army.

At times my innocence approached stupidity. One of my assignments during that fateful week was to comb the neighboring company mess halls in search of a pie stretcher. Determined to vindicate myself for the heinous potato caper, I set off intrepidly, asking one mess sergeant after another if they had seen the gadget, and in so doing made a complete fool of myself. The whole world knew there was no such thing as a pie stretcher, except me. Realizing that I possessed a suspicious nature (my mother trained me) and wishing to rid myself of it, I suppose that I just wanted too much to believe. Years later Eleanor Roosevelt sagaciously observed that it would be better to be fooled, which is human, than to be suspicious, which is common. At that moment, her admonition wasn't working well for me. For whether innocent, naive, or just plain dumb, I was deeply mortified. Nor would that spell the end of my pervasive naiveté. It surfaced repeatedly in training and on the battlefield. I just wasn't aware of the way things are, nor was I worldly-wise.

At Camp Roberts (referred to as the "asshole of California"—an appellation, I would later learn, given to all basic training camps) it was customary to rise *very* early, fall in, do calisthenics, fall out, eat breakfast, fall in again, and set off marching somewhere—anywhere, it didn't matter. We marched and paraded incessantly, and got dusty and tired; with two inches of dust covering everything within view, there was no escape.

Fortunately, we were dismissed early each afternoon when the July heat became unbearable. After a welcome shower most recruits sacked out or played cards, the games blossoming spontaneously, like wildflowers. I had been resourceful enough to bring some art materials along, so I'd head back into the low rolling hills and paint in the late afternoons. It was one of my favorite times to work outdoors, with the shadows lengthening to lend drama to the voluptuous golden hills, barren as they were. It might be stretching things a bit to suggest that this was a landscape painter's paradise, but it was better than nothing and provided me with the therapy necessary at the time. I think, in retrospect, that I was making an attempt to retain my identity, and in doing so I produced a couple of successful things. One painting was selected by a New York publishing house to be reproduced as a Christmas card for sale in the army exchanges. It depicted a basic training exercise in which "enemy" planes dropped sacks of flour, which I thought terribly exciting. Little did I realize then the terror of real bombing and strafing.

When basic training ended, a miracle took place: Gordon and I were both assigned to Fort Ord, California, to the same division, regiment, company, and even barracks. We were full-fledged privates now, with the right to wear myriad emblems and insignia, which I proudly sewed onto my drab olive green uniform. Always fond of colors, shapes, and designs of any persuasion, I enjoyed my new attire and felt like a seasoned veteran. Basho's familiar *haiku* would have been appropriate: "In my new clothing I feel so different, I must look like someone else."

Fort Ord sprawled out from its main base, across the ocean highway, and onto the sandy beaches forming the northern rim of Monterey Bay. In the distance, the colorful towns of Monterey and Pacific Grove were visible; behind them lay Carmel and Pebble Beach. The area was filled with history. Sir Francis Drake once anchored in the bay; Monterey was the site of California's first state capital; the peninsula was the locale of some of John Steinbeck's novels.

General Joseph "Vinegar Joe" Stilwell was in command of the Seventh Army and my regiment, the 32nd Infantry. The good general would soon dramatically alter the course of my life.

Gordon and I were seldom apart, and as artists we were subjected to our fair share of heckling. A familiar cry reverberated in our ears: "Hey you, get your asses over here on the double." The Seventh Army fielded a football team, and we were required to attend the games, which, as a sports fan, I looked forward to eagerly. When we arrived at the first game, however, after having been packed into trucks like sardines, Gordy and I drew Military Police duty and were sent off to patrol the town. Not only didn't I see one damn play of that contest, but the two of us had to disarm a violent, drunken soldier wielding an ugly-looking knife, and my colorful jacket was cut to shreds.

I tried out for the Fort Ord basketball team and just barely made it. On the eve of our first game some big bozos landed on me, and my ankle was fractured badly enough to put me in the hospital. While I was laid up, Gordon made a number of contacts in the neighboring art-conscious communities, notably Carmel; when he met Carol Steinbeck, the reigning president of the Carmel Art Association, our destinies took a new turn. Carol, writer John's estranged wife, lived nearby and was a close friend of the Stilwells; with the general, she was engaged in planning a million-dollar club for enlisted men only. The club would be generously decorated with paintings, sculpture, and murals, and the general was in search of soldiers with artistic talent; I was assured that it was just a matter of time before we were selected to paint murals. Gordon related this to me at the hospital in a manner so casual that it sounded like a routine, everyday occurrence, but it was all I could do to keep from leaping out of my bed, at the risk of reinjuring my bum ankle.

It was some time before our transfer orders arrived, and in the interim I was released from the hospital and sent on maneuvers to Jolon, California. There my rifle was stolen by some nifty thieves working in cahoots with civilians in Pennsylvania. Since this was not known at the time, I faced a court-martial for this most serious crime of all—a soldier and his rifle parted; I was a veritable basket case with worry. As it turned out, I was only ordered to pay for the rifle and strongly admonished. When the crime ring was exposed some years after the war, the army refunded the money. The regular-army soldiers involved in the racket would steal the rifles while on maneuvers, hang them high in the numerous oak trees, and return much later to collect the weapons. Then they would ship them off to their eastern contacts, where the guns were sold for hunting rifles. Somewhere along the line the ploy was discovered, and the culprits apprehended and imprisoned.

The majority of men in our outfit were army regulars, which to most of us neophytes was a euphemism for street-corner bums. Their values were unique. A noncommissioned officer could be tossed into the guardhouse or stockade, stripped of rank, and humiliated—only to be back on the job within the week with all stripes restored. Getting drunk and disorderly, fighting, damaging property, being busted and spending the night in the local jail were all a routine part of the old army tradition, like a badge of honor or a symbol of being tough. The bulk of the pre–Pearl Harbor types we soldiered with had just returned from Oahu, Hawaii, and were the most hard-nosed, uncouth, bullheaded, and intolerant idiots alive. They had little incentive or desire to be anything beyond what they were at the moment, and generally were so preoccupied with drinking that the mess sergeant had to lock up the vanilla extract. Similarly, the infirmary kept all medicinal supplies under lock and key, since these creeps guzzled anything that was wet as long as it had an alcoholic content, and "footlocker booze" was well publicized by grim tales of illness and death resulting from swallowing the stuff. With the mural commission in mind, I was enthralled at the prospect of waving bye-bye to the bunch.

At last orders arrived from General Stilwell's headquarters assigning Gordon and me to the venerable Presidio of Monterey across the bay. The presidio sat on a rather unspectacular promontory offering a modest view of the harbor, John Steinbeck's beloved Cannery Row, the Fishermens' Wharf tourist attractions, and the lovely, unspoiled city of Monterey. We would billet at the presidio but do our work in town at Colton Hall, which had been California's first state capitol. Our assignment was laid out for us clearly: we were to prepare three panels, two 8 feet square and one 8 feet by 24 feet, depicting the history of exploration and conquest in South America, California, and the United States, respectively. Gordon and I were very enthusiastic about the work, and in finishing the panels added our names to those of Magellan, Vasco de Gama, Balboa, Sir Walter Raleigh, Pizzaro, Vizcaíno, Cortez, and others appearing in the mural. It was Gordon's idea, naturally. To this day we speculate upon the countless numbers of persons who must have walked away bewildered and perhaps a bit humbled by not being able to recollect those famous early explorers Mellor and Reep.

On the precise day of our transfer to the presidio, Pearl Harbor was attacked. Gordon and I sat in General Stilwell's outer office within earshot of the intermittent shouting, cursing, and arguing taking place between the general and Colonel "Pinky" Dorn, his aide. Understandably fearful of what lay ahead, they were heatedly discussing the advisability of placing the entire west coast of the United States under military rule. In the midst of this vigorous debate, Colonel Dorn took time out to greet us warmly and provide us with peremptory passes that would permit us to go to and from the presidio in order to proceed with our work on the murals. No mere war was about to prevent "Vinegar Joe" from getting his privates' club completed on schedule.

Gordon and I had Monterey to ourselves, since the potent passes signed by Stilwell did their magic with consummate ease in a town that was now off limits; we saw only an occasional GI on some sort of errand. At the nightly USO dances, attended by Gordon, Joe Kalina (another artist working on a separate project), and me, all the beautiful young ladies were ours for the evening, 50 girls to three guys. I was tagged so much I thought I was Fred Astaire, and as proof of the overwhelming effect it had on me, I fell in love with the most persistent tagger; ultimately, I married her.

I saw General Stilwell only occasionally after that; he was soon whisked away clandestinely, to pop up later in the China-Burma sector. But during that period I learned how he maintained an almost magical control of his men, largely through the agency of *caring*. As an example, the city jail lay beneath our work quarters in Colton Hall, and the general routinely came by to check on his men who had been tossed into the clink. The men loved him for his concern and interest in their welfare, and he took pride in being their champion. Stilwell once observed, "The private carries the woes of one man; the general carries the woes of all."

Striding down a Pentagon hall a few years later, I saw the general for the last time. An old soldier, tired and worn, clad in a drab and unadorned uniform, walked toward me. His eyes were fixed straight ahead; his steps were measured, almost mechanical. It was the famed "Vinegar Joe," back from *his* war and the political battles he had faced in his courageous denunciation of Chiang Kai-shek. Almost blind, he had persevered to become the most telling authority on Chinese-American relationships, so misunderstood at the time. His gallantry in leading his troops was legend; it is doubtful that a less self-demanding man could have survived his ordeal.

We must have looked a strange pair; Stilwell so plain and me in a dazzling new uniform, decorated everywhere possible. I was eager to remind him who I was and to tell him of my accomplishments. I talked of the mural assignment and of having dinner with his wife and family in their Carmel home some four years earlier. He did not discuss his experiences; he was like a father pleased to learn of his son's accomplishments. I noticed an inordinately small circle of silver stars pinned to his shirt collar. That was the general: courageous, sensitive, humble, a man one couldn't fail to admire.

The murals were nearing completion when a bulletin arrived an-

To the brave men who fought so gallantly to vanquish a tyrannical enemy, and to the artists, photographers, and writers who were also there

nouncing that test interviews for Officer Candidate School would soon be conducted. Gordy and I agreed that if we took the test and one of us passed, the other could complete the murals. Frankly, we didn't think either of us had a chance, for we had no clue as to what took place at such interviews. Nevertheless, we joined the horde of anxious applicants at Fort Ord to nervously await our turn.

The crux of my interrogation surfaced when I was asked to name five countries in South America. When I did so, the panel of grim-faced colonels seemed upset; they stared incredulously at me and impatiently asked if I had heard the question. So I repeated my answer; at this juncture I had no idea that they were testing my emotional stability. The baiting continued. Finally, in desperation, I rattled off the names of five *more* countries. That ought to hold them, I thought; it seemed inconceivable that these dumb bastards wouldn't be able to verify at least five of the ten names I had given them. The colonels acted dumfounded, exasperated; their role-playing was worthy of an Oscar, but inwardly they must have been pleased to think they had such a knowledgeable candidate. How were they to know that for weeks prior to the exam I had been poring over maps of South America in research for the murals?

When the results were posted I was overjoyed to find my name at the top of the list. In a few weeks I would be off to the Engineer Officer Candidate School at Fort Belvoir, Virginia, and if I succeeded in becoming an officer, Pat and I could marry. Gordon remained to complete the central panel of our mural and did so with distinction, possibly better than if I had been there to assist.

The OCS drew its men from throughout the nation, from streetwise kids in metropolises to raw-boned youngsters fresh from the farming belts. I found the various dialects interesting and at times, perplexing: "Bahston" and "New Yawk" seemed obvious corruptions of the language yet comprehensible; the southerners' drawl and colloquialisms required patience and careful listening. We worked so hard during the day, running from one class to another, that there was little time for fraternization or games. The competition was fierce. With my heart set on gaining the income necessary to support a bride, I studied far into each night and fell asleep totally spent. At one point I nearly blew up my group at the demolition exercises, but aside from that fiasco the training progressed without incident, and I was commissioned a second lieutenant in the Corps of Engineers, United States Army. I was busting with pride and seemingly invulnerable.

The day after graduation, Pat and I were married in a little chapel on the Belvoir post. We spent our honeymoon night in Washington, D.C., and left the following day for the Ozark Mountains of Missouri and Fort Leonard Wood. In the months ahead I would train recruits, all black, to become engineers. It was my first opportunity to teach, and despite having to pore over each subject in advance, due to my lack of experience, I enjoyed the assignment immensely. From there I was sent to New Orleans, ostensibly to be trained at the Andrew Higgins Boat School for service in the Amphibian Brigade. I worked diligently, excelling in the navigation courses (though just barely getting by in marine motor maintenance), and was retained as an instructor. I would one day train as a member of a commando team in that proud brigade.

Pat and I turned these assignments into a honeymoon, fighting cockroaches in one-room apartments but blissfully happy and grateful to be together. Although I didn't realize it at the time, my days of training were ending—the real war lay ahead.

CHAPTER TWO

Official War Artist

When the Andrew Higgins Boat School closed in the late spring of 1943, I was reassigned directly back to the place I had come from, Fort Ord in Monterey, California. It was a stroke of the greatest good fortune, because this was the home of my bride of five months and our familiar stomping ground. I had courted Pat for almost a year, and only the deep poverty all privates suffered had prevented us from marrying sooner.

I was now a member of the Third Engineer Amphibian Brigade, which soon assumed the name of the Third Engineer Boat and Shore Regiment. More specifically, I was a navigation wave leader being prepared for assault in combat. Our mission would soon be to recapture the Alaskan islands of Attu and Kiska, which had been occupied by the Japanese. I was training as part of a unit that would reconnoiter the shores for mines prior to actual invasion. Once it was determined where a landing would be attempted, we would clear the area of the mines. At least that's how the scuttlebutt had it.

The regiment I was assigned to was "frozen." That meant there could be no transfers out of the unit. None. All information we were given was top secret. Presumably, we all knew where we were going and what we would be expected to do. But while stimulated by the assignment ahead, I wasn't truly happy at the time. A couple of my immediate superior officers were riding me hard, for what reasons I'll never know; we were all under great tension, and people react differently under such conditions. I had worked alongside one of the officers at the boat school at Camp Ponchartrain, New Orleans; he had seemed pleasant and friendly at the time. Perhaps he wasn't very secure in his new role. He and the other character giving me a bad time spent their free hours together and were usually half crocked. As things turned out, it didn't matter very much.

Our unit had been dispatched to Indio, California, in order to practice firing at target sleeves towed aloft by tiny Piper Cub airplanes. We had developed skills with the invasion barges, but none of us had any experience firing the machine guns that would be mounted in the bow of each craft. On May 27, 1943, I was lying prone on the firing line and blasting away with my machine gun when a soldier approached and asked if I happened to be Lieutenant Reep. When I nodded yes, he handed me a telegram, adding that it was urgent.

> CONFIDENTIAL. THE WAR DEPARTMENT ART ADVISORY COMMITTEE IS CONSIDERING YOU FOR OVERSEAS ARTIST ASSIGNMENT. BEFORE WE SEND YOU DETAILS WE WOULD LIKE AN EXPRESSION OF INTEREST IN SUCH AN ASSIGNMENT FROM YOU.

After rereading the message in virtual disbelief, I leaped into the air to dash to the nearest telephone. This was surely a dream come true. How could anyone have invented such a wonderful assignment? In my haste I tripped over the soldier sprawled out next to me, and almost fell into his line of fire.

Inexplicably, the War Department in Washington had had great difficulty in discovering my whereabouts and had almost given up on me. If my call in reply to their telegram had not arrived in the nick of time, the assignment would have gone out the window. Peremptory orders were to be cut in Washington, and a nine-day leave en route to New York was considerately granted.

Apart from the enormous thrill I felt at the prospect of becoming an "official war artist-correspondent"—what a splendid title, I mused, I was departing from a pretty sick situation. The arrogant officers who were my immediate superiors and who took pleasure in reminding me of that circumstance repeatedly, were in disbelief. They had devised all sorts of ways to make me uncomfortable and were now about to lose their favorite whipping boy. Further, had I remained in that outfit and continued under their command, the condition could only have worsened.

With puerile glee, I went to great lengths to carefully outline my new assignment to them, concluding that I would be promoted to captain at once. They were utterly nonplussed—no, they were devastated. That last little fillip was an outright lie, of course, but I simply couldn't resist adding to *their* misery, for a change.

It was June when I got my orders.

> The Secretary of War directs that Second Lieutenant Edward A. Reep, 01107648, CE, 3rd Engineer Amphibian Brigade, proceed from Fort Ord, California, to New York, N.Y., for temporary duty of approximately 10 days in the Office of the District Engineer, New York Engineer District, 120 Wall Street, thence on further temporary duty to station outside the continental limits of the United States, temperate climate, Shipment 00 - 724-H. He will be available on call of the Commanding General, New York Port of Embarkation, Brooklyn, N.Y., and/or Hampton Roads Port of Embarkation, Newport News, Virginia, and upon receipt of notification that transportation is available he will proceed to the proper port and report to the Commanding General, that port, for first available water transportation to destination. Upon arrival at destination he will report to the Commanding General for temporary duty of six (6) months or more. Upon completion of this temporary duty he will return to his proper station, Fort Ord, California.

After a brief stay at Los Angeles, where I bade both wife and family adieu, I entrained for New York to be briefed, outfitted, inoculated, and otherwise readied for the wondrous adventure ahead. Although my only clue to where I would be sent was that little notation of "temperate climate," it seemed likely that I'd wind up in the North African theater of operations.

In New York, Reeves Lewenthal, a member of the War Department's Art Advisory Committee and director of the Associated American Artists—an innovative gallery that offered original art at affordable prices—was my gracious and helpful host. He introduced me to the renowned Thomas Hart Benton and Reginald Marsh, among others. I was petrified in their presence, yet proud to be numbered among their colleagues, young and inexperienced as I was. In the days to follow, either at social affairs or in various art gallery offices, I met many noted artists, writers, and musicians, some of whom had been my demigods for years. I recall spending an afternoon with Reginald Marsh and accompanying him to his studio to see his current efforts. Just a year or two earlier, while attending art school, I had studiously examined his work in books and on museum walls. Now, it seemed strangely unreal to be in the tiny studio of the great man. Yet when he asked me to join him in a sketching session at Coney Island, working from the beach characters that filled his paintings, I nervously trumped up some sort of excuse out of fear that he would discover how raw a recruit I was. Whether true or not, I didn't consider myself a good draughtsman, notably when the subject matter included people, so right then and there I vowed even more deeply to one day learn how to draw.

I had been given the run of supplies available at the vast Brooklyn Port of Embarkation, and the sky-high stacks of materials, equipment, and photographic supplies startled me to the point of confusion. I had never seen such quantities in my life. In addition, I had a voucher for $1,000 to spend wherever I wished, presumably for more personal and sophisticated art materials not procurable at the military supply warehouses. I blew the entire sum at a single art store in New York that featured Winsor-Newton art materials, among the finest manufactured. I loaded up on paint, bought out their supply of exquisite Albata sable brushes, and spent the balance on the best of rag papers. (Later, this single act on my part would prove to be the luckiest move I could have made, for I was able to keep our entire unit in materials until their own supplies arrived.) If there was a paradise on earth, surely I was living in it at the moment.

The days in New York turned into weeks as I waited somewhat impatiently, completely outfitted and briefed, for something to happen. I wanted to get started; the incessant partying was growing stale, and I was accomplishing very little of consequence. I had visited the historic sites in and near Gotham and had attended some Broadway plays and musicals. I had a magnificent Leica 35mm camera with all the necessary accessories, and in my comfortable Madison Avenue hotel room had become expert at using the light meter, filters, and self-timer. To fight off boredom, I'd sketch in the streets in the evenings when the crowds thinned. The deep canyons formed by the incomparable skyscrapers fascinated me, as did the nutty night people wandering about or hustling some poor sucker. I did a few self-portraits and some tiny still lifes in the hotel room, the latter suffused with nostalgia. I was becoming unbearably lonesome.

Finally, providentially, my overseas orders arrived.

CHAPTER THREE

The Voyage

In the early fall of 1943, amid much confusion, I was herded onto a Liberty ship along with 500 enlisted men and about 50 other officers. We would become part of a convoy numbering approximately 55 ships, and our destination was North Africa. Once having cleared the port of embarkation, we would be joined by an escort of sleek destroyers. Our ship had successfully completed her shakedown voyage, a solo roundtrip to Bombay, India, so we were reassured that she was seaworthy. Many of the cargo carriers, tankers, and other vessels in our convoy were rusty old derelicts resurrected from shipyard cemeteries to aid in the all-out war effort.

The horde of enlisted men were crammed into the forward hold, and the officers fared only to slight advantage. Separated from the enlisted men by the strict army rules against fraternization, we were packed like sardines into a makeshift room belowdecks that measured just 24 by 12 feet. Fred Zinn, the only civilian passenger aboard, graphically described our quarters:

> We are four deep—I am number three from the bottom, and as the fellow above me has a particularly sizeable set of buttocks there is a trifle less than eight inches between the bottom of him and the top of me. Our beds are canvas strips laced onto pipe frames and the canvas creaks horribly everytime one turns over. There is about an eight foot alley between our bedroom and the cargo so we are not as badly congested as the enlisted men in the forward hold. The blankets that we brought aboard make a little additional padding and life preservers are pillows. This all doesn't sound too comfortable, but all in all it probably could be worse. Some of the fellows who brought Val-pacs so

they could hang their clothes up neatly in their staterooms are feeling a little hurt about things, but I have heard very little griping.

Fred Zinn and I became very close friends during the 26-day trip. He was a portly fellow who had seen service in World War I some 25 years earlier, and was headed for an undisclosed destination as a civil affairs official. He was well informed and inordinately intelligent; one of the most caring men I have ever had the pleasure of knowing, he became the enlisted men's mother and father, as well as their champion and father confessor.

Because the men received little news from home and had far less idea of their fate than the officers, Zinn established a daily bulletin, which was eagerly read each morning. He personally gathered and edited the material and printed the newsletter by hand, working in the ship captain's stateroom long into each night in order to post it where the men could read it the following morning. Fred also kept an accurate diary of his adventures and put it together in a stapled pamphlet, crudely written but effective and reliable. I drew an equally crude cover for his modest publication, which as a layman in art he thought wonderful. The title of his masterwork was "The Camel on the Iceberg, or Three Weeks on an Australian Tugboat." His sharp sense of humor made his profound comprehension of human nature even more attractive, and his bulletins and pamphlet (which I rely upon to reinforce my narrative) kept the majority of men loose and laughing at our situation.

He was especially concerned about the food the troops were served; he tried to see that their meals were as well prepared as possible and that each soldier received his fair portion. Fred Zinn's ample waistline was clear evidence that food was a vital part of his daily routine. We ate two meals a day, one early in the morning and the other late in the afternoon. It was horrible stuff, mainly steamed and utterly tasteless. I particularly detested the powdered eggs. However, apart from the fact that I knew I didn't like it, I paid little attention to the food. Not so the irrepressible Zinn, who unearthed a number of revealing inequities. The 500 enlisted men were devouring 600 meals, yet those at the end of the long lines were often coming up empty. It seems that the army majors, whom Zinn must have held in small regard, were snitching food, and that practice was taking its toll. When supplies threatened to run low, he discovered massive stacks of C-rations in the ship's hold, but it was explained to him that those were for prisoners of war on the return trip. If a crisis had arisen, however, Zinn would likely have led a charge of hungry enlisted men to storm the hold, justifiably.

Everyone knew that we were on a long voyage in an exceptionally slow convoy. The officers I lived among had been drawn from the higher echelons of civilian life; they included a Wall Street banker, a telephone company manager, a college professor, an orphanage superintendent, a bank examiner, and assorted executives from the business world. They had been assembled as officers of what was originally termed AMGOT, which stood for American Military Government of Occupied Territories. Some were lend-lease people; others were carefully trained for the dangerous work of the Office of Strategic Services (OSS) and prepared to parachute behind enemy lines if necessary. Comically, when it was discovered that "amgot" was a very dirty Turkish word, the group's name was altered to simply "Civil Affairs Officers."

The captain of our ship and his officers made all major decisions, and they were final. For protection from submarine and air attack, he had a small naval gunnery crew aboard which manned the cannon on the bow and the 20mm antiaircraft weapons. Along with the other junior grade army officers, I was trained to fire the antiaircraft guns should the emergency arise. I enjoyed my brief training immensely, watching the red tracers streak high into the clear blue sky to create arching, graceful, parabolic divisions not unlike a monstrous spider's web. I envisioned myself shooting down the hated Red Baron single-handedly.

Each junior officer was assigned to be "Officer-of-the-Day" at least once during the voyage. The OD was responsible to the ship's captain only and had a guard detail to work with, consisting of a corporal and sergeant of the guard plus a handful of men. I listened routinely to the daily charge of duties because I didn't wish to be embarrassed when my turn came to assume command. Little did I realize how vital the information I was nonchalantly absorbing would become.

We were two weeks out of port when enemy submarines were sighted. No action ensued, and as a matter of fact we army men didn't learn of the lurking German U-boats until the following day. The weather was mostly pleasant, and we were blessed with a succession of bright sunny days that always terminated in spectacularly colorful sunsets. I painted and sketched daily, without exception, making a valiant attempt to record all the activities taking place above and below decks and the ominous, rolling endless sea. When squalls or storms did send us below deck, I concentrated on activities such as men gambling (a crap game could last for days on end), washing their clothes, or just knocking off some sack time in their hammocks. In those crowded quarters, the poor ventilation and my intense concentration necessary on my subject matter made me prone to seasickness; hence I prospered far better on the nicer days when I could work on deck in the open air. The men were always showering or bathing in tubs on deck and proved willing models. It seems that everybody really wants to get in a picture, despite the good-natured roasting of those standing by. The gunnery crews held daily practice, and I futilely attempted to capture those red tracers in the sky. It made me reflect upon Rembrandt's observation that he wished he had a tube of "light." The army officers slept on deck and conducted language classes at the stern. Since they were deep into Italian, it was obvious that their hush-hush orders had them pegged for Sicily or Italy. They were extremely cooperative subjects, too.

The days passed, one much like another. Now and then a sleek destroyer sliced by at a crazy tilt, majestic, graceful, and downright comforting. We waved to the men aboard, they waved back, and we cheered them robustly. I continued painting and produced dozens of small watercolors and even more drawings. Despite my credentials as an "official war photographer" with all of the privileges attached, I knew little about the equipment issued so generously to me, so I shot hundreds of photos mainly for practice. In this fashion I became very comfortable with my expensive Leica (strange that it was manufactured in Germany) and kept it hanging about my neck at all times.

We tried to keep the restless men occupied by staging boxing matches, for they were getting very little exercise and were growing lethargic. If we could arouse some interest in the matches, there would be training sessions, the anticipation of subsequent wagering, and the events themselves to amuse the men. The mere anticipation worked to perfection, and enthusiasm for the program of bouts built to a fever pitch. But when the actual fights began, we discovered that the participants could weather only one-minute rounds, even in three-round matches. The men were grossly out of shape.

One stroke of good fortune befell the listless, weary soldiers. It was now October and the World Series was being played back in the States. Zinn appointed me his sports editor and reporter, making me responsible for posting the daily scores as they were received by the ship's radio. Understandably, excitement rose as the series went along, and betting was more prevalent than ever.

At last we sighted and continued through the majestic Strait of Gibralter, but while it was refreshing to see land, we knew that we were entering very dangerous waters. The rumor mill, working overtime, had us heading for Oran, North Africa, and because we were so close to land and land-based enemy aircraft, the ship's captain became jittery about lights on deck and in the passageways, and any smoking whatsoever, especially in the late afternoon and evening. We were cautioned that on a clear night a flame lighting a cigarette might be seen by a plane 50 miles away, and the seasoned captain wasn't about to reveal the position of *his* ship to the enemy. All of the ships in the convoy were zigzagging continuously to make themselves less vulnerable to submarine attack, and one night we almost collided with a massive tanker that cut crazily in front of our bow. Our ship's engines were jammed into full astern, amid whistle tooting from both vessels and frantic shouting and cursing from both crews.

When it was my turn to be the Officer-of-the-Day, finding little else to do beyond maintaining contact with my sergeant and his guard detail, I gathered my art materials and went to work painting the lovely Mediterranean Sea from a vantage point on the rear deck. The setting sun was a veritable ball of intense vermilion that thatched the turquoise sea with chunks of flaming reflections.

Then, in an instant, all hell broke loose. Dive bombers, undoubtedly German Stukas, appeared low on the horizon, streaking at us out of the sun's glare. They were upon us in seconds. The first pass missed as they flashed by to wheel and return. The noise was deafening, and for those of us receiving our indoctrination into the war, every strike seemed aimed directly at *us*. The ship rocked and continued to reverberate long after each bomb had exploded and the planes had passed by. The naval gunnery crew was pouring ack-ack high into the sky at the Jennies, seemingly floating overhead, but the heavy bombers were doing their damage. I was absolutely certain that we were going down. The corporal of the guard appeared to inform me that the ship's captain wanted me to report to him post-haste, so I hightailed it for the bridge, my art materials scattering helter-skelter. It was a damn good thing that I had become so well versed in my responsibilities, because I *knew* the captain of the ship was in full command. My baptism by fire was at hand. What had been a story heretofore, or perhaps a newsreel, a picture where someone else was involved and I was merely a spectator, had suddenly become real and I had duties to perform.

My initial orders were to "batten down the hatches" and see to it that all soldiers, enlisted men and officers, were below decks. I passed along my orders to the guard detail and tore after all of the men on deck, commanding them to get below. Then I returned to work feverishly with my little complement of men to get those damn massive hatch covers on. The bombs continued to fall, the flashes of their explosion illuminating the atmosphere, as the light of day had all but vanished. The ship was complaining bitterly as if retching in agony; it turned, rattled, and shook violently while its cannon and shell fire banged away. There was a constant roar in my ears; to make matters worse, shrapnel was pinging on the steel decks. If I hadn't had duties to perform, I would have been terrified. As it was, I was far too occupied to be frightened.

We were almost done with the hatches when enlisted men began reappearing on the deck, and I could hear the captain shouting down from the bridge to get those goddamn soldiers below where they belonged—and, he added, no damn smoking either. With the guard's help the soldiers were corralled and sent right back down passageways and ladders that others were attempting to climb. Finally they were all where the captain wanted them, and I was summoned to the bridge again. There was another problem: the army officers were clogging up the working passageways below decks and getting in the way of the ship's crew. The officers had reasoned wisely that if the ship were struck forward, they should quickly go aft, and vice versa; thus they had concluded that the best place to be was next to the bulkhead. My colorful orders were to "move their asses away from the bulkhead doors."

Before I could carry out my mission, I was literally seized by a smallish redheaded army captain who in no uncertain terms questioned my authority to make everyone stay below. When he saw that I was not about to change my viewpoint, he ordered me to report to the major in command of the military personnel. I was heading that way anyhow, so together we went below. Sure enough, the army officers were huddled against the bulkhead door.

The redheaded captain spoke first, even before the major uttered a word. "Lieutenant, the major wants those enlisted men on deck, where if we're struck they'll have at least a 50-50 chance at survival." The major interrupted, remaining remarkably calm in view of all that was taking place. He asked me why the enlisted men couldn't be on deck, and I answered that I didn't know why but had my orders and that was that; further, I had come below to see that the officers cleared the area where they were now standing. I explained that they were blocking the passage and interfering with the efficiency of the ship's crew, and that these were my orders from the captain of the ship. The major listened attentively but then repeated what the army captain had said and ordered me to allow the enlisted men on deck. I stiffly replied, "Major, sir, my orders are to see that all enlisted men and army officers are to be kept below decks, and that the army officers remove themselves from the area of the bulkhead doors since they are clogging up the passageway and causing the ship's crew distress in their work." I was calm and succinct, but there was a tremor in my voice that is omnipresent when I get into a tight spot.

The little army captain was furious and turned to me, screaming, "Lieutenant, do you realize that a major in the United States army has given you a direct order that you have refused to obey?" That did it. I seized him by the collar with both hands, both thumbs sticking hard in his throat; as he resisted, I pinned him against the bulkhead and lifted him a good foot off the deck. It effectively shut him up, for in truth he was gagging. It was my turn to scream: "One more word out of you and I'll slap you in the brig—right now."

Not another word ensued. The officers moved quietly away from the bulkhead, and the enlisted men stayed below. When I returned above, night had fallen and it was pitch black. The eerie silence was gently pierced by the short conversations of the gunnery crews at work at their posts. There was no more firing, even in the distance. It was over. Several of our convoy's ships had been damaged; five were sunk.

I went searching for the precious art materials I'd spilled on the rear deck where I had been painting when the attack began. That was two hours before; to me, so totally occupied, it was a mere moment, but it seemed like an eternity to most of the army men. Some of them reported later that they had felt like rats in one of those old-fashioned traps people used to dunk into a pail of water.

Curiously, to this day I'm not certain that Liberty ships even *had* a brig. In my distress I must have picked up that word, plus a few other phrases and maybe mannerisms, from the war movies I'd seen. As for the redheaded captain I almost strangled, I was to see him but once again, in an officer's club in Algiers. He was a proud new father then, and he offered me a cigar. Nothing was said about the incident aboard our ship.

Fred Zinn's account of the bombing appeared punctually in his daily bulletin, but it was clear that he had only a vague idea of what I had been subjected to. As I reread his pamphlet recently, I came across this passage:

> There are aboard others who might be called unwanted children as they belong neither to the large officer group nor with the troops. One of them is Lt. Reep, whom I like particularly well. By the way, he was Officer-of-the-Day yesterday and as such had the responsibility of handling guard last evening. He acquitted himself very well, particularly in one instance where he had to countermand an order of an officer who ranked him (the one I don't like) and by example contributed quite a lot toward keeping the men from running a temperature.

CHAPTER FOUR

North Africa

The following letter preceded my arrival in North Africa. It is dated 11 April 1943, or two months prior to my inclusion as a member of the art unit. A copy was provided to me in Italy, many months later, by one of my fellow artists, wisely reasoning that I might like to keep it among my memorabilia. After all, how often would a general of the armies (George Marshall) and a commanding general in the field (Dwight D. Eisenhower) take time out in the thick of a world conflict to concern themselves with a mere art project? Marshall's letter to Eisenhower is placed here to provide a background for the unexpected events to follow.

> In our recent exchange of radiograms on the subject, you indicated your approval of a proposed plan to send a group of professionally qualified artists to your theater to obtain an historical record of the war in the form of drawings, paintings and other graphic media. Such a group for your area is now being selected and its leader, Mr. George Biddle, will be sent to you by air to arrive in the latter part of the month. Mr. Biddle is both an artist and the Chairman of the Advisory Committee which is assisting the War Department in the planning of this work.
>
> The project as a whole has been placed under the charge of the Chief of Engineers, who requests that if consistent with your headquarters organization the unit be attached to the Engineer section of your special staff for administration and supply.
>
> It is requested that Mr. Biddle and his unit be provided with adequate facilities and opportunities and accorded latitude commensurate with the military situation; and that their work be forwarded from time to time as completed to the Chief of Engineers.

After safely debarking at Oran—a Mediterranean seaport in northwest Algeria—and getting the feel of solid terrain under my feet, I almost felt like a full-fledged war artist. It mattered little to me that the war in North Africa had ended, or that for the next few days I would simply wallow in the mud of the camp while awaiting assignment. The art materials and photo equipment I carried in my personal gear were sufficient to allow me to function in a limited fashion, which was probably just as well. It would be far better to begin modestly; when the rest of my supplies arrived I'd be fully prepared to tackle more ambitious things. Nevertheless, I was terribly anxious to begin and strained against the inevitable, typical, exasperating delays. Then I learned that the ship carrying the bulk of my art supplies and all that wonderful, sophisticated equipment issued to me back in Brooklyn, had been sunk in the Mediterranean when we were attacked by the Luftwaffe. I had no idea if or when replenishments would be forthcoming. With my grand plan a bit cracked and in jeopardy, I returned to shooting photographs and producing small watercolors similar to those I had done on shipboard.

We were assigned to tents in a muddy field that seemed surrounded by outdoor latrines. Hordes of soldiers were being "processed" for new assignments, each requiring appropriate equipment. My new orders finally arrived, so I lugged my gear to one of the waiting boxcars that formed a quaint and colorful train. The cars were the famous World War I "40-and-eights," having derived their affectionate title from the fact that each car carried 40 men and eight horses. We rattled along over the bleak North African land, stopping often and for interminable periods of time, which gave the soldiers an opportunity to barter with natives who clustered eagerly about, anxious to peddle their wares.

Two very unpleasant experiences befell me at that time. One was a bout with dysentery just prior to boarding the train; I had to be carried to the field hospital, doubled up with my knees pressed hard against my chest. The second involved the trading and bartering by soldiers aboard the "40-and-eights," which gave me a glimpse of the ruthless yet understandable behavior of military troops in a foreign land.

At every stop I'd whip out my sketch pad and attempt something. I had no way of determining how long a stop would last, and no one else seemed to know either. I'd simply work away until the shrill whistles warned that we would soon be on our way. I also discovered that I could keep working until the train started to move, for it took so long to get going that a fast walk could overtake it. The natives, especially any number of officials in tasseled red fezzes and resplendent blue uniforms, served as willing and exotic models. They lent welcome accents of color to the barren landscape.

Meanwhile, the wheeling and dealing was taking place at every boxcar door. We would grind to a halt in what appeared to be a vast wasteland with nary a soul in sight; then suddenly, as if by magic, the natives swarmed about us. Nearly all of them wore dramatic *jalabas*, large white robes made of lightly woven fabric that hung loosely from their shoulders and scraped the ground. Under this outer garment they carried their life's possessions, neatly concealed from view. Their myriad trinkets held great appeal for the soldiers anxious to send something home to their sweethearts or family. The Arabs' robes were jokingly referred to as "mattress covers," which I thought humorous until I discovered how they possibly acquired their name. All of us had been issued new mattress covers back at Oran, and now they were being used as a principal bartering item, since it was common knowledge that they were coveted by the Arabs. The fact that soldiers had no legal right to use their government-issue equipment in this fashion wasn't about to stop the lively action. As a consequence, as we neared Algiers, this hot commodity was mysteriously disappearing from the boxcars.

Recognizing that their precious supply was dwindling, some of the men initiated a cruel prank designed to fleece the natives. They timed their transactions so finely that the actual handing over of the bartered goods would coincide with the departure of the train. The haggling could be dragged on and on if need be and thereby easily controlled. As the train began to move and as native and soldier alike kept one hand on his merchandise and the other on his customer's—the Arab walking faster as the train gathered momentum—the bartering grew desperate. Then the soldier, never relinquishing his frim grip on the lengthy fabric and in perfect harmony with the accelerating speed, would ruthlessly jerk back both articles, leaving the startled native empty-handed. It was a contemptible act, and as an American I felt deeply ashamed.

Little did I suspect that awaiting my arrival in Algiers would be the devastating news that the Congress of the United States of America had eliminated the budget for the art program. Civilian artists stranded in various theaters of operation were to be sent home, while soldier-artists would be reassigned to military duty: "Edward A. Reep . . . letter orders 12th June 43 corrected to assign officer permanent station your JQRS for duties which will be appropriate to his qualifications and training . . . was military artist under war art project, which has terminated." The entire art budget amounted to a mere $125,000, a pittance contrasted with the $77 million appropriation from which it was being carved. I was distraught.

In Algiers, without assignment, I was billeted with other officers in an unusual structure, possibly a quaint old home turned into an office building and now serving as sleeping quarters for a foreign army. Everything was makeshift, with beds simply jammed alongside one another. We were so terribly cramped that our equipment had to be stored under our beds, but at least we were under roof and dry, and enjoyed the unique advantage of indoor toilet facilities. (My bewilderment at the bidet was typical of most American soldiers who had never seen the darn things before.)

I was about to be treated to my first taste of real human suffering in warfare, for I was not only bunking with fresh recruits from the States but with wounded, suffering men returning from action. Even the furious dive bombing at sea with all of its frightening aspects hadn't brought me to grips with bloodshed or agony.

The aviator sleeping next to me had been shot down in a flaming plane, and how he survived is one of those miracles that defy explanation. He was sound in mind and body save for his eyes, which had been severely burned into a cruel open state. Unable to move what remained of his eyelids, in order to sleep he covered his anguished, reddened eyes with soft damp pads. Yet I never once heard him complain, and though we held endless conversations I never asked what had happened. I must have assumed that he didn't want to talk about it. I came away with the distinct impression that he felt lucky to have survived and to be on his way home.

On 24 October 1943 my brief career as an artist-correspondent appeared to be over with my assignment to the publications division of the Psychological Warfare Branch (PWB), Allied Forces Headquarters in Algiers, there to commence work not as a painter but as a commercial artist. I did my best to bury my pride and dig into the new task ahead.

Without changing billets, I walked to work daily in the relative calm of the early morning. At that hour before the shops were open, the streets of Algiers were empty of people and vehicles, and I welcomed the tranquillity as a respite from the crowded, tumultuous conditions that existed during business hours. I poked along surveying everything in sight, enjoying my introduction to a foreign land and grateful that I'd studied French, the principal language of Algeria, in high school.

The vast majority of the buildings along the way seemed to be rooted deep into the earth, their quasi-basements lining the sidewalks. The walls of the ground floors were inordinately thick in the manner of early European churches and castles. Light reached the basements through recessed subterranean windows that allowed passing pedestrians to peer into them. The windows caught my eye because they appeared to have been literally carved out of the massive walls that framed them.

One morning I happened upon a pathetic situation. In one of these window niches a native girl lay curled up, asleep and stark naked; she couldn't have been more than 14 or 15 years old. I had never experienced anything remotely close to this in America and was startled and perplexed. Why was she sleeping outside in the cold damp atmosphere? The nights could be as frigid as the days were hot, and she had apparently spent the night there. Could she be an orphan or a runaway? Had she been abandoned? Was she deranged? My heart bled for her, but what could I do?

I hurried on, too embarrassed to stop, turning to look back only to reassure myself that what I had witnessed was real. I noted that the child was very pretty with dark black hair tumbling around her rich reddish-brown face and shoulders. Although she seemed slender, she didn't appear to be malnourished or starving.

Upon arriving at the PWB offices I phoned the police and reported what I had seen, careful to pinpoint the location. I offered a full description of the young lady with expectation that they might possess some measure of history on her. I implored them to investigate and do something to rectify this horrible inhuman situation; they assured me they would attend to the matter immediately and thanked me for my interest and concern. I returned to my work, now much delayed, but felt better about myself and the world I lived in.

The following morning the poor little waif lay asleep in the same place, the identical window where I had seen her the day before. I phoned the police again. Perhaps, I reasoned, they had failed to find her yesterday and were awaiting this morning to try again. But for several days thereafter I found the forlorn child asleep in that window or another nearby. She was always nude and, I concluded, homeless. Then she disappeared and I was to see no more of her, although the vision of her will never leave my consciousness.

My superior officer and head of the Algerian branch of PWB was Captain John Ferren who, unbeknownst to me at the time, was a fairly well-recognized American painter in the contemporary idiom. I knew him only as my boss, and we had few conversations. A rather distinguished-looking fellow with thinning reddish-blond hair but sporting a full and terribly British red mustache, he was having a whale of a good time with an attractive young lady in the British army. Years later, when I was a member of the Art Center School faculty in Los Angeles, John was hired one summer as a resident artist. We established a marvelous rapport, laughing as we exchanged our private stories of the war. It was evident that he had enjoyed not allowing me to know that he too was a painter, for in Algiers in the fall of 1943 my career as an artist was only beginning, and I hadn't built any reputation among artists. I suspect that John felt we had very little in common at that time.

My immediate superior was a likable character named George Krikorian. "Krik" was a short swarthy man, energetic and very astute. A camera, his trademark, hung around his neck at all times, and he was a genius in relying upon it in every phase of his work, even illustrations. I can't recall that he drew or painted anything, for with scissors in hand he could cut up and reassemble photographs into the most creative arrangements imaginable. Krik had been art director for the *New York Times* and as a consequence enjoyed a fine reputation as a first-rate professional. He knew how to work with people and extracted the most out of me. Under his wing I did all of the hand-lettering, drawing, and painting for the unit.

We worked in relatively primitive conditions. If I did a large painting or illustration, it would be transferred to an enormous lithographic stone by hand, in preparation for reproduction. Skilled native craftsmen swarmed about these giant stone slabs, working on their hands and knees on sandy floors, since the stones weighed hundreds of pounds and were far too heavy to manipulate. The results were fantastically faithful.

We were engaged in producing propaganda to be read by our enemies and the civilian populations of occupied countries. For the most part, our production consisted of small leaflets to be dropped from airplanes, initially over France, Sicily, and Italy. The more elaborate posters would be used to encourage peasants to continue farming and at the same time reassure them that the Allies were on the way. At times we were merely trying to cement relations, to let them know that we stood in admiration of their accomplishments and their heroes. For example, we did a leaflet attesting to the high esteem Americans felt for the renowned Italian conductor Arturo Toscanini. In a very positive sense we were attempting to build good will among Italians for the approaching American, British, and Australian soldiers. One leaflet I particularly liked working on dealt with Australia. On one side was an outline drawing of the Australian flag, with directions in Italian for children to color in the appropriate shapes with red and blue. The reverse illustrated and briefly described various animals—such as the emu and the koala bear—and Australian aborigines. Any child would have been fascinated.

We also produced a brochure publicizing the speeches of Stalin, Churchill, and Franklin D. Roosevelt. This document was entitled "Trois Discours" and was targeted for France. Other leaflets were designed to encourage Italian and German soldiers to surrender; these mere scraps of paper would serve as "safe conduct" passes. Another read "Die Hiemat Braucht Dich" (your homeland needs you) and was ticketed for the Wehrmacht. We posed a French woman holding an Arab child for the illustration, and I lettered the caption in Old English. We were trying to make the leaflet appear very German, hoping to make Jerry homesick enough to desert his ranks or just worry him to all get out by reminding him of his loved ones. That's about as rotten as we got.

On the other hand, the German propagandists poured out predictably consistent pornography and outright lies in an attempt to terrorize Allied soldiers or turn one against another. If ever an American soldier needed reassurance that we were far more civilized and honorable than our enemy, he had only to compare propaganda leaflets. The German leaflets were suffused with sex, bigotry, and deceit: all Allied leaders were corrupt Jews, notably politicians and bankers; Negroes and Jews at home were sleeping with our sweethearts and wives while we were engaged in a useless, futile war where we would needlessly die in battle.

We ought to surrender at once and avail ourselves of the generous, caring, lovable protection afforded by the Jerries, who were prepared to place us in comfortable detention camps to ride out the conflict in safety. This would occur under the rules of war established by the Geneva convention, which would be dutifully observed. Photos of British and American prisoners of war were reproduced as evidence to one and all that they were happy and productive, exercising and playing games, and well fed and safe. After all, the supermen would inevitably be the victors, so why prolong our agony or risk death?

The stupidity and arrogance of the technically ingenious German surfaced once again. The stuff backfired. In their fervent appeals to the American soldiers, in particular, the Germans had employed British advisors—but British spelling and phraseology is a virtual foreign language to an Iowa or Carolina farm boy, and when purported to be written by a contented American prisoner of war, it fell like a lead balloon. They used current film stars such as Loretta Young to symbolize our wives and girlfriends, the ideal American beauty, whose portrait had obviously been spirited from a Chevrolet advertisement. The ploy was thoroughly transparent.

If the Jerries had had an inkling of the effect of their propaganda on the American forces, they could have saved considerable time, effort, and expense. For example, the "Georgia" series consisted of six separate leaflets which revealed a showgirl, unquestionably taken from a German cabaret, in various stages of undress. By the time she had been maneuvered about, retouched, and reconstructed, she bore little resemblance to an American woman; nevertheless, she was supposed to agonize our boys by making them homesick and hungry for female companionship and a warm bed. But instead of causing the deep suffering the Germans contemplated, the leaflets entertained and amused us. Also, they gave us something to do. Anyone familiar with the American psyche knows we are inveterate collectors. It matters little what the item is; we collect beer cans, baseball cards, and cigar bands as well as stamps and coins; worthless or valuable—who cares? No sooner did the Georgia leaflets flutter to earth then we were running about gleefully yelling, "I've got two Georgia No. 5s—anyone got an extra No. 3?"

German propaganda asserted further that our leaders were gangsters and cutthroats who were misleading the common man and operating for

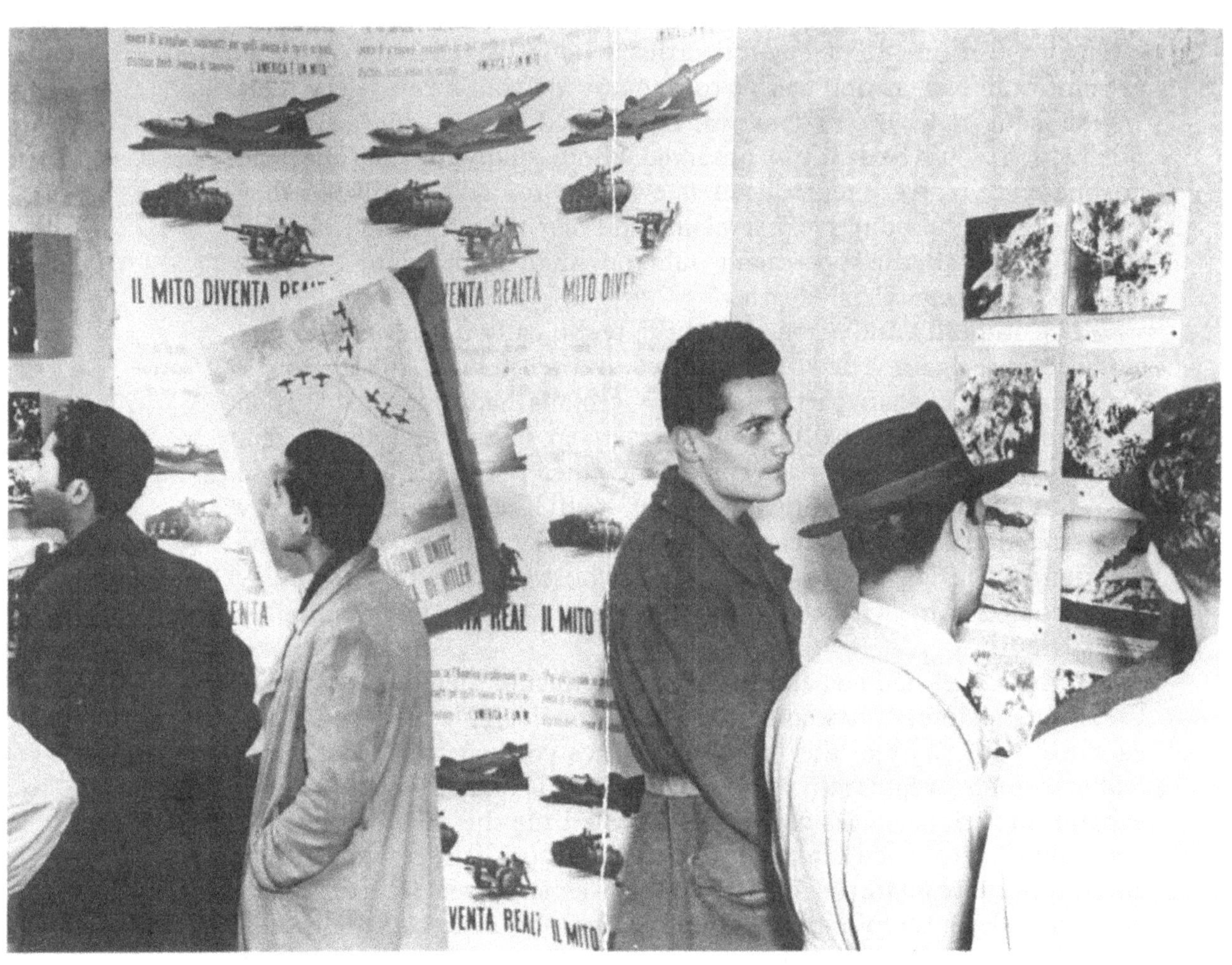

Italians browse in a Roman shop filled with Allied propaganda leaflets and posters, some designed by me. This was an effective way to let the populace learn more about the Allied forces, our intentions, and, at the same time, what would be expected of them—a nation in defeat.

personal gain, but the argument was so oversimplified that in no way could it be taken seriously. In our counterpropaganda it became relatively simple to expose German lies with factual evidence, often in the form of photographs that could be substantiated. The maniacal utterances of Adolf Hitler kept us amply supplied with new and effective ideas. I did one large poster based upon Der Fuehrer's speech delivered over Radio Tedesca to the Italian populace on 28 September 1942. Hitler had boasted, "America might as well produce umbrellas as airplanes, pincushions as armored cars, and toothpicks as cannons." Then he arrogantly added, "America is a myth." Beneath those words on our poster I painted a most formidable-looking superfortress airplane, Sherman tank, and artillery cannon. Across the bottom of the poster, under the ominous pictures and in very large, bold capitals, I carefully hand-lettered "IL MITO DIVENTA REALTÀ" (the myth becomes a reality). I was fighting the war furiously with my paintbrush. Oh, how I detested that crazy son-of-a-bitch.

Soon we turned to even more vivid and painfully obvious subjects, such as the continuing German retreats and casualties in Russia. The tide of battle swung over to the Russian "winter soldiers" concurrently with the increased Allied bombing of Germany and the waning attacks upon Great Britain. The simple graphics of our tiny leaflets sent chills up our backs; it was plain that the total annihilation of German industry and major cities was only a matter of time.

The poster that gave me the greatest sense of gratification was devoid of violence. It simply encouraged the Italian peasant farmers to continue to work their land. The caption read, "Italiani! Il Cibo E Un Arma Per La Vittoria" (food is a weapon for victory). When we finally invaded Italy and had an opportunity to tour the great cities, we discovered Italians excitedly milling about shops where my posters were abundantly displayed, digesting every word and carefully scrutinizing every illustration. There was little doubt that our propaganda leaflets had been effective.

CHAPTER FIVE

The Art Program Is Saved

In early December of 1943, during a routine day at the Psychological Warfare Branch, I received a message to report to General Eisenhower's headquarters first thing the following morning. Bright and early the next day, brimming with excitement, I waited impatiently in the corridor outside of the general's office. Ike soon appeared, running up and down the hall vigorously and stopping abruptly to execute a neat sit-up or two; he was dutifully carrying out his daily program of calisthenics in the tradition of all well-trained soldiers. As quickly as he had appeared, he vanished, and a colonel stood in his place, beckoning me to enter the outer office; the general would be with me in a moment or two, he said. I was not only filled with anticipation and nervous as all get out but terribly perplexed and just a wee bit frightened. Why in the world was I here? What did this important, busy man want to see me about? My mind raced.

I was certainly fond of General Eisenhower; that was a plus. I admired him as we admire our favorite actors and sports heroes. In person, however, things could be different. Would he measure up to the lofty standards I had accorded him? I had little idea of how luminaries might behave in their private moments or behind the scenes, and not one shred of evidence as to the general's private attitude toward society. He couldn't be a hypocrite—could he? The hell with it, I'd soon find out.

Sitting there anxiously, I recalled my goofy experiences with the only famous person I'd met, Orson Welles, and his intention to take credit for my work. But Ike seemed pleasant enough in his public appearances, smiling, confident—someone you could respect and trust. He had already made a smash hit with the soldiers in North Africa by countermanding General Patton's unrealistic orders that all members of the armed forces wear thick black ties in sweltering heat. Added to the five layers of fabric in our shirt collars, the ties meant no less than eight layers drawn tightly about our necks. To worsen matters, we watched the British soldiers moving about in relative comfort wearing open-collared short-sleeved shirts and walking shorts. Ike's immediate orders were to remove the ties and unbutton the collars.

The colonel reappeared and led me into the general's spacious office. On a smallish table near the door lay numerous papers spread out for my examination. I tendered my most polished salute as the general strolled toward me. "Lieutenant Reep" (my God, he knew my name!), he simultaneously inquired and ordered, not waiting for a reply, "we're reestablishing the art program with army artists only. The civilians are going home. Now—there are five artists awaiting assignment, and there will be five divisions going into Italy. You will head up the group, pick a division, and assign each of the others to a division." Obviously, rank was the sole determinant (I was the only officer-artist at the time; the others were sergeants); certainly experience had nothing to do with my new role of responsibility.

I looked over the names of the other artists; I knew none of them personally. Next I scanned the list of divisions: the 45th, 34th, 3rd, and 36th Infantry and the 1st Armored. I chose the armored division for myself for two reasons: it would prove distinctive, and I hated to walk. Without hesitation or reason, I distributed the other names. When I looked up, General Eisenhower was gone. The colonel thanked me and ushered me out. Once in the hall, I had all I could do to keep from shouting and jumping for joy. I was once again a real artist-correspondent, and I loved the title. Filled with exultation, I raced back to spread the good news among my colleagues at PWB.

Special orders reassigning me to Headquarters, 1st Armored Division, were issued on 7 December 1943. On this same date two years earlier, General Stilwell had commissioned me to paint murals for the soldiers' club in Monterey, California. For numerologists or those who simply believe in lucky numbers, the most infamous date in American history, Pearl Harbor Day, was my lucky number.

Orders flew thick and fast after that. The army had taken command of a raft of artists and had little idea of what to do with them. The Engineers had originally been responsible for the artists, but all that changed with our assignment to the various division headquarters. Finally it was concluded that although we were bona fide members of fighting divisions, we would be placed on "detached service" and *attached* to Headquarters, Fifth Army Historical Section. It was all very complicated but in time worked out very well. Whereas Secretary of War Stimson had originally given his blessing and clout to the art project, Congress may have tied Stimson's hands, but Generals Marshall and Eisenhower were now in command and fully responsible, and when they gave orders to the military, those orders were carried out pronto. For example, a memo emanating from Ike's desk, dated 10 December 1943, included instructions to "draft letter to CG Fifth Army (with assistance and concurrence Engr, AFHQ) informing him that these men are being sent out at the personal direction of General EISENHOWER for the purpose set forth in attached memo." Note the capitalization of the general's name. Things were beginning to fall into place.

The "attached memo," written in longhand on what was labeled an informal routing slip, was sent along by R.H. Burrage, a colonel in the Corps of Engineers. He too was taking no chances with this thing failing, and dropped a couple of names into the hopper.

> Lieut. Reep will show you a letter which tells the story of the present status of the War Dept. Art Project.
>
> Lt. Reep will need some advice and assistance as to how he may have some boxes of art equipment shipped to and stored in Naples, and possibly also in arranging for a little space where the 5 artists may work as they get opportunities to get back from the front. The project has the interest and support of the Sec. of War and of Gen. Reybold.
>
> Any assistance you can give Lieut. Reep and T/Sgt. Siporin in reaching their Divisions will be appreciated.

To complete the cycle of good news, the bulk of my painting materials, thought sunk with the Liberty ship in the Mediterranean, were discovered floating off African shores, rescued, and safely delivered to me when I reached Naples. They had been superbly packed in air-tight, waterproof containers totally saturated with Cosmoline, a petroleum grease.

Upon arriving in Naples, I immediately reported to my new commanding officer, Colonel John D. Forsythe, and received a "chewing-out" in the finest tradition of the military. What in hell did I do to deserve this, I thought. Who was this old goat? A year or so later, after Colonel Forsythe and I had become warm friends, I asked him what had prompted that riproaring indoctrination. "I chew out every shavetail when I first meet them," he replied. The dressing-down was only a small part of the major plan to let new lieutenants know how lowly they were in the echelon of officers.

On the night of 9 September 1943, Colonel Forsythe had led the 142d Infantry Regiment of the 36th Division onto the beaches of Salerno, where his men faced bitter resistance from seasoned German soldiers. The battle seesawed for days. Forsythe was a tough old army regular yet was shortly removed from his command—perhaps deemed too old for the assignment—and reassigned to head up the Fifth Army Historical Section to which we artists would be attached on a temporary basis.

Forsythe held artists in low regard when first we met, calling us "ham-and-eggers" when he initially bawled me out. Coming from California, I knew that the "Townsend Plan," a pre–Social Security proposal that had failed, was considered by men like Forsythe to be a system where freeloaders, referred to as ham-and-eggers, could live luxuriously in a welfare state. To its detractors, this California-bred pension plan was a menace to all of society. The colonel had concluded that all artists were lazy and useless, and now he was saddled with a gaggle of them. Much to his credit, he must have apologized for that absurd notion about a dozen times. Maybe the bitterness of being relieved of his command had not at the outset fully vanished from his mind; he had to have been deeply scarred.

Colonel Forsythe was all army and crusty as dry toast. Miscast in his new role as the leader of a bunch of writers and artists, he struck me as being bewildered at first. Since we were pea green, too, and had our own hurdles to get over, we began our work in polite harmony. Whatever the colonel's disappointments or frustrations, he knew how the army functioned in peace and war; as a consequence, he quickly organized his historians and artists into an efficient unit.

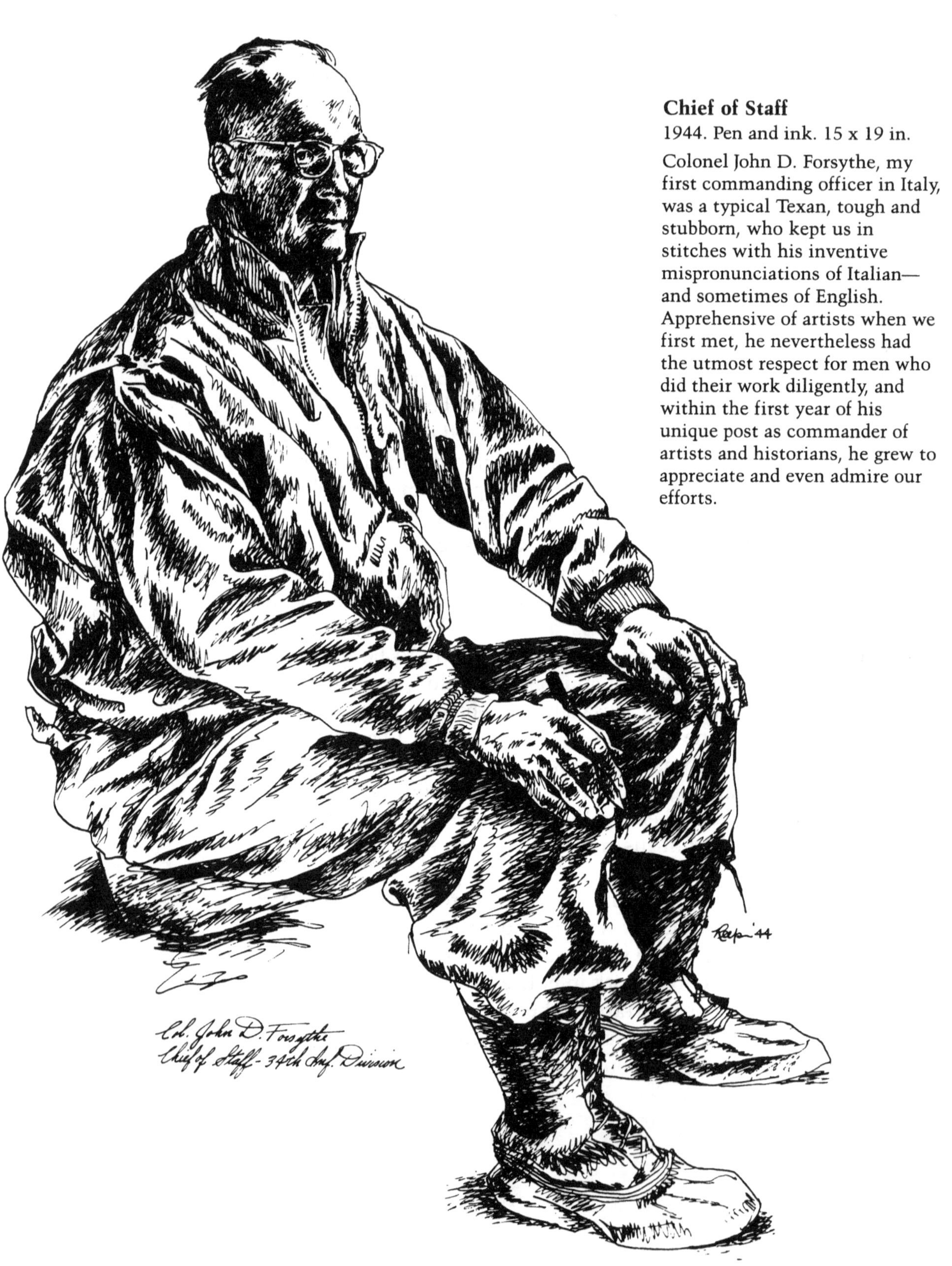

Chief of Staff

1944. Pen and ink. 15 x 19 in.

Colonel John D. Forsythe, my first commanding officer in Italy, was a typical Texan, tough and stubborn, who kept us in stitches with his inventive mispronunciations of Italian—and sometimes of English. Apprehensive of artists when we first met, he nevertheless had the utmost respect for men who did their work diligently, and within the first year of his unique post as commander of artists and historians, he grew to appreciate and even admire our efforts.

My first official act would win the colonel's favor, but in no sense of the word was it done for that reason. One of the four artists in my charge, Rudolph C. Von Ripper, had long since become a proven fighting soldier and artist. Although he was technically under my wing, I had little control, if any, of his movements. Nor was it necessary. "Rip" was a one-man army in himself, having fought in several wars, soldiered and painted with the 34th Infantry, and been wounded in Sicily. Only upon occasion would he report back to the Historical Section to deliver work, to visit, or to see what the rest of us were doing. It was due to my having met Von Ripper and been impressed by tales of his dangerous missions that I vowed to do something similar right away. Hence, the first time I got my hands on a jeep, I tore wildly toward the front lines.

Maybe I was young and foolish, even ambitious. Nevertheless, I was accustomed to painting outdoors and on location and was eager to get going. The other three artists seemed content to work indoors in makeshift studios that at one time must have been elegant Neapolitan apartments, but I couldn't get started there without subject matter. When I finally made arrangements to get a jeep and drive up to the front lines, it wasn't particularly surprising to find that the others had little enthusiasm for my preposterous notion. Somehow I managed to talk the most unlikely of them all, Mitchell Siporin, into accompanying me. As we drove along Mitch asked me where we were going, as if my announcement back at the Naples studio was in jest. I answered that I wasn't really certain, but I just simply wanted to get up front. Soon we heard artillery fire growing louder and more intense. Mitch panicked—"What the hell are you doing? Let's get the hell out of here!" He was trembling with fright. Today I realize that his responses were more natural than mine, for I had no idea what I was doing. On that day, we did turn back, and maybe it was just as well. I was probably scared as hell too and simply putting up a brave front. Mitch never ventured near the front lines again; violence was totally antithetical to everything he revered. Despite this he contributed many noteworthy paintings and even more elaborate drawings that dealt with his perceptions of soldiers in rest areas, their relationships with the Italians, and the plight of our often homeless and hungry "hosts."

I immediately returned to the front, however, this time unaccompanied. My first painting depicted a group of infantrymen from the 3rd

Division heating up some coffee while seeking protection in a giant shell crater. They were dressed in those heavy woolen GI overcoats so common in the early going, and they were dirty, tired, and unshaven. The landscape about them was virtually barren save for the blackened, leafless trees that I soon discovered were a trademark of the battlefield. In the near distance lay the shell-torn town of Mignano couched against Monte Rotondo, both key objectives of the early fighting in Italy.

I went on to San Vittore, where a fierce battle had ensued. There I found a German machine-gun position, sat in it, and imagined the enemy vainly trying to prevent the Americans from advancing up the street it overlooked. Bursting with curiosity, I examined with great care everything that was left of the machine-gun nest, not even remotely conscious of the possibility that it could have been booby-trapped. Fortunately for me, the Germans had been blown out of the place, and those who were not wounded or killed had departed in such haste that they'd had no time to set a trap. After completing the painting, I gathered grim souvenirs of the scene, to the awe of my colleagues. I would learn my real battlefield lessons later. Meanwhile, either my innocence or my naiveté allowed me to do some very foolish things and come away scot-free.

When I returned to the Historical Section with my first two efforts, Colonel Forsythe was ecstatic. Now he had two artists at the front, Von Ripper and me. Since Rip was rarely about, I became the colonel's connection with the battle he savored. I really wasn't in any position to give orders to the other artists even if I had wanted to, so Forsythe found plenty for them to do in the wake of the fighting, and I was relieved of that concern. Meanwhile, he had gained full trust in me, and in turn I became devoted to the "old man"—an army term used only when one has full respect for a commanding officer. After the war we exchanged Christmas letters until his death in 1980. The only times I disliked Colonel Forsythe were those when he'd challenge me (it was a virtual order) to a round of cribbage during the late evening hours. He loved the game, hated to lose, and—in order to make certain that he would win—loaded my canteen cup with gin. Many a night I left his tent dead drunk and a big loser.

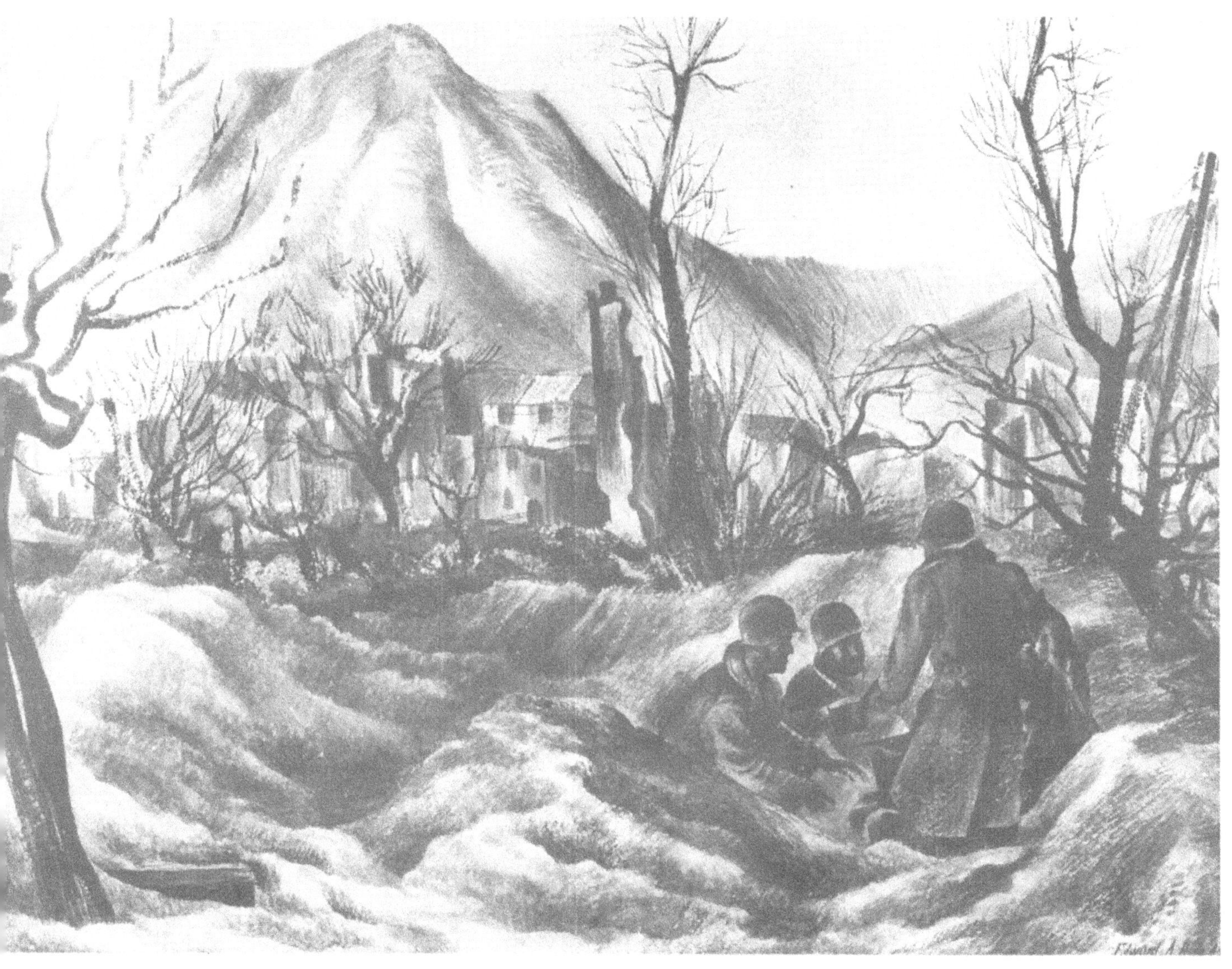

Coffee Break

1944. Watercolor. 13 x 19 in.

Soldiers stop in a shell crater for a hot cup of coffee. Mignano and Monte Rotondo are seen in the distance. The dugout at the lower left was formerly occupied by men of an artillery unit. This painting was executed during my early days in Italy, when all was new and I was familiarizing myself with the image of the battlefield primarily by studying its wake.

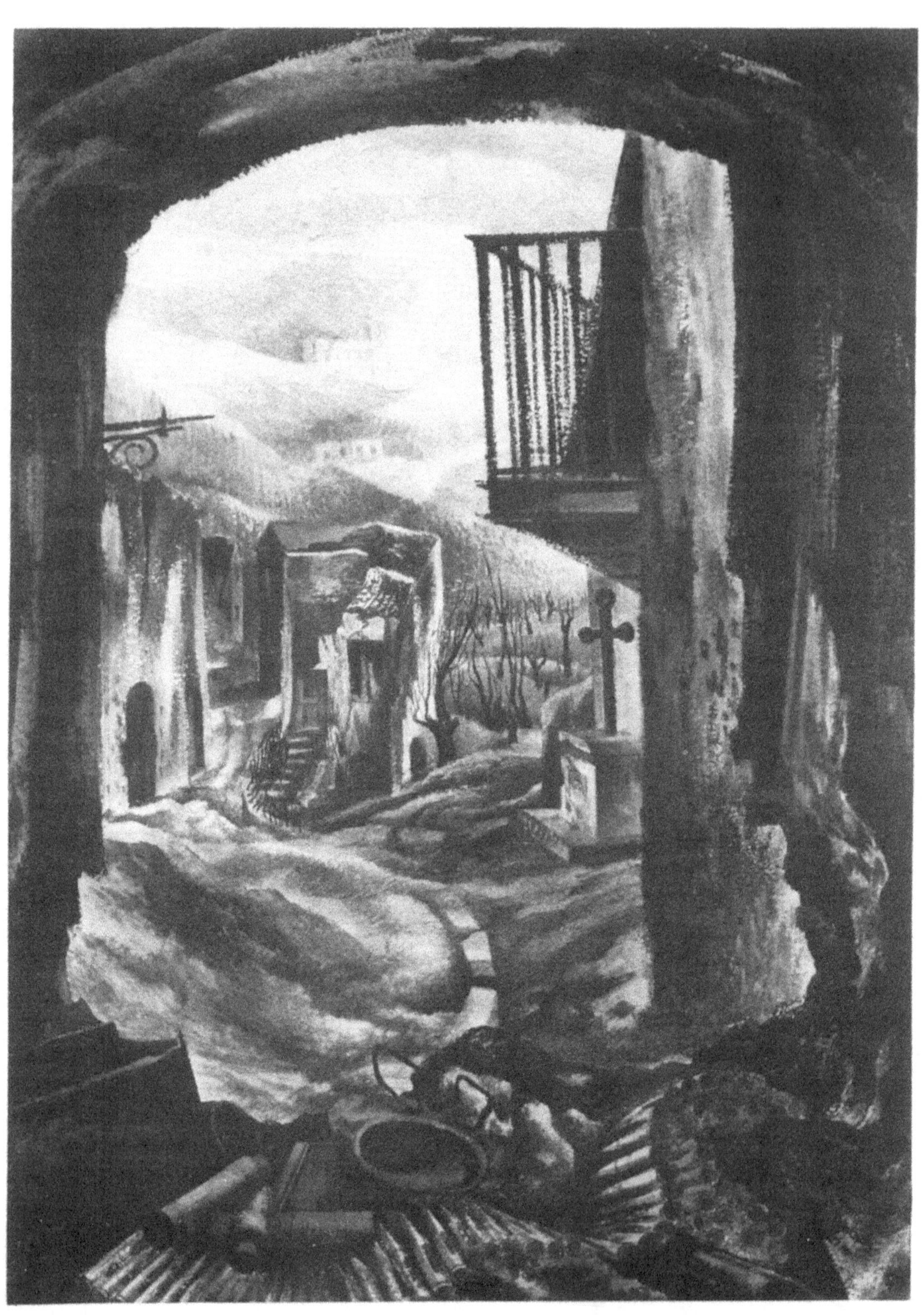

A Machine Gun Position

1944. Watercolor. 16¾ x 22¾ in.

According to the official army caption, a Jerry machine gunner was eliminated by a hand grenade thrown by a member of the 36th Division, and I then occupied the position of the gunner and painted this view as seen from the wine cellar he had occupied. I'm not certain, however, when the fighting took place at this precise location; it could have been days earlier. Raw, inexperienced, and very impressionable, I did sit in that nest and envision the oncoming troops. The German canteen cup, shells, and other scattered equipment gave evidence of the grenade's explosion, but as far as I was concerned, I was fighting the battle right then and there.

CHAPTER SIX

The Artists

The original group of artists that came together in Naples was composed of Master Sergeant Mitchell Siporin, Technical Sergeants Savo Radulovic and Frank D. Duncan, Lieutenant Rudolf C. Von Ripper (he had been promoted to second lieutenant for his outstanding service on the battlefield), and me. Technical Sergeants Ludwig Mactarian and Harry Davis joined us about a year later. I want to tell you about all of them in order to present a clearer picture of what different combat artists do, particularly in view of their varied backgrounds, ages, and persuasions.

Rudolf C. Von Ripper was our senior member in terms of age and experience. He was the ultimate soldier-artist in World War II, and possibly in all of recorded history. Born in 1905 in Klausenburg, Austria, he was the son of Edward Maria Von Ripper, general in the Austrian army, and Clara, Baroness Von Salis-Samaden. He was thoroughly educated and traveled, a linguist, scholar, soldier, and artist of note; his versatility as a combat artist is unparalleled. Some readers may look askance at that bold statement, especially those acquainted with the monumental depictions of one battle or another during the Renaissance or work from the earlier Oriental dynasties. But with all due respect to the gamut of paintings pertaining to warfare throughout history, I know of no other artist who was both a consummate draughtsman and at the same time a fearless and effective warrior.

In his book *Brave Men*, Ernie Pyle says of Von Ripper, "He was so fabulous, a man might have been justified in thinking him a phony until he got to know him." Pyle devotes over three full pages to Rip's exploits as a fighting man, in several wars.* But Pyle, as a layman in art, cannot

*Ernie Pyle, *Brave Men* (New York: Holt, 1944), 138-40.

fully attest to Von Ripper's brilliance as a draughtsman and painter.

Meeting Rip was an event all by itself. By the time he officially reported in to the Historical Section in Naples, he had been hit by four enemy machine pistol slugs, in his upper lip, hand, fingers, and shoulder. Since his lip was now malfunctioning, he drooled constantly and spoke with a lisp. One eye was already useless from an injury in an earlier war, and there he stood as living proof of the many wild tales he loved to tell. He was no shrinking violet, that was certain. If you liked him, as I did, his adventures were fascinating and most often narrated with an ingenious ploy to prevent his appearing vain: he would brag in great detail about the difficulties and risks of a particular mission, always referring to an accomplice as he glorified man and deed. Only as a tagline would he add, "And I did it too." In this quaint way Rip held his listeners' attention without arousing a shred of envy, and our admiration swelled.

Anyway, envy was out of the question; there was only one Von Ripper, and how in the world could anyone begin to emulate his life? His family was titled, which made him a baron right off the bat. As a teenager he had fled home to take jobs in the sawmills, as a garbage collector, a coal miner, and a performing clown in the circus. At 14 he took up arms with the German youth in an attempt to prevent further crimes on the part of the defeated armies returning home from World War I. Before he was 20, he had volunteered for the French Foreign Legion and was wounded in action. In 1936 he was a gunner in the Spanish Loyalist Air Force; his plane, along with his entire squadron, was shot down and his leg riddled with 16 bullets, yet he lived to crawl away from the wreckage. In all, he had been wounded in combat some 20 times.

Von Ripper's life alternated between painting and getting into the thick of battle; more simply, he was an artist and a soldier. He had been educated at a Jesuit school in Vienna and a humanistic gymnasium in Salzburg and had studied art at the Art Academy in Dusseldorf, Germany, and privately in Paris. Leaving Austria in 1938 after recognizing the futility of resisting the Nazis, he fled to America and within five years became a citizen. Too old for the World War II draft and soundly rejected by the regular army, he wangled his way into service via the Red Cross as a litter bearer. Ultimately, this led to his acceptance into the army as a hospital laboratory technician; later still, he was transferred to the army's art program and sent to North Africa as a combat artist.

I didn't know Rip in North Africa but played a minor role in his life by leaving him assigned to the 34th Division that morning in General Eisenhower's office. Though I was unaware of his record at the time, he had already proved invaluable as an interrogator in Sicily. In Naples, where I first met the fabulous man, he had produced some striking paintings and sketches and, while recuperating from wounds suffered in Sicily, was setting to work in the relative calm of our rear area quarters, to develop them into more elaborate works. I was in awe of him. Even the titles of his paintings were intriguing; "And the Earth Bled of a Thousand Wounds" was, in my estimation, the most spectacular. His pen-and-ink drawings were like jewels, virtual masterpieces that could hold their own against much of the greatest art. I felt more than ever the neophyte and wondered if the time would come when I could rival such magnificent work.

Since Von Ripper was highly educated, extremely cunning, and daring, one would imagine him to be terribly serious. Yet he possessed a lighter side, and he and I always found time to horse around. He was 39 and looked, in my eyes, closer to 89, beaten around the edges as he was. (Ernie Pyle thought he looked younger, but Ernie was older than Rip, and that explains a lot.) I worked alongside Pyle briefly in Caserta, Italy, where he sat in bed, drinking heavily, while he ground out his tales. Pyle looked to me like a man going on 200 and Von Ripper resembled a beaten-up antique—but then, I was only 25.

I used to infuriate Rip because I was physically much stronger. He was always testing those around him, accenting his narratives with good-natured slaps and jabs that invariably led to shoving and light jostling. When I'd had enough, I'd wrestle him to the ground and sit on him. He'd turn beet red and curse me—the expression that always broke me up was "stchoopid idiot." When someone blurts that out with a perpetually drooling lip and gutteral accent, the result can be disastrous; you had better get out of the way or risk being sprayed.

During intellectual discussions of war strategy and a thousand other things, Rip displayed his brilliance. He spoke fluent French, Italian, Spanish, and German—the last in all dialects, which allowed him to be enormously effective on patrols into enemy territory and again in later interrogation. His English, while solid in sentence structure and vocabulary, was virtually extruded from that misshapen mouth and at times difficult to understand. I'd caution him to speak more clearly and improve his enunciation, pointing out that for a member of the United States Army his speech was disgraceful, but despite the fact that he knew I was ribbing him, he'd call me a stchoopid idiot again, waving his arms frantically and pushing me around. That's when I'd take him down and sit on him again—and we'd laugh.

Rip was stubborn like no other person I have ever known, which brings me to one final story about him. Rip enjoyed a deep friendship with a character all fighting men knew as "Stan the Doughnut Man." Stan worked for the Red Cross, delivering doughnuts and hot coffee to our frontline troops. How he got around was a dark mystery, but Stan was often set up and serving when the first assault troops arrived. He was a nonviolent person, and to accomplish his miraculous deeds he needed not weapons but fast transportation. My requirements were somewhat different, for I was always getting into tight spots and felt the need of some form of personal protection. The sidearm I carried was old and unwieldy, a Colt 45 that I couldn't have shot effectively even had I been a marksman. So one afternoon on the Anzio beachhead, Rip, Stan, and I came together for a brief moment. Rip had just returned from one of his adventures and brought back a coveted P-38 German pistol along with a huge, spanking new "Indian" motorcycle that he had "found." Stan eyed that motorcycle as if it were a gift from heaven, and I wanted the pistol in the worst way. But Von Ripper had other ideas, and his mind was set: the motorcycle was for me, and Stan must have the pistol for self-defense. We argued for some time but to no avail. Stan departed with the unwanted pistol, and I drove off with that infernal machine. About an hour later, not having had any experience with motorcycles, I ran off a dusty Anzio road heading straight for a great tree, jumped off the monster, and left it writhing on the ground against the trunk of the tree. Rip alone was pleased with the transaction.

Shortly after the end of the war I received a postcard from Rip, which I treasured. It read: "Dear Eddie—I have a wife, a car and a house—what more is there?" A few years later, exhausted and worn, he was dead. I think he was in his late forties. It is difficult for me to comprehend how so much had been crammed into one short lifetime. Ernie Pyle neglects to mention Rip's home-front action following World War I; counting that, he had participated in no less than four separate wars.

Savo Radulovic was another member of our art unit in Italy, and we would become inseparable in the years ahead. He and I shared—and survived—experiences of every description and relied upon each other in every sort of crisis. Our relationship was founded upon mutual respect but developed into a deep brotherly love.

Savo was born in Niksuch, Yugoslavia, in 1910 and arrived in America in 1921, a citizen through his father's U.S. citizenship. Starting at 17, he toiled in the Illinois coal mines for three years and later in the Detroit steel mills. While visiting his sister in St. Louis, he decided to stay on, and with his hard-earned savings attended the School of Fine Art at Washington University. He eventually won a Carnegie Fellowship to Harvard and was exhibiting his paintings in museums and galleries when he was inducted into the army.

Quiet and unassuming in spirit and deed, Savo had the remarkable ability to project a silent admiration for those in his presence. In other words, he made people feel comfortable and happy. He called me "*Tenente*" (lieutenant) until I became a captain; then he resorted to a more elaborate salutation and affectionately addressed me as "Mon Capitan." Like Von Ripper, Savo was older and more worldly wise than I, and a good deal of our relationship depended upon good-natured kidding; rank meant little to us.

If there was booze to be found, anywhere and at any hour, Savo would track it down. He was like a magnificent hunting dog except that instead of pointing to the prey, Savo would get a twinkle in his eye as he caught the scent. He had about as much command of the Italian language, or lack of it, as the rest of us, with words of necessity or convenience mastered and verbs remaining largely unconjugated. We relied on gestures most of the time, although when Savo needed a drink neither gestures nor the spoken word was necessary. He could exchange glances with a *paesano* at 50 yards and in no time they would be merrily toasting one another with something wet.

His love for liquor kept me continually amused and entertained even when I wasn't wholly participating in the festivities. We held long, relaxed conversations about everything imaginable—our work, the war and its political ramifications, and our earlier experiences as civilians. Compared to Savo, I was a mere neophyte when discussing his favorite subject, world politics and intrigue, and as a consequence felt rewarded to be in his company. Unlike many drinking men, he became gentler and more soft-spoken as the booze and discussion wore on endlessly.

Radulovic was a powerful man whose physical strength was totally concealed. Rugged in frame and square jawed, he sported a generous, handsome mustache and resembled the typical Hollywood prototype of a Yugoslavian peasant. He was gentle, insightful, and compassionate; he genuinely cared about the plight of his fellow man. His paintings, somewhat crude and always bold, came directly to the point, conveying emotions and messages in the purposely evident manner of primitive paintings and melodrama.

The worst thing that ever happened to Savo took place when we landed at Anzio shortly after the initial wave. The beachhead had been secured and was now being subjected to intermittent shellfire. As we docked, we could see the little towns of Anzio and Nettuno nestled together, much like the tiny communities of Monterey and Pacific Grove on the California coast I loved. But this was Italy and the Tyrrhenian Sea, and for the moment it was deceptively quiet and beautiful. The long docking area stretched out into the sea like a great index finger, and under the bright sun American ships were busily disgorging their cargoes. Suddenly, the silence was broken; "Anzio Annie" began lobbing in her massive shells, those that struck the water producing towering geysers reminiscent of Old Faithful in Yellowstone National Park. (I would return to study those amazing columns of water and there execute one of my most exciting works. Although it was not as aesthetically pleasing to me as I could have wished, it did capture the spirit of the beachhead.) Anzio Annie was the affectionate name given to a great German cannon mounted on a railway flatcar (the 280mm railway gun was also known as the Anzio Express). It could be brought into range, unleash its awesome charge, and then return to a point well out of Allied artillery retaliation. The shells sailing into Anzio were more of a nuisance than anything else, creating little damage or destruction.

Savo was very jittery. He had lovingly packed a precious bottle of good booze in his musette bag, which was slung over his shoulders to lie flat on his back. As he descended the steel ladder of the great landing craft, the musette bag caught on a rung of the ladder, breaking the bottle, and the liquor spilled out upon the embossed steel steps, puddling and dripping in tiny, muddy streams from one step down to the next. Watching poor Savo trying desperately to salvage the dripping booze from the steps and the saturated musette bag was heartrending. Working feverishly, he placed his canteen cup under one dribble and then another, and no sooner did the cup fill to an inch or so than he downed it on the spot. What safer place to store the precious stuff than in his belly? I was torn between laughter and tears but remained stonefaced out of respect for my buddy.

After the Anzio experience, Savo and I went on many missions together, virtually to the end of the Italian campaign. Near the final mopping up of German forces in Italy, he went off by himself and took part in some pretty extensive battles, carrying ammunition up muddy hills under intense enemy fire. My youthful if not downright reckless spirit had influenced Savo to work in dangerous frontline positions, but he undoubtedly felt the need to do something tangible to help win the war. Subsequently, he was awarded the Bronze Star for gallantry in action.

The best way to describe our relationship is to say that we leaned upon one another for courage, comfort, companionship, and approbation. The liquor kept Savo loose and at times did me some good, too. In those days a snort or two was all I needed to gain a heady feeling, and the occasional drink momentarily washed away the war. Savo continued to uncover strega, cognac, vodka, and (mainly) *vino*; bourbon and scotch were rarely available. It mattered very little; if there was a dram of alcohol in it, he found it and downed it.

One night in Livorno (Leghorn) on the west coast of Italy, the two of us had the ravaged city to ourselves. Whatever structures the Wehrmacht had neglected to destroy were blown asunder by Allied warplanes, and the city was in shambles. We made preparations to settle in somewhere within the city and took pains to case the area, noting the more elite sections. Our plan was to paint and sketch or generally gather material in the city and its suburbs, possibly for two or three days. There were handsome canals everywhere one turned, with exciting massive walls and unique architecture that held inordinate cosmetic appeal for an artist. We soon discovered an elegant building that suited our tastes and took full possession. It had formerly been a very elaborate, posh apartment house for the Italian upper crust. We moved our sleeping bags and equipment into what was once the master bedroom and made ourselves comfortable. There was no roof overhead, as it had been cruelly blown to

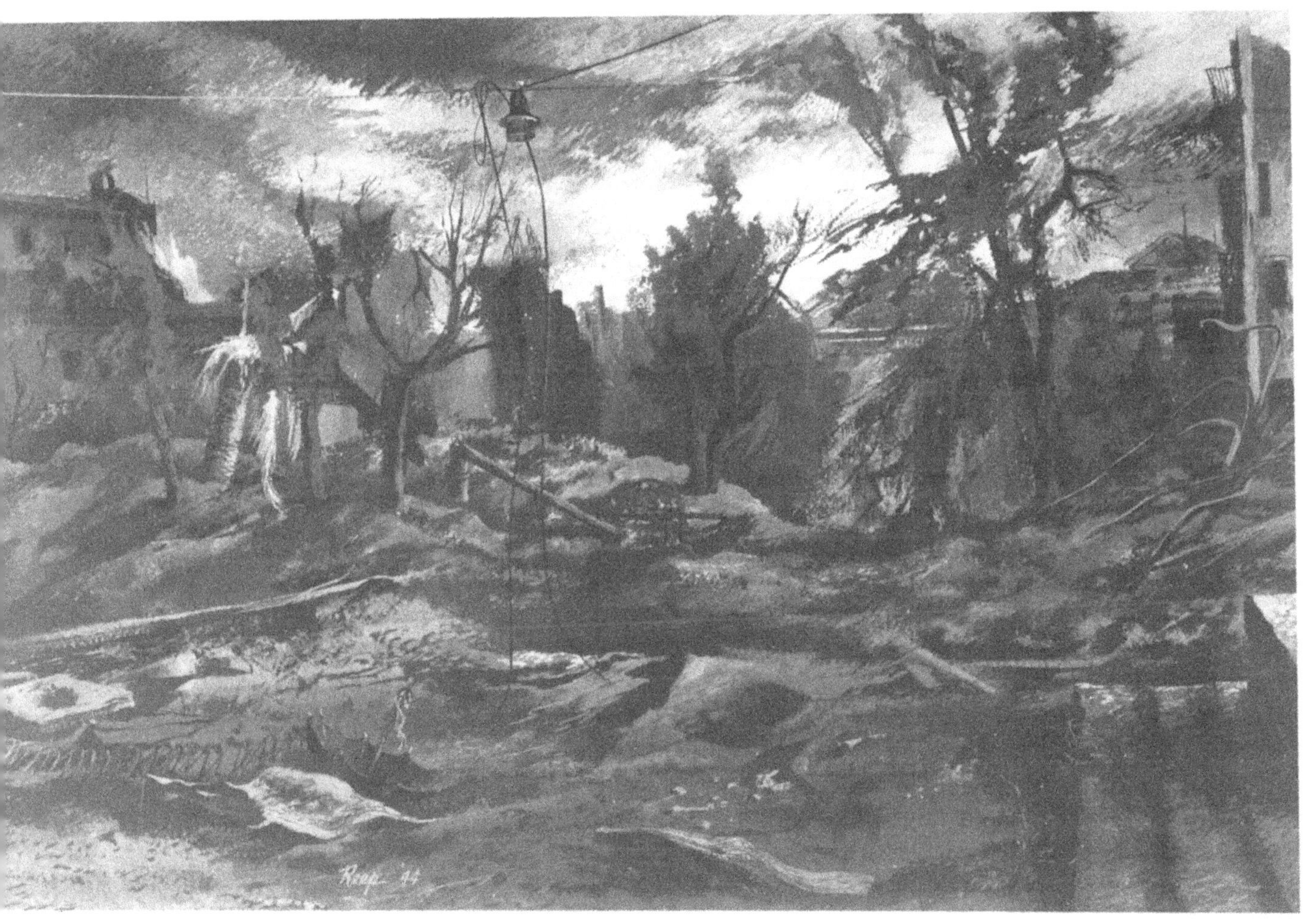

Piazza in Leghorn
1944. Gouache. 15 x 22½ in.

Repeatedly bombed and shelled, Leghorn was reduced to rubble. Although Germans and Italians had constructed elaborate air-raid shelters for the protection of the populace, the city itself lay helpless. Devastation was everywhere, and it was apparent that the enemy had long since given up hope of restoring it to usability. Nevertheless, I sensed its former elegance and could not resist spending a couple of days there in an attempt to capture something of that former ambiance. The old saw that the artist sees beauty in ruin held true: twisted steel, shattered glass, broken concrete, macabre tree forms, and dangling wires all suggest strange patterns and movement.

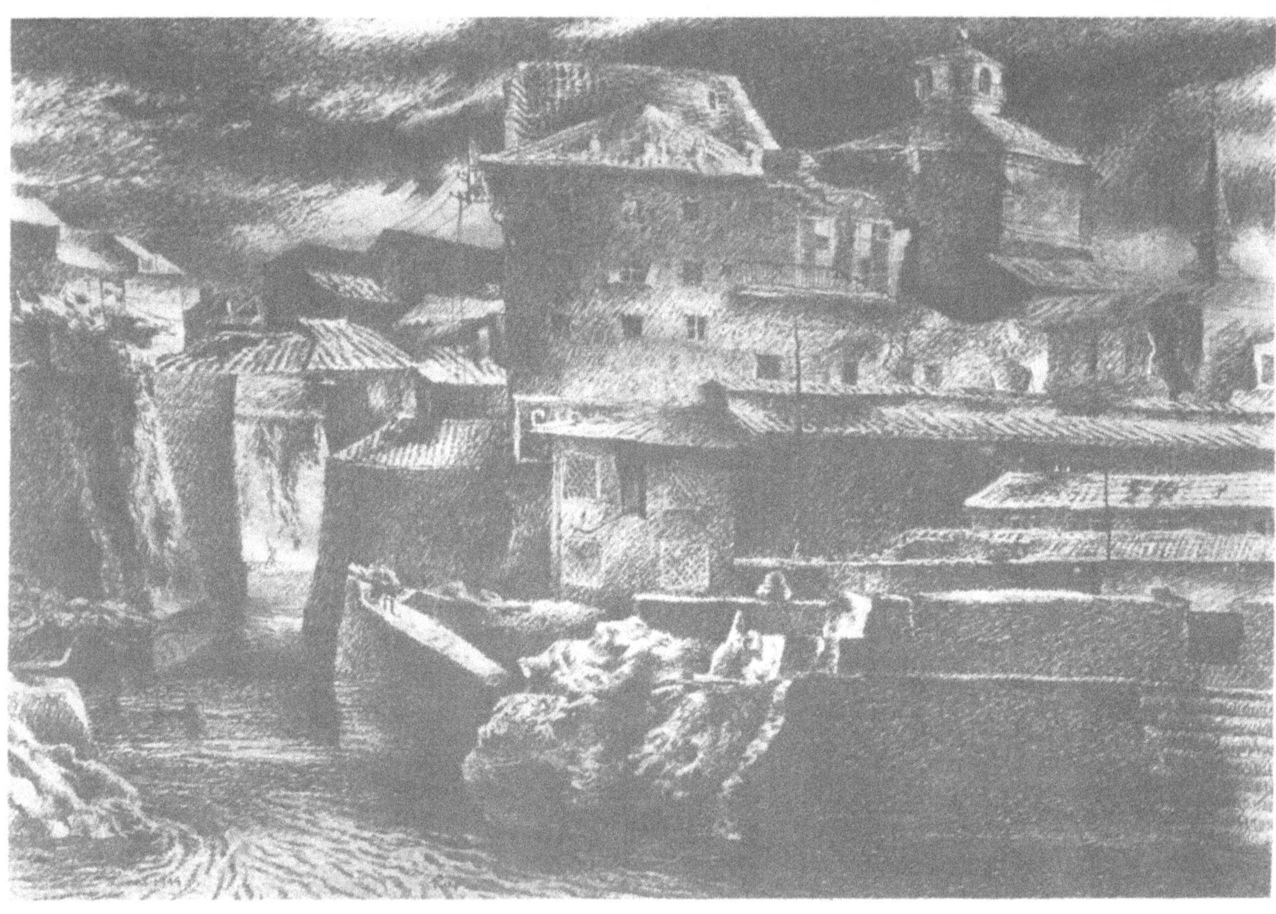

Leghorn Canal

1944. Pen and ink and watercolor. 13 x 19 in.

Pictured here is one of the many canals in the city of Leghorn. These canals formed the greater part of the harbor, necessitating bombing within the city itself. When the city was captured, signs of life were nowhere to be found. Only after German shelling ceased some months later did soldiers and civilians begin to appear on the deserted streets.

The pen drawing was applied over a rich sienna wash of watercolor to suggest the brick walls of canals and buildings.

bits, nor did the plumbing or electricity or any other household conveniences function. Nevertheless, we happily spread our sleeping bags on badly misshapen bed frames and placed various pieces of furniture about the room to serve our needs. As the more dutiful member of this premature "odd couple," I set about sprucing up our new abode. Savo didn't take to housekeeping, and though I was his superior officer, he graciously allowed me to do all of the menial chores for us both. For example, one night as we moved forward as part of a massive convoy with only blackout lights visible (the tiny blackout lights allowed us to see the vehicle ahead, while offering maximum security from enemy observation), *we* drove steadily for precisely 23 hours and 45 minutes—that is, *I* drove for that interminable length of time; my sergeant had never learned to drive a vehicle.

Once we were settled comfortably into our lavish Livorno quarters—not unlike another screwball couple, Laurel and Hardy—we surveyed our luxurious accommodations as if checking into a suite at the Waldorf-Astoria. The expensive furniture was broken and propped in place against the remnants of sophisticated wallpapers valiantly clinging to the walls. Carved wooden crown moldings where the ceiling used to be and lavish trim about the remaining doors and windows added to the ambiance of opulence. And there was color, or at least pieces of it, here and there—a pleasant switch from the monotonous, olive drab of our equipment, vehicles, and uniforms. At bedtime after a terrible meal of C-ration spaghetti or stew or some similar concoction the army issued with pride (all food tastes horrible when eaten for the hundredth straight meal), Savo lovingly placed his bottle of cognac on the Louis Quinze nightstand by the side of his bed. "Tenente, Tenente, let's have a little nightcap."

Savo's eyes twinkled brightly at the prospect, for this was the best part of the day. The only thing he savored more than just plain drinking was to have a companion join him and discuss world politics. I obliged him and had one drink (in no way could I keep up with his enormous appetite), we chatted, and I fell asleep. Then I was awakened. "Tenente, Tenente, what's that noise?" Savo heard shellfire in the distance. "It's getting closer. Do you think we ought to move? Listen Tenente. We'd better have another drink."

The shellfire could have been our own, but it was far away. Savo's effort to appear frightened was little more than a lame excuse to have another nip. "Go to sleep, Savo, we've got a big day ahead of us—you know I don't want another drink. I can't take it like you. Besides, who the hell is going to shell us in this miserable, Godforsaken abandoned city?"

When Savo tried for the third time, I cursed him and told him in plain English that I needed to get some rest. But my resistance broke because I sensed that it would comfort him if I shared one more drink, and I was right. He was pleased, took one long pull; turned over, and relaxed. We slept.

The morning light poured in from our open-air ceiling to awaken me. It was going to be a fine day, and it was time to get moving, so I tried to arouse my companion. "Out of the sack, old buddy, hit the deck, let's go. Come on Savo." I shook him gently and he finally awakened. I was impatient and as always eager to get started on another masterpiece.

He arose slowly. I went to the jeep, returned with our precious five-gallon can of water, and finished washing. Savo filled his helmet with water and attempted to wash his hands and face, dragging his towel through the muddy puddles of spilled water gathered on the wooden floor. Savo looked worse than the towel and very unsteady on his feet. Then I noticed that the bottle of cognac was empty. He had consumed an entire fifth during the night. "Tenente, I feel terrible. How do you feel? My stomach is killing me. You don't suppose that spaghetti was bad, do you?"

Through all our adventures, we worked hard and laughed at ourselves and our plight. We ran from bullets and mortars. We were once pinned down by mortar fire for an entire afternoon and into the night, and through all this we kept producing art.

The most sensitive artist in our unit had to be Mitchell Siporin, who was born in New York City in 1910, the same year as Radulovic; only Von Ripper was older. With respect to his experience as an artist, Siporin towered above the rest of us, for his early commissions had included illustrating for various national publications and exhibiting throughout the country. Unlike the others, Siporin had quickly achieved national prominence by winning major awards as well as being listed in *Who's Who in America*. In collaboration with Edward Millman, he executed large frescoes for the lobby of the St. Louis post office, covering more than 3,000 square feet of wall space. His paintings were a part of the permanent collections of the Metropolitan Museum, the Whitney Museum, and the Museum of Modern Art—three of the leading collections in America. Siporin had a very strong influence on all the artists in our unit, and there is little question that we profited by his example.

Mitch was a small roly-poly man with jet black hair and dark complexion, and one of a kind in many respects. He saw life as a stage and theater for his art and missed very little, viewing not only the great sadness and turmoil but the humor as well. He used to come to me for "fatherly" advice, taking a great deal of pleasure from the act. It was his way of letting me know that the army had turned his world upside down; still, the idea that a younger and less experienced man was in charge of the unit didn't seriously affect him or his work. He was a good sport with respect to the work we were asked to do and the conditions under which we functioned, and we enjoyed one another's company.

For the most part he was a self-contained man, very private, working in tiny cubicles and generally curled about his current project. It was a perpetual love affair: the piece Mitch was working on and Mitch the artist were one. Whenever we moved on to new quarters, whether building or tent, the question of where each artist would work had to be solved. When I was there, I'd call the men together to draw straws for preferred working spaces, but never once did Mitch participate. He would back off obligingly and seem happy with a leftover, less well-lighted area. It worked out well, for he seemed to prefer the more neutral light of the darker corners. Also, the harsh, bright light near the windows may have hurt his eyes.

After that one abortive try, there was no way to get Mitch to go to the front lines. He openly admitted that he would be too frightened to work; the notion of creating art on the battlefield was preposterous to him. Instead, he covered the rear or rest areas and any activities where soldiers functioned away from the front. He possessed a keen perception of the relationship between our soldiers and the Italian *paesanos*, often capturing them mingling in work and play. He sought out and recorded the strange and ludicrous events; the mix of Indian, British, Brazilian, American, and other troops; and the agony of refugees. Virtually everything Siporin touched and documented was transformed into a veritable jewel, superbly executed, the message clear and singularly personal. Apart from the intangible things we were to gain from working with Mitch, we learned much from the way he approached each work, his technique, and notably his deft use of casein paint and his handling of pen and ink.

For example, in the study of chiaroscuro, (the management of light and dark moving through an image), I had learned my art school lessons reasonably well and felt informed. As a student I had almost lived on landscape locations for four years of Saturdays, and there the sun was my sole source of light, creating shadows that I reasoned were the absence of light. That was one of the few romantic observations that I believed in at the time that makes sense to me to this day. When the sun played upon an object or person, it seemed a relatively simple matter to work out a convincing shadow pattern, so to my pragmatic mind, that was that. There was little need for experimentation; those truths were proven and incontestable. Dealing with artificial light indoors or out, even when there was more than one light to contend with, was a matter of applying foolproof formulas to solve the problem. I had a lock on this—until I ran into Siporin.

The message was delivered to me in a subtle, rather circuitous manner, but I don't think Mitch was conscious of its significance. One day when he was huddled in his darkish corner, embracing his drawing the way a guitarist surrounds his instrument, I politely asked him what he was up to. "Nothing much" was his answer. Upon reflection, probably out of courtesy, he added, "Some heads." "Heads?" My rejoinder must have been tinged with incredulity, for he looked up and asked if I'd like to see them.

As he slowly uncoiled and displayed the drawing, I saw three large heads of helmeted soldiers staring blankly into space. The compassionate faces were not those of individuals but representations of all soldiers, everywhere, at any time and in any army. Siporin's work evoked a timelessness permeated with sadness that played heavily upon the viewer's sympathy. After all, this was war, and wasn't everybody suffering?

As I studied the compelling drawing, there seemed to be something very peculiar about the lighting. One head was illuminated from the left, a second from the right, and the third head directly from the front. Horrors! What a tragic error.

Gaining courage, I asked Mitch if I might make a comment about his work, and he nodded approvingly. All artists must learn to respect one another by first asking whether criticism is welcome, preferably of a constructive nature with the opening wedge couched in propriety.

"Well, you see Mitch—that is, uh, you have these three heads in a singular statement"—I paused in my attempt to form words that would be convincing and yet not too pedantic, and then proceeded to run down the long list of possible lighting errors that were obvious to the well-trained artist. Mitch listened in apparent fascination; taking courage from his silence, I coughed up solutions, remedies, and myriad helpful suggestions. In conclusion, I returned to the original tragedy, that his three heads were lighted differently.

Mitch looked at me with a knowing smile, deceptively nodding his massive head in approval. I took heart—but his ploy merely concealed his reaction.

"So what?" That was all he said.

So what, indeed. Where were the rules—the laws? By whose edict were all artists bound to conform to such absurdity? What difference did it make if he had rearranged the light conditions to suit his purpose? What an ass I'd made of myself. I have never forgotten the incident, or the priceless lesson.

Siporin knew who he was and what he was doing. Consistent with the awareness of public relations that most prominent persons possess, even when behaving peevishly or being downright antisocial, their actions are measured for their effect upon an audience; such a game plan, once imagined and then learned, is designed to create a distinctive image that may prove helpful in their careers. Siporin was no exception. On another occasion when we were engaged in a lengthy, intellectual discussion that was going nowhere, I strode away from him with my patience exhausted. After a few steps I turned and, looking him squarely in the eye in utter frustration, I said, "Mitch, you are truly a character." "Am I?" he replied hopefully.

The last I heard of Siporin, he was happily married and had become head of the department of art at Brandeis University.

Frank D. Duncan, also a member of the original art group in Italy, had attended the Yale School of Fine Art for six years and garnered a number of awards for painting. Enigmatically, his work in the Italian theater of operations, confined to watercolors only, recorded a scenic tranquillity that seemed disparate from the real conflict taking place. He was a gentle man, likable and very quiet. His early years in the army had been filled with myriad accomplishments in the art sector, commissions that ranged from murals to decorative projects for various army clubs and other facilities. He had been a prizewinner in an all-service competition; prior to that, he had exhibited in New York galleries.

Born in Chicago in 1916, Duncan moved to New York, where his interest in painting was born. He was drafted soon after his graduation from Yale. Like Siporin, his work was confined to activities in the rear areas, but unlike Siporin, he rarely featured people in his paintings. He discovered beauty in scenes of military equipment amid ruins, blossoming trees, and pastoral landscapes. His work might well be called documentary, but it always contained a rich poetry in its delicate framework. Nearing the end of hostilities, Duncan became more interested in subject matter associated with the armies at the front.

About halfway through the campaign, we were fortunate to welcome Ludwig Mactarian to the Italian group of artists. Soft-spoken and unassuming, he was by far the most introspective of the artists. Coincidentally, he was born in 1910 and came to America in 1921, the same as Radulovic; the difference was that Mac came from Armenia. He had been exceptionally well trained, in the manner of the classic Renaissance painters, at the renowned Art Students League in New York and had exhibited work throughout the country prior to the war. His major claim to fame was having assisted Reginald Marsh with his fresco secco murals for the New York customs house. He had also executed a mural for an Arkansas post office.

Mactarian's finest works depicted ravaged buildings abandoned in the wake of battle. The mutilated terrain fascinated him, as did makeshift army structures and Bailey bridges. His keen eye for detail filled his casein paintings and pen-and-ink sketches with personal, somber overtones that were characteristic of the man, yet they remained faithful to the subject matter in a unique, almost surreal, fashion. Mac (he simply detested his first name, Ludwig) was a confirmed bachelor in his early thirties, and while pleasant and cooperative at all times, he appeared to lead a lonely life tinged with a pervasive melancholia. He rarely spoke of his earlier accomplishments. Shortly after the war he was found dead in his single-room apartment in New York. The cause was never revealed.

The last artist to join us in Italy was Harry Davis. In a belated sense, Davis's experiences as a war artist paralleled mine, for though the Italian campaign was winding down and the Jerries were on the run, he jumped right into the thick of the work to establish himself as a very significant, intrepid member of the unit. Old Colonel Forsythe would have been justifiably proud of Davis, for, despite being raw and uninitiated, he made the adjustment to working on the battlefield with remarkable ease and produced stirring frontline depictions of some of the bloodiest engagements high in the Apennine Mountains.

Davis was well trained, too, an accomplished draughtsman who had mastered the handling of the human figure. Born in Indiana, he had attended the John Herron Art School in Indianapolis, going on to win a coveted *Prix de Rome* in 1938. This enabled him to study for one year in Rome, and that led to two years of extensive travel throughout the European continent before he returned to Rome to execute a fresco for the cortile of the American Academy. Later he taught courses in painting at Beloit College in Wisconsin and continued exhibiting widely in museums and galleries prior to his entrance into the armed forces.

His production as a war artist took form rather slowly at first, although he was able to crank out paintings with a prolific ease. Suddenly, picking up from the vast amount of work that the other artists had produced, Harry accelerated in unbelievable fashion. He sought out dangerous combat zones and quickly picked up Siporin's magical pen-and-ink approach, which was well suited to working under the conditions we faced. Not only did he become involved with gut-level ground warfare and perform at enormous personal risk, but he was also able to incorporate the soldiers as primary subject matter. Only a consummate draughtsman could have accomplished this with the high quality he was able to achieve. For a late arrival, he contributed an astonishing number of meaningful drawings and paintings.

A few years ago I was invited to jury a major art exhibition in Indiana. To my delight, both Harry Davis and his wife, also an artist, were very ably represented and walked off with a number of awards. Today he is at work on various commissions; the last one I recall pertained to the documentation of historical sites throughout the midwestern states.

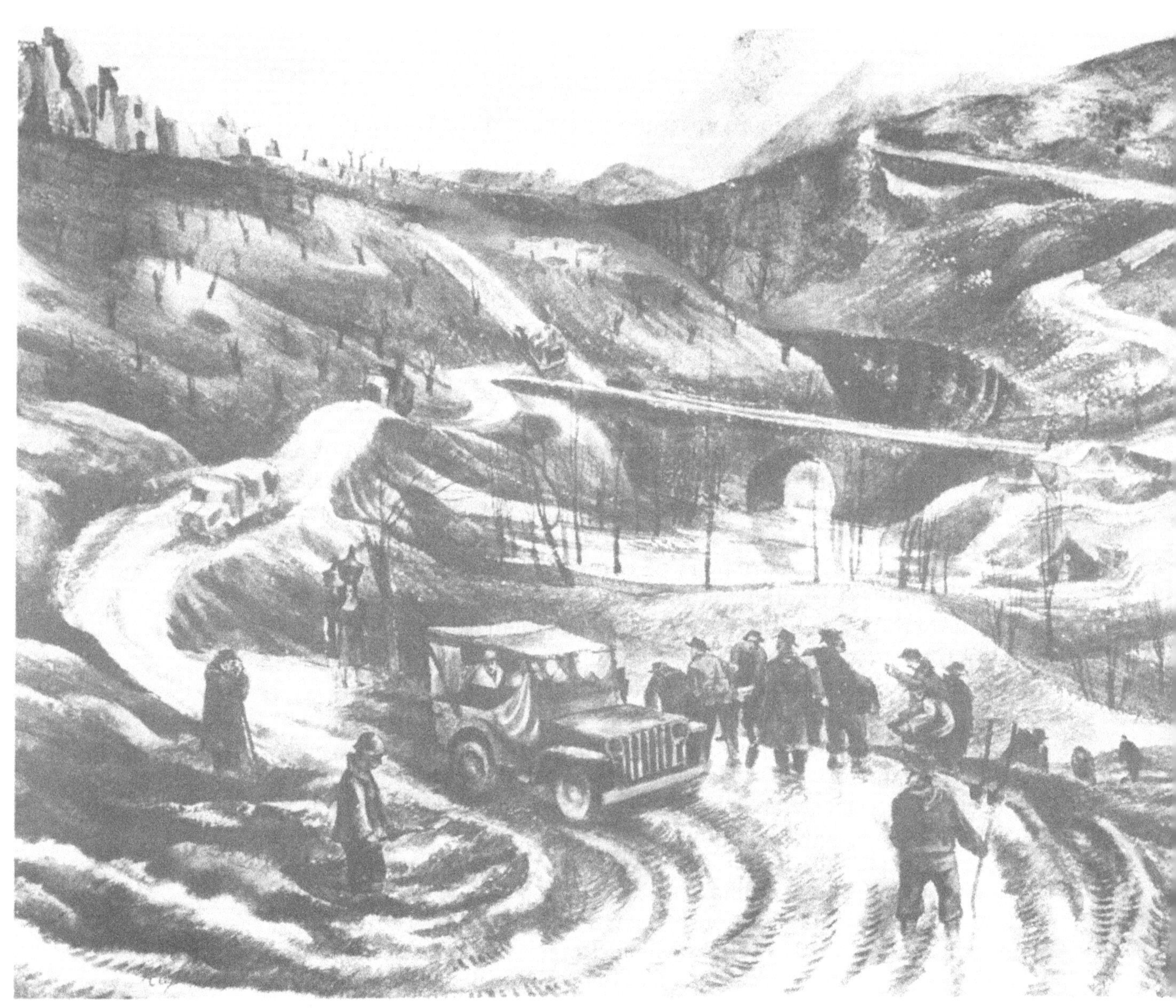

Back Road to Cassino

1944. Watercolor. 17 x 22 in.

Winding mountain roads and rugged terrain are typical of the Italian countryside we fought for, each rain producing new hazards and washouts. With the aid of Italian civilians, American GIs are here at work in the rain in an effort to keep the roads open. Since I was working in watercolor, which is not possible in a steady downpour, this painting was done in the back seat of a covered jeep similar to the one shown on the road.

CHAPTER SEVEN

Painting Begins in Earnest

After my initial attempts at painting in the footsteps of various battles, I began to acquire a feel for my assignment. In January 1944 the fighting in Italy was stalemated at what was termed the Gustav Line, and there it would remain for the next several months. Built by the Todt Organization and aided by civilians and prisoners of war forced into service, it ran from Mt. Scauri on the Tyrrhenian Sea, west of the Garigliani River, to the Gari River, and continued to follow the west banks of the Gari and Rapido rivers to Cassino. From there it extended along the forward slopes of the hills behind Cassino and northward to Mt. Marrone, where the Eighth and Fifth armies joined. The Gustav Line was some 35 miles in length. Our forces consisted of British, French, and American troops. On the left or southern flank were three British divisions, the 5th, 46th, and 56th, plus their 23rd Armoured Brigade. The right flank was occupied by two units of the French Expeditionary Corps, namely, the 2nd Moroccan and 3rd Algerian Divisions. At the center and heart of the line facing Cassino, the sector I concentrated upon, were two American infantry divisions, the 34th and the 36th.

The commanding hill of Monte Cassino, along with adjoining hillside promontories and in particular the hallowed abbey of Monte Cassino, gave the enemy an advantage that was not easily overcome. Heavily fortified, the Germans held out tenaciously against repeated assaults; it was revealed after the conflict that not one but two belts of German fortifications awaited our troops. The abbey, a Benedictine monastery, lay directly in the path of the Allies, preventing us from advancing

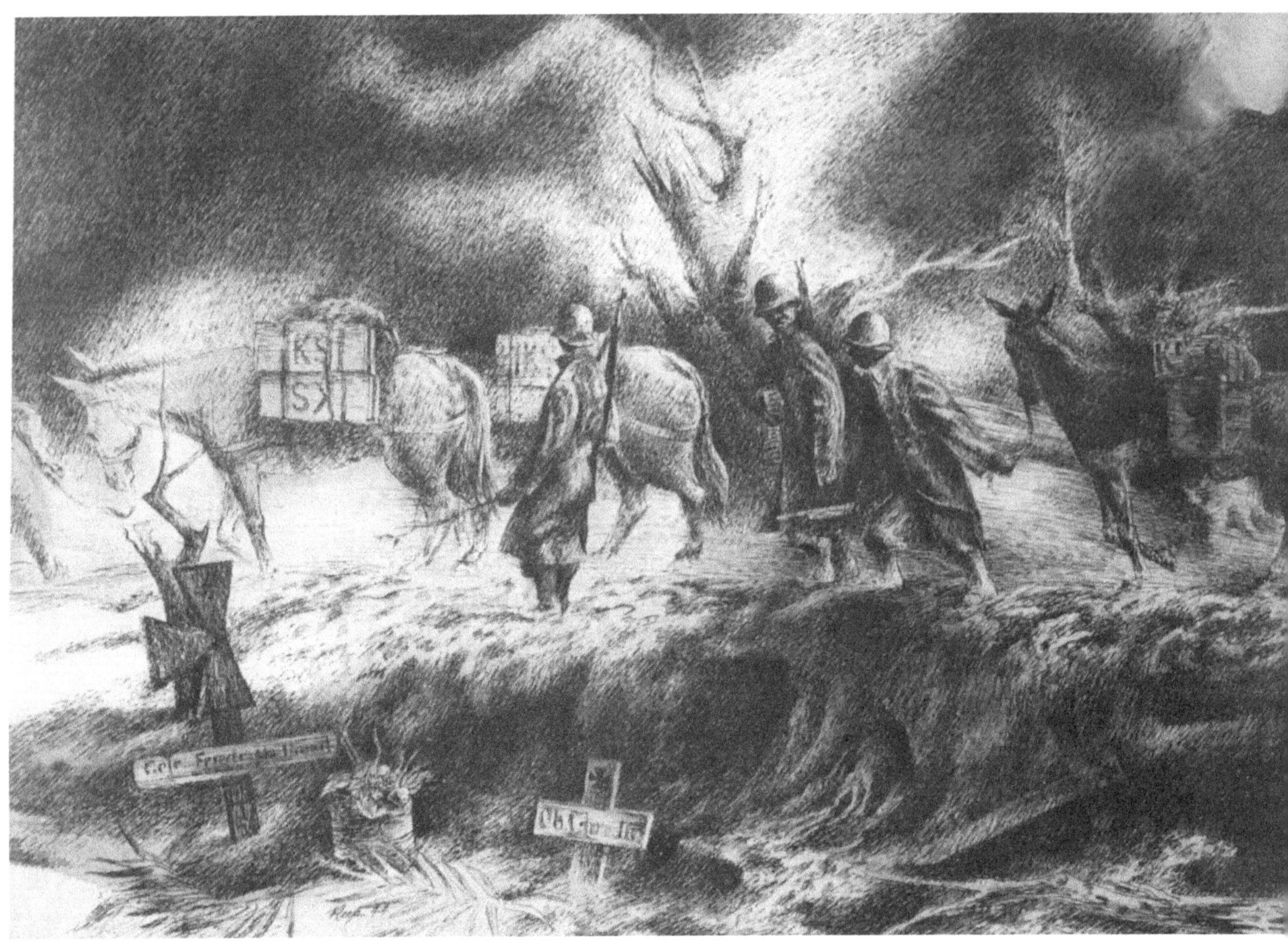

Pack Trains to Cassino

1944. Pen and ink and watercolor. 15 x 21 in.

Passing a German graveyard torn apart by German shells, soldiers and mules pack supplies to the troops isolated in Cassino by no-man's-land, which is impassable during the daylight hours. This early effort exhibits my lack of experience in dealing with unfamiliar subject matter. At this point, excited and wary of everything, I would dramatize my work with strong contrasts of light and dark and invent menacing, eerie shapes. I could hear artillery fire in the near distance as I drew but was in no personal danger. I was unconsciously preparing for the time when I would work exclusively at the front.

through the verdant Liri Valley or gateway to Rome and the north. Our forces believed the monastery was being used as an enemy observation post, an ammunition dump, a fortification, a refuge, and a headquarters for personnel, but so far it had been spared our fire because of its designation as a historical monument.

At this juncture I was billeted in the Royal Palace of Caserta, originally built for King Charles of Spain. This magnificent structure, with its own opera house and library, not only served as army headquarters but also housed a horde of civilian reporters, photographers, and various USO performing groups. It was all very exciting to me, a young unknown working alongside so many celebrated persons. Each day I'd venture forth to some picturesque area and return with sketches and small paintings. I captured the devastated bridges and buildings as well as the unusual scars of battles ended. Then I discovered pack trains of foot soldiers and mules, tank units, and replacements moving toward the front, and I joined them for a day or two. I was adjusting to field conditions slowly, finding my footing and developing a modus operandi. I lived out of a jeep from the motor pool (eventually I would have my own), washed in my helmet with water from a five-gallon can I lugged around, and slept on the ground in my bedroll. This was a giant step for one who, in civilian life, had rarely been camping and detested hunting and fishing.

My first painting actually involving the enemy was fairly benign. One day I looked high up into the sky to observe two German reconnaissance planes streaking over the tiny mountain village of Cervaro. At once our ack-ack began thundering away, creeping up on but not quite catching the planes, which left long, graceful vapor trails followed by the great white puffs of our antiaircraft fire. While I was in no danger, it was a stirring experience to be so close to the real war.

Not long after this, Savo Radulovic joined me in a visit to the battlefront overlooking the Liri Valley and the abbey of Monte Cassino. I set up my gear on a modest promontory from which I could view the entire valley with its flat plains stretching out as if beckoning to the Allies: "Come on ahead—Rome is awaiting your arrival." Savo busied himself with his camera (he rarely painted or sketched on location), shooting everything in sight on this clear sunny day. We scanned the hills occupied by the enemy but reasoned that even if they could see us, they wouldn't waste ammunition or jeopardize their own positions by firing directly at us. Nothing could have been further from the truth; German mortarmen had zeroed in on us and began peppering our hillside. We raced for cover, stumbling, falling, and searching for any decent protection. The mortars that found our little hilltop were lovingly called "Screaming Meemies," ingenious Jerry weapons that fired one round after another in rapid succession. They whistled in on their victims with a lengthy cacophony of unearthly screams, but we were fortunate to have fled slightly before being "bracketed in." I am reminded of that day whenever I use my beloved Leica camera because in my haste to seek cover, I fell and tore the leather cover from it. Although frightened, we returned from the small ravine in which we had taken cover and continued with our work, for I needed a firmer grasp on the subject matter. Then we departed in haste.

I was becoming accustomed to staying up front for several days at a time. Upon returning to the relative safety of the palace, there to complete work and catch my breath, I'd compare notes with the other artists and reporters. It was at the Caserta palace that my friendship with Ernie Pyle was born and there that I learned how he functioned, going to the front for short periods and returning to complete his syndicated, eagerly awaited stories. Ernie, freely admitting that he was scared half to death most of the time at the front, was a true champion of the lowly GI, for his tales were filled with the kind of human interest that informed and entertained the folks at home.

Virtually all of the USO-sponsored Hollywood personalities coming to Italy stayed at the palace. They were given VIP treatment as one would expect, and dined in an exclusive mess hall with the chicken colonels and generals. Humphrey Bogart and his wife of the moment, Mayo Methot, passed through, and although I never caught their performance before the troops, I was witness to a backstage incident that caused all sorts of gossip. Many of us junior officers, dining in our adjacent mess hall, could see the turmoil and confusion when Bogey slapped his wife at the dinner table. In my continuing innocence, my Marquis of Queensberry world, I thought him a first-class bum after that; still, Mayo was said to be drunk and making a fool of herself.

Joe E. Brown, the lovable comedian who had built his reputation on the enormousness of his mouth, visited us along with his entourage,

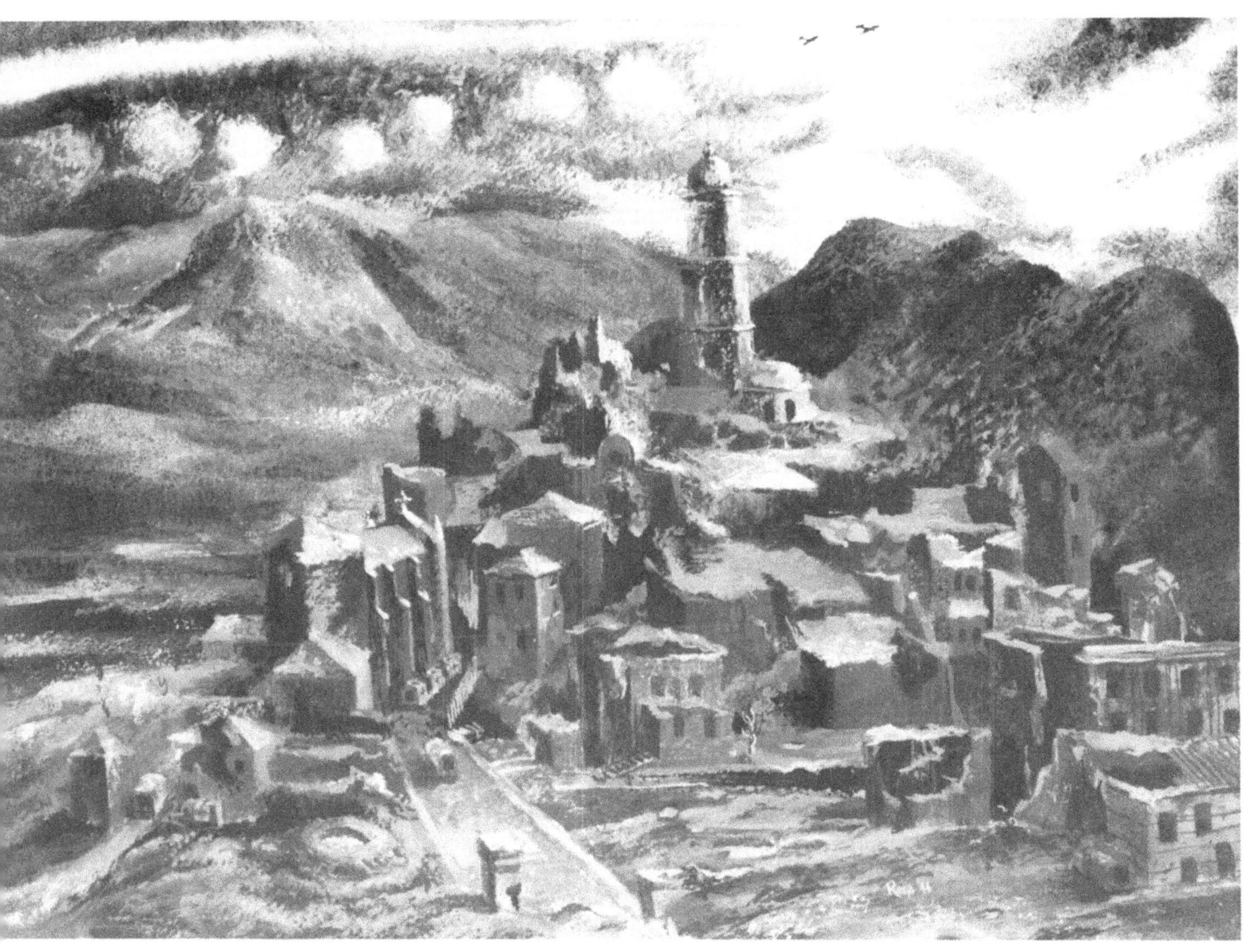

Ack-ack over Cervaro
1944. Gouache. 15 x 23 in.

I had painted abandoned enemy positions but hadn't confronted the Germans in action until I saw two reconnaissance planes blazing by the mountain village of Cervaro. Their white vapor trails and the puffs of our pursuing antiaircraft fire were so striking couched against a darkening cool blue sky that I determined to build a painting around the event. Working rapidly in watercolor, I painted until the light of day had vanished, then returned to the Historical Section to complete the work, using a semiopaque watercolor (gouache) for more detailed portions. Amid the rubble of Cervaro are several Red Cross vehicles, a church, and the dominating building. My goal was to capture the ambiance of that fleeting moment between night and day.

including Mike Frankovitch, Harry Barris (a former Bing Crosby Rhythm Boy), and an orchestra; it was a big group and very popular. I sat just behind the orchestra during their performance and looked out upon the audience of army personnel—men and women, officers and enlisted men. My purpose was to draw the troops from a new and distinctive vantage point, but the unaccustomed din nearly did me in. What a horrible life to be a musician in a band, I thought.

Soldiers were sprawled everywhere, even occupying trees stripped of their foliage. They hung and clung and draped over those blackened limbs like strange Neanderthals, cheering wildly at every twist of the performance and, naturally, at the pretty girls. The troops were hungry for entertainment, and the performers worked hard to please their appreciative audience. Harry Barris took my home phone number and upon his return, true to his word, called my wife to report that he had seen me and that I was well and working diligently. It seems like very little at this telling, but it was a very moving event in my life then, a deeply appreciated contact with my loved ones. There can be little doubt that the USO did a valiant and important job in boosting the morale of our troops.

In February 1944, when I'd been in Italy for almost three months without ever considering taking a day off—there was so much to do and such abundant subject matter from which to work—I received a letter from an old art school buddy, Andy Aldridge. He was on duty with the air corps near Bari, just a few hours away. It seemed as good a time as any to take a break, as our forces were still going nowhere. As a consequence, one of the few times I took advantage of my position as an independent, freewheeling soldier-artist responsible mainly to myself, I decided to visit Andy. Naturally, Radulovic joined in, and we headed south instead of north to the front.

Andy Aldridge was a painter at heart but, having found eating essential, had turned to commercial illustration for his livelihood. He was a long, stringy fellow with a ready smile, tough as a coffeehouse steak and full of mischief. Andy and I had formed a two-man touch football team in college, where we reigned undefeated. Together, we had dreamed of becoming Van Goghs.

Savo and I drove directly to Bari, a charming seacoast city on the shores of the Adriatic Sea in southern Italy. We had been forewarned of the rampant thievery of American vehicles, so our first order of business

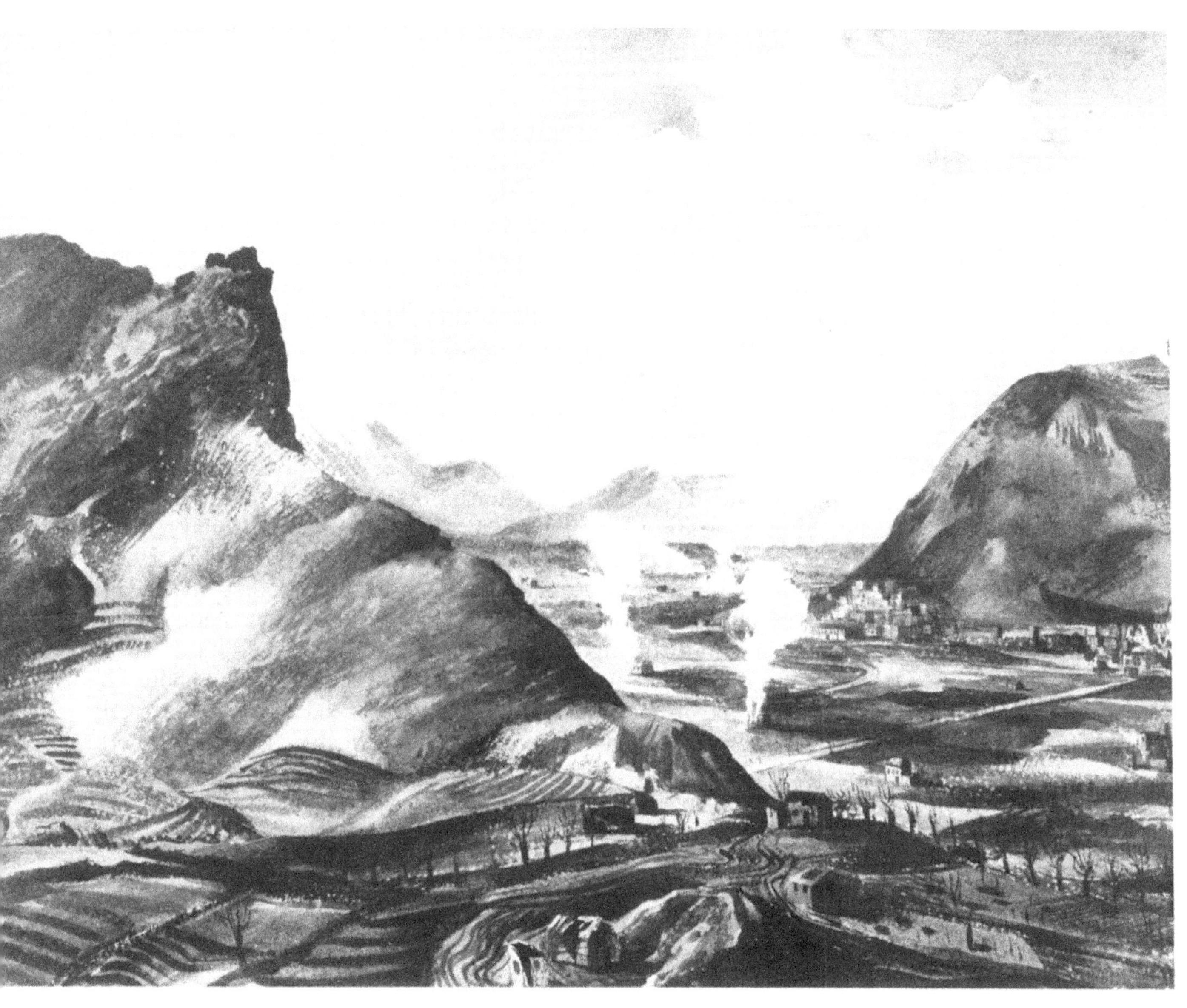

Rapido River in Purple Heart Valley
1944. Watercolor. 16½ x 22½ in.

The Liri Valley sprawled out before my eyes, lovely, fertile, beckoning our forces on to Rome. From my vantage point I could see the venerable Abbey of Monte Cassino to the high right. Shelling from both sides occurred throughout the day and night; the Jerries even lobbed "Screaming Meemies" at me in a pitiful waste of ammunition.

Monte Cassino was the major block in the Allies' futile attempts to penetrate the Gustav Line, where we had been stalled during the initial winter in Italy. Later, Mark Clark suffered enormous losses at the Rapido River, making "Purple Heart Valley" an apt name.

was to locate a safe place to park the precious jeep. No American troops were stationed in the city at the time, which made matters worse. We hired a *paesano* to watch over the vehicle—perhaps a questionable move—and to further ensure its safety we commandeered help from a group of able-bodied Italians and together lifted and squeezed the car into a loading alcove in such a manner that it would have taken an equal number of men to remove it. I also stripped the engine of its rotor and a few other essential parts before seeking accommodations.

While waiting at the hotel desk, we found ourselves surrounded by a group of young Italian boys who were avidly pimping for their sisters, their explicit terms spiced with lewd gestures. That night, dead tired and soundly sleeping, I was rudely awakened by one of these characters asking if I wanted *"fickey-fickey"* with his sister. I'm not sure how that colorful phrase is spelled, for it isn't in my Italian dictionary, but it certainly wasn't difficult to comprehend. I shouted at the *piccolino* to get the hell out of my bedroom and let me sleep, and wasn't disturbed again. There were roughly 10 or 12 beds to a room, and the boys made routine rounds throughout the night.

In the morning, Savo must have had second thoughts about the night-long propositions, for he came to me and asked for a loan of exactly 300 lire (which amounted to three dollars, American): "There's this little girl," the look in Savo's eyes was a dead giveaway that he was happy, "that I would like to—well, you know, Tenente—can you spare the money?" He was always circumspect to the point of mild embarrassment in such matters, relying mostly on facial expressions to get his message across. In order to have a bit of fun at his expense, I asked where this special lady was at the moment. He pointed to a tiny room at the end of the hall, only a trifle larger than a closet.

Now I was getting into the act and living the experience through Savo, although as envious as I was of his romantic escapade, I didn't really want to participate. First, there was that personal resolve to remain faithful to my wife; second, I wasn't about to risk contacting one of these nasty venereal diseases so prevalent at the time. So I did the next best thing and went down the hall to the tiny room, opened the door, and peered inside. There on the bed, sprawled out and stark naked, was a raven-haired *signorina* beckoning me in with a coquettish grin.

"Buon giorno, signorina, come sta?" My pidgin Italian was at its best with salutations, good morning, how are you, I inquired. I was trying to be blasé but could feel my face redden.

"Ah, Tenente—avanti. Come sta?"

"No—grazie." She had asked me in and I had graciously declined; instead I asked how much money she wanted.

"Oh, tres cento lire." My intention was to pay her and depart. I walked to her bedside, placed the 300 lire on a small table, and was about to walk out when, alas, my resistance cracked. First I smiled at her and then gave each nipple a little pinch. After surveying her delightful body carefully, I turned again to leave. The dear girl was both anxious and perplexed.

"Dove va? Dove va?" Her tone was almost frantic as she asked where I was going. Her workday was just beginning and she was apparently eager to get started. I was deeply moved by the sincerity in her voice. Once again I thanked her politely and added that her customer would be right along.

Now at last things began to make sense to her. Who was this strange American officer she had wondered, who entered her boudoir, doled out the asking price, and prepared to leave? Then she brightened and began to talk a mile a minute. I could understand little except the word *dottore;* apparently she had me pegged as one of the army doctors who customarily made the rounds of the local brothels in an attempt to control venereal disease. I nodded, kept a straight face in order not to disillusion her, and left hurriedly to summon Savo, who was waiting impatiently.

Halfway down the hall I got another bright idea. A small transom window provided light to the little room. I found a chair to stand on, and with my camera held high over my head I attempted to take several shots of Savo's activities, which I thought would prove amusing. When finally we visited with Andy at the air base, amid much laughter I told him of my foul deed, which is invariably funnier in the telling than the actual event. Andy volunteered to get the film developed, for by no means would I dare to have it processed through my official channels. Perhaps it's just as well that Andy apparently never got the job done. I never heard about the results, at any rate, nor did I ever tell Savo of my dastardly act.

Back at Fifth Army headquarters in Caserta, scuttlebutt persisted that we would shortly be attacking Monte Cassino, perhaps by the middle of the month. Prior to the Bari hiatus I had been painting in the general area for some time, on ground where the bitter fighting had taken place in the initial struggle for Cassino in mid-January. The Rapido River was the hub of one of the most costly Italian battles in terms of casualties; Mark Clark's old infantry division, the 36th, had suffered the greatest losses. There had been much talk about that ill-fated assault, and General Clark took a lot of flak, justified or not.

Then the astonishing news broke that Allied patience had collapsed and the abbey itself would be bombed by our aircraft, that it was deemed militarily crucial to eliminate the enemy's hold there at all costs. So on that epochal day—for it must be noted that we were about to destroy a bona fide historical monument, which all knew was contrary to the rules of war—I hurried to the banks of the Rapido River to secure a grandstand seat and document the memorable event.

It occurred to me at that time that battles are often fought in relatively good weather, for it was a lovely morning when I looked skyward to discover wave after wave of our Flying Fortresses, Marauders, and Mitchell bombers passing overhead. Everyone cheered wildly—for a moment. Then we saw something unbelievable and terrifying: there were bombs raining down directly at us, the Americans—our own planes were dropping bombs on us! For the moment I was so transfixed I didn't even consider taking cover. I hadn't realized that from the ground one can actually *see* bombs leaving their bays. Now some soldiers were screaming at me to take cover, and in a moment I was stretched out prone in a deep ravine alongside them. The earth shook violently as the bombs exploded. Luckily no one was killed in this goof-up.

Farther ahead the abbey was being blown to bits. I set up my gear and painted an *alla prima* watercolor that would have warmed Van Gogh's heart. In art parlance "*alla prima*" means at one time or at one sitting, but I prefer my own definition: "that which starts with emotion and ends with emotion." Smoke rose from the bombs bursting on the lower hills and from the massive monastery. My brushstrokes were crude, brusque, tortured. No reworking of this painting was necessary; the frenzied statement would be finished concurrently with the action, and besides, the area was filling with clouds of dust and smoke to make vision impossible. The abbey was now in shambles. Retrospectively, I think of myself as some sort of a nut to have been able to function under those conditions.

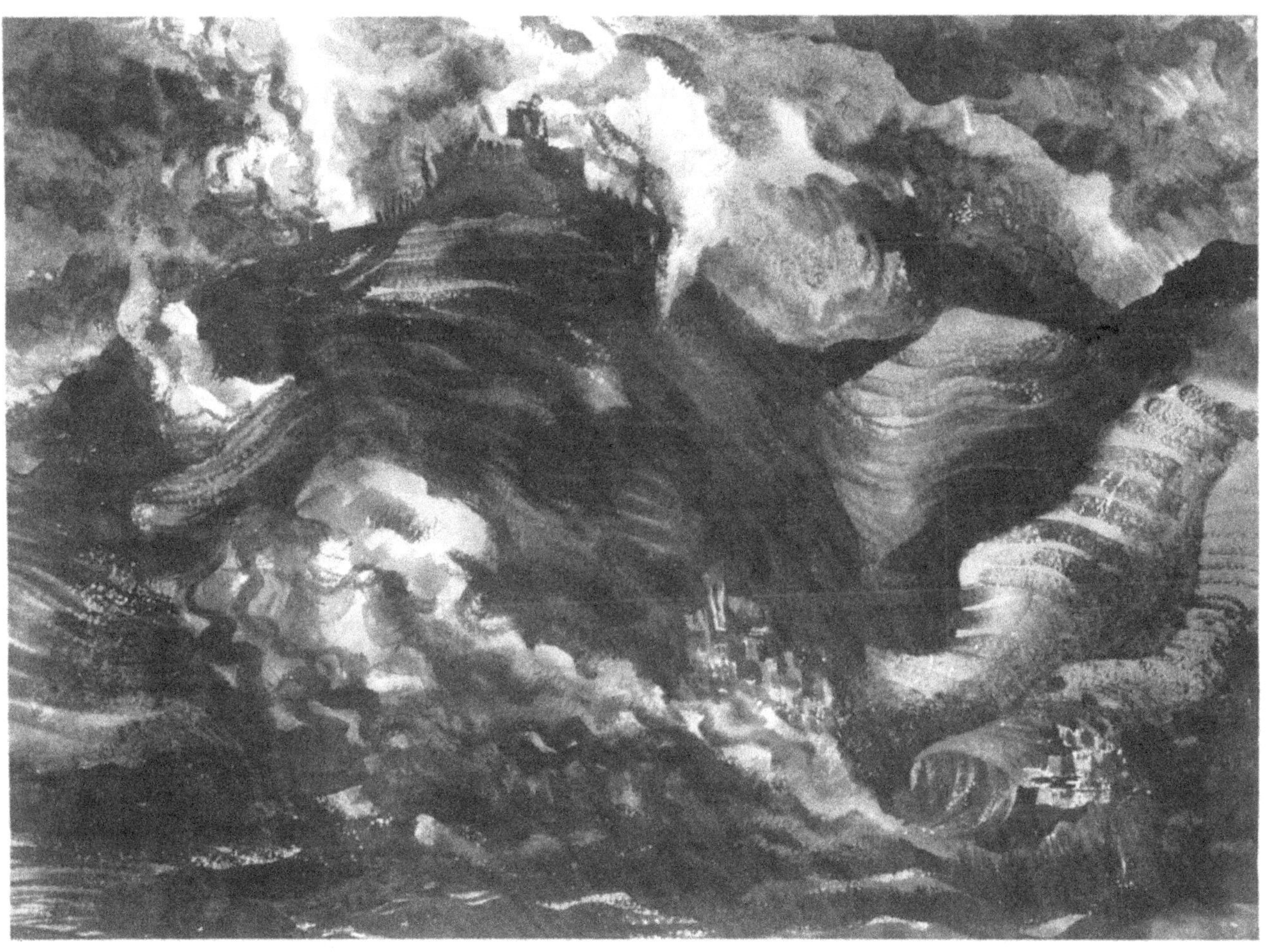

Bombing of the Abbey of Monte Cassino
1944. Watercolor. 17½ x 22½ in.

As we battled northward, with Rome as our next great goal, the central features blocking our path were the Rapido River and Monte Cassino, upon which stood the famed monastery. On 15 February 1944, Allied bombers dropped over 450 tons of bombs on the abbey, a historical monument. Winston Churchill later wrote: "There is controversy about whether it [the abbey] should have been destroyed once again. The monastery did not contain German troops, but the enemy fortifications were hardly separate from the building itself."

Certainly those fighting a vicious, ruthless enemy saw in the bombing the opportunity to move forward at last and defeat the Germans. As a soldier-artist, sitting on earth trembling with each great explosion, I never gave a thought to the propriety of the bombing. My concern lay totally with the documentation of the historic event.

Whenever I'd propose a tour of the front to Colonel Forsythe, the problem of transportation arose and had to be solved. Until now I had been hitching rides to and from the front lines, but I realized from the start that my work would be severely hampered and precious time lost if that impediment persisted. The motor pool, consistently reluctant to let its beloved vehicles stray from sight for even a morning or afternoon, became virtually paranoid when it came to checking one out for an overnight journey. Added to that, they insisted that I use one of their so-called experienced drivers, who for all I knew might never have seen a car in civilian life. Even after the proper requisition forms were filled out and the myriad official signatures of approval affixed, the papers still had to be taken to the motor pool, there to face the bureaucrats and their admonitions. Any bumptiousness in my manner would immediately scotch the deal; I was obliged to proceed cautiously. As a consequence, half a day would be shot with that rigmarole.

In a stroke of unparalleled good fortune, my motor pool jeep broke down on one of my sorties and had to be towed in for minor repairs. After several phone calls back to the army headquarters motor pool, I got permission for the field maintenance mechanics to repair the vehicle. During the interminable waiting—not unlike the experience we all suffer in civilian repair garages—I browsed about the maintenance yard. Off in a remote corner of the vast dirt compound lay a battle-scarred veteran of the war: namely, the beat-up carcass of an abandoned jeep. I asked why it was there, who owned it, and what was to be done with it. With disbelief that any sane person would be silly enough to show any interest in that derelict hunk of scrap metal, I was assured the the vehicle was over the hill and useful only for cannibalizing whatever spare parts it might still yield. I asked if I might have it, my manner casual and lighthearted as if I weren't taking my own request very seriously; indeed, we all laughed in unison at this preposterous idea. The mechanics pointed out in vivid detail what was wrong with the old jeep, adding that it didn't even have tires. They gave it to me.

Once the characters working in the maintenance yard knew how determined I was to have my own wheels and how vital it would prove to my assignment, they were on my side, so we began to lay plans for renovating the crate and getting some tires. They promised me that the next time a jeep appeared in need of new tires, they would save the old rubber for me. In the interim, *if* they could find any spare time (that was one thing we all had plenty of when the fighting came to a halt), they would try to get the motor running. And like all good mechanics, once having decided to engage in this charitable project, they accepted it as a challenge not only to their abilities but to their cunning as well. Everything would have to be done under cover; none of their superiors could get wind of it or the jig was up. In the noble tradition of the real American GI, it would be contrary to army regulations and stand as a defiant act against the hierarchy.

Each day for about a week I checked in with the mechanics to see if there was any progress, and sure enough, when some high-ranking officer ordered new tires for his jeep, the old ones went smack onto mine. For the life of me, I couldn't see what was wrong with them, with that durable rubber and the treads still thick. By this time the men had my jeep running well enough to allow me to drive it away, so amid loud cheering, razzing, and a thousand reminders that the thing would undoubtedly break down at any moment, I headed triumphantly out of the yard for a joyful return to the Historical Section. There I painted my wife's name on the lower metal portion of the windshield—in Greek, for what reason I'll never understand. None of the members of the section were of Greek origin, and my wife and I weren't Greek. But our new commanding officer, Chester Starr (Colonel Forsythe had been recalled to the States), was a brilliant Greek scholar and knew how to spell the name "Patsy" phonetically. And it *was* unique.

As the months passed, my Greek *Patsy* improved like old wine. Whenever I passed a frontline maintenance unit, I'd turn in and talk them out of a replacement part or two until ultimately, the jeep was totally rebuilt and almost as sound as a new model.

One of the greatest personal tragedies I suffered during the entire Italian campaign was the demise of the *Patsy.* I had driven into Pisa as far as possible and parked the jeep behind some ravaged buildings. It was pretty much out of sight of the enemy, although I knew their observers on the top floor of the historic Leaning Tower had probably seen me. I could plainly see them peering through their binoculars as I drove up, and I knew they could witness my actions even more clearly. They were there in violation of the rules of war; they knew that the Allies would not destroy that magnificent structure, one of the most delicate and charming pieces of architecture I have ever seen.

Leaving *Patsy* safely under cover, I followed our communication wires into the heart of the city. The Arno River bisects Pisa: the Jerries occupied the northern sector and the Allies the south. For protection and cover our soldiers were using the sewer system as a means of moving about, an ingenious and elaborate way of avoiding detection by the enemy observers in the Leaning Tower.

Once in the heart of the city, I took photos, sketched, made notes, and foraged about in a wondrous bookstore. I found several large editions of Cervantes' *Don Quixote,* illustrated by the famous Gustave Doré, and "liberated" a few of them to take back to the men in our section. Alas, when I retraced my steps to where my jeep was parked, I found that those damn Jerries in the tower had mortared it to death, and it lay as a total loss. I was distraught. Though there wasn't much I could have done about it anyway, I did recall hearing some rather persistent shelling as I was heading into the town but had paid little attention to it at the time. Now, I gathered together the pieces of my art equipment and salvaged whatever precious materials remained, notably the brushes, and then laboriously worked my way back to army headquarters by shank's mare and thumb. I was back where I had begun, and the thought of starting up once more with the motor pools made me ill. I resolved to go after another jeep as soon as practical.

By that time, however, my work patterns were well established, and my superior officers had enough confidence in me that checking out a vehicle was a far less complex exercise than before. In my favor, Allied materiel had stockpiled to such a degree that many units now were in possession of their own vehicles, a rarity in the early going. But there was no way that the brass would assign a jeep to anyone on a personal basis or for extended periods, certainly not to a lowly lieutenant.

I intensified my search and struck pay dirt in the zaniest fashion. Visiting one motor maintenance unit after another, lamenting my fate and meeting rejection again and again, I had virtually given up hope when an empathetic sergeant called me aside and asked *where* —he stressed the word—I proposed to use a jeep if I had one and *where* I would be seen with it. I replied that I spent most of my time at the front and upon returning to the rear it was always to the Historical Section of Fifth Army Headquarters, adding that the historians and artists were invariably located in some remote, offbeat area. I prayed that was what he wanted to hear.

He then revealed his deep secret accompanied by a proposal. A couple of potted GIs had swiped a general's jeep. At first they thought of it as a prank, since they detested the general with a vengeance. It seems that he was pompous and overbearing, treating all enlisted men and junior officers like vassals or, in truth, like the second-class citizens they actually were in the army. Once they had gone that far, however, there was no turning back, no way to restore the vehicle without the risk of being caught in the act, so they hid it away deep in the junk of the salvage yard. If I could get the damn thing out of there without being detected, it would afford them some peace of mind, and the farther away I would drive it, the better.

There remained one problem. The general was extremely proud of his jeep and had installed a million extra gadgets on it, mostly superfluous ornamentation. The thing smacked of a teenager's obsession with his first automobile or a Hollywood cowboy's Cadillac replete with silver embellishments and steer's horns. What's more, it had his insignia and rank emblazoned everywhere; he was the sort to have stars sewn on his underwear and pajamas, or at least that's how he was described to me. All of this ornamentation would have to be removed—again, clandestinely, for anyone detected removing these things could be accused of theft, and the Lord only knew what kind of punishment the alleged culprit would face.

I jumped at the opportunity to get the jeep. It mattered little to me how or where I came by it; hand me the keys and I'd drive it away. So in the dead of night I drove that memorable jeep out of their yard into freedom—freedom from motor pools forever. The men had repainted the vehicle completely, and it looked spanking new, not at all like my first relic. We promptly christened it the *Patsy II* and once again lettered the name in Greek.

It lasted throughout the conflict. Back at the historical section, Colonel Starr was so pleased with my good fortune that he had the vehicle assigned to our section permanently, which meant that it would be maintained and repaired on a regular basis or as required. Starr never knew how I procured this jeep—and never asked. When the war ended and my forays to the front ceased, our section was assigned an official driver who took personal pride in its care. I think even the general would have been pleased.

CHAPTER EIGHT

The Anzio Beachhead

In late January of 1944 the Anzio beachhead was established, and it was there I got my first taste of sustained combat or—to be more explicit—my indoctrination into sustained peril. Heretofore it had been my custom to visit a frontline position for a few days or possibly a week or two at the most, sketch or produce small paintings, and then return to the relative calm of the rear-area Historical Section to complete the paintings, rest a bit, and prepare for the next artistic assault.

Anzio (in ancient times Antium) and the twin city of Nettuno were once-popular seaside resorts located about 30 miles directly south of Rome. The Allied forces, initially halted at the Winter Line in mid-November of 1943, and presently stalled at the more formidable Gustav Line, were attempting to penetrate the sophisticated German defenses from the rear with the ultimate goal of moving up the Italian peninsula to Rome. After much deliberation, Anzio had been selected as the place to strike and establish an Allied beachhead.

Sergeant Radulovic and I arrived at Anzio shortly after the initial landings, and were baptized with sporadic bursts of Jerry artillery. This was in sharp contrast to the experience of the first waves of Allied troops that went ashore; they had met no resistance whatsoever, as the Germans had been caught napping. Even their numerous pillboxes and assorted defenses, so skillfully designed and strategically deployed, lay unmanned. From recountals by the men with whom I lived in the months that followed, I gathered that the first troops to land encountered only a couple of drunken, astonished "supermen" wandering the streets of Nettuno.

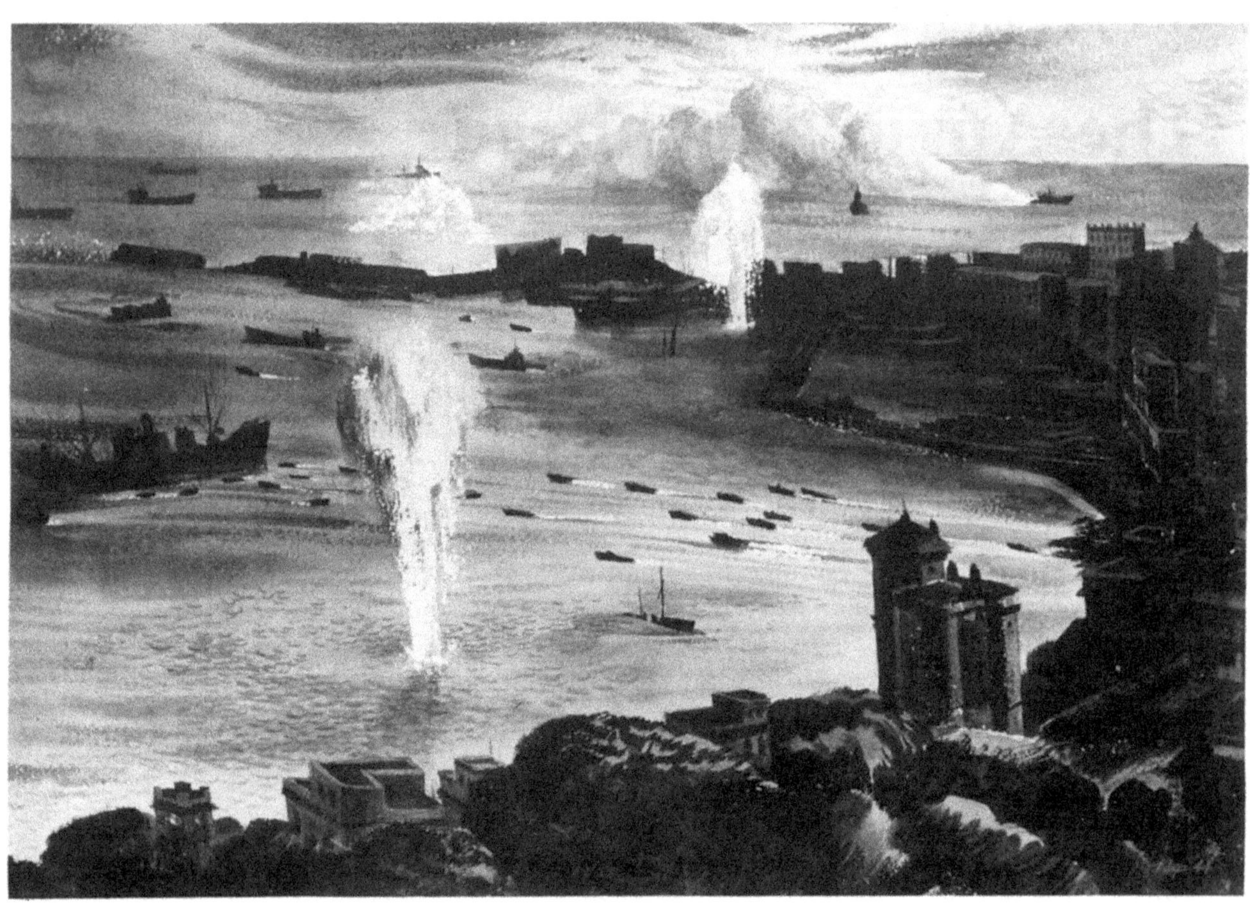

Anzio Harbor

1944. Watercolor. 15½ x 22¾ in.

The Anzio harbor, a beehive of activity at all times, is subjected to German bombardment. Wakes of small landing craft stripe the water as they race to unload the transport ship to the left. In the distance, other ships await their turn to dock; a smoke screen is being laid down to conceal them from enemy observation. I was fascinated by the great geysers sent up by enemy artillery, and would foolishly sit on the docks waiting for them to strike in an attempt to record their shape and movement.

The headquarters of Commanding General Mark Clark nestled in relative safety deep in the ancient catacombs of Nettuno, an underground labyrinth that defied description. The offices and sleeping quarters at that remarkable command post were little more than elaborate caves, dimly lit with tiny electric light bulbs suspended from snaky black wires that clung to the dirt walls and ceilings. For all of the safety it afforded, merely visiting for a moment gave me an eerie feeling; it would have been a great place for Dracula and his friends to avoid the sun. Whenever I needed a vehicle (this was prior to *Patsy*), I was obliged to report to the caves' motor pool. Later on, this necessity would lead to my most embarrassing moment of the entire Italian campaign.

Anzio was different from other battlefields in many ways. There was no escape from the constant fire of long-range enemy artillery and the occasional Luftwaffe fighter-bomber raids. We were sitting ducks for the Jerries and under continuous observation from their vantage points in the surrounding hills. Consequently, everything possible on the beachhead was underground—the orderly rooms, supply services, and other administrative "offices." Wires ran along the ground and then quickly dipped into a dugout via ventilators made of what appeared to be giant mailing tubes. These protruded from mounds of earth piled over the dugouts for protection, forming quaint little "T" shapes that listed at different angles. Radulovic didn't find this weird place to his liking and soon hitched a ride back to the Historical Section via one of the countless vessels transporting daily supplies to the beachhead. I chose to stay on because there was so much to learn and the subject matter for my work was so enticing. I was a veritable modern-day Ulysses being beckoned by the Sirens, only I was *electing* to let those wicked sea nymphs have a go at me. I must emphasize that there is a vast difference between being ordered by a higher authority to do something and being able to decide unilaterally whether or not to chance it.

I was fortunate to secure a ready-made, improved, first-class foxhole fully equipped with an ingenious trap door, and was discreet enough not to ask why it was unoccupied. This little hole in the ground, roughly the size of a typical kitchen table, served as my home for the next two and a half months. I didn't know who dug that marvelous foxhole, but he sure knew what he was doing. The stout beams overhead were raw tree trunks or mammoth limbs measuring a foot in diameter, which were reassuring to view but would not have proved effective against a direct hit. Nevertheless, I had cause later to remain forever grateful for the protection my underground home provided.

In the evening I'd curl up in my earth nest and pore over my sketches and notes by candlelight, or write letters, or *listen to music.* Somewhere along the way I'd picked up an old telephone receiver and now had it suspended from the rafters. It perpetually dangled in my way, but despite banging my head into it again and again, it was my contact with the outer world and I was grateful for its comfort. In the dark of night I'd steal toward the field commander's generator and hook up my wire to his radio line. In this manner I could listen to the same programs as he, which were graciously provided by the enemy and delivered by the infamous Axis Sally. With soothing melodies and a plainly seductive voice, Sally provided us with popular tunes and not very convincing chitchat. We were periodically informed that the "jig was up" and we ought to surrender to the superior German forces, who would see to it that we would be cared for under strict adherence to the International Red Cross and Geneva convention guidelines. We would receive VIP treatment by the inevitable victors, and as prisoners of war we could safely ride out the remainder of the conflict to eventually return home safe and sound. It was all baloney, propaganda served with soft dreamy music intended to make us lonely and homesick. Instead, we looked forward to the programs; we found them amusing, and besides, they gave us something to discuss the following day.

At times the music would abruptly stop. We knew when this was going to happen because the sound would weaken beforehand, which meant that too many soldiers had tied into the generator. This made the commanding officer furious, and he would scream at his orderly to get his ass outside and pull those damn wires. The next day the orderly would warn me not to tie into the generator and would explain in vivid language how irate the old man became, adding that we would all face disciplinary action sooner or later—but that never came to pass. In retrospect, I realize that our wires could have been confiscated and we might have been severely reprimanded or punished, but we weren't. The old man was warning us that if an emergency arose while his power was

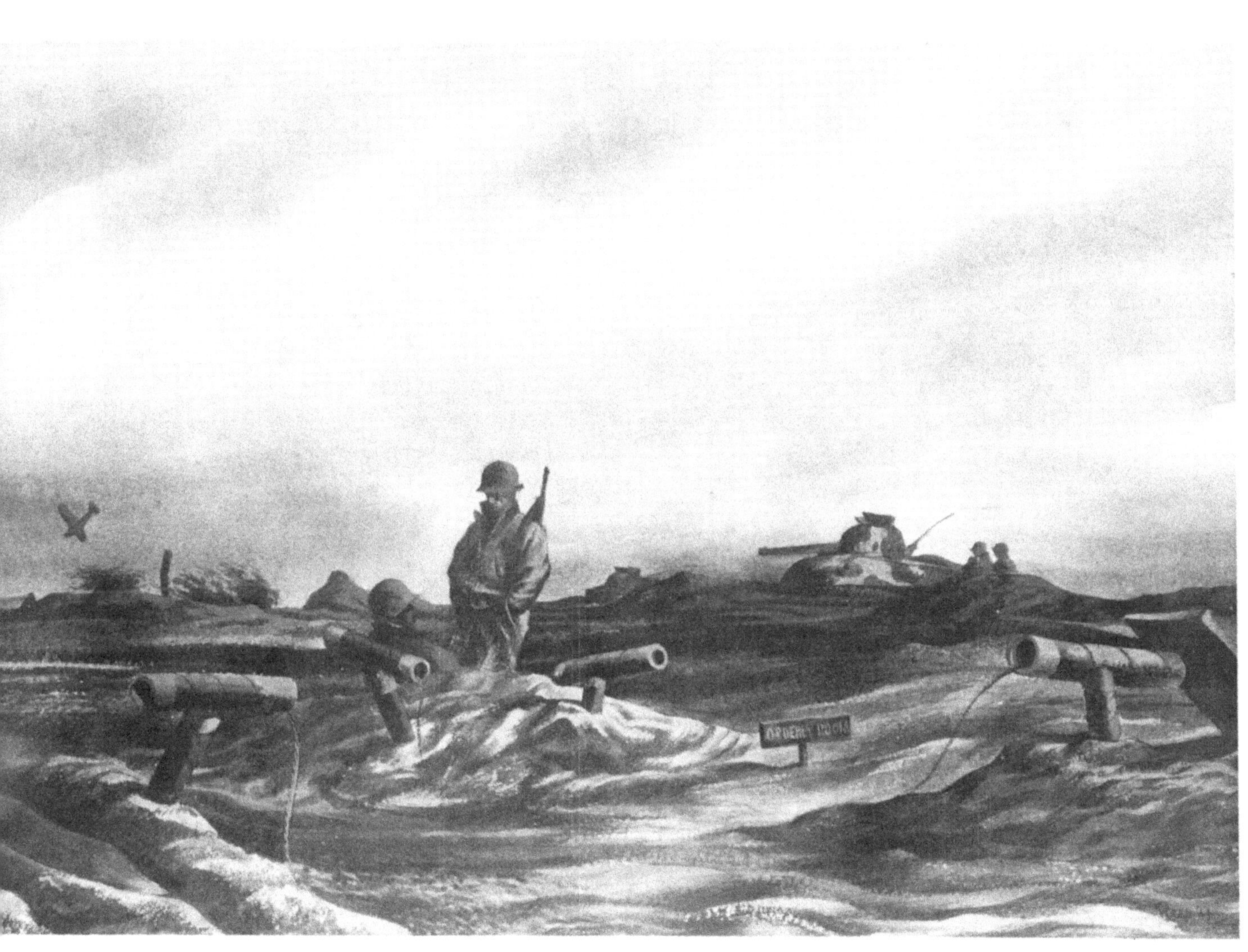

Orderly Room at Anzio
1944. Watercolor. 14½ x 23 in.

A vital part of the "Anzio Underground" was this orderly room. Note the telephone lines going down through the ventilator pipes to provide communication between dugouts. The pipes are actually cardboard casings that once housed artillery shells, an example of the American soldier's ingenuity. On the horizon, tanks can be seen half buried in the earth, while a Piper Cub skitters about overhead—the eyes of our army.

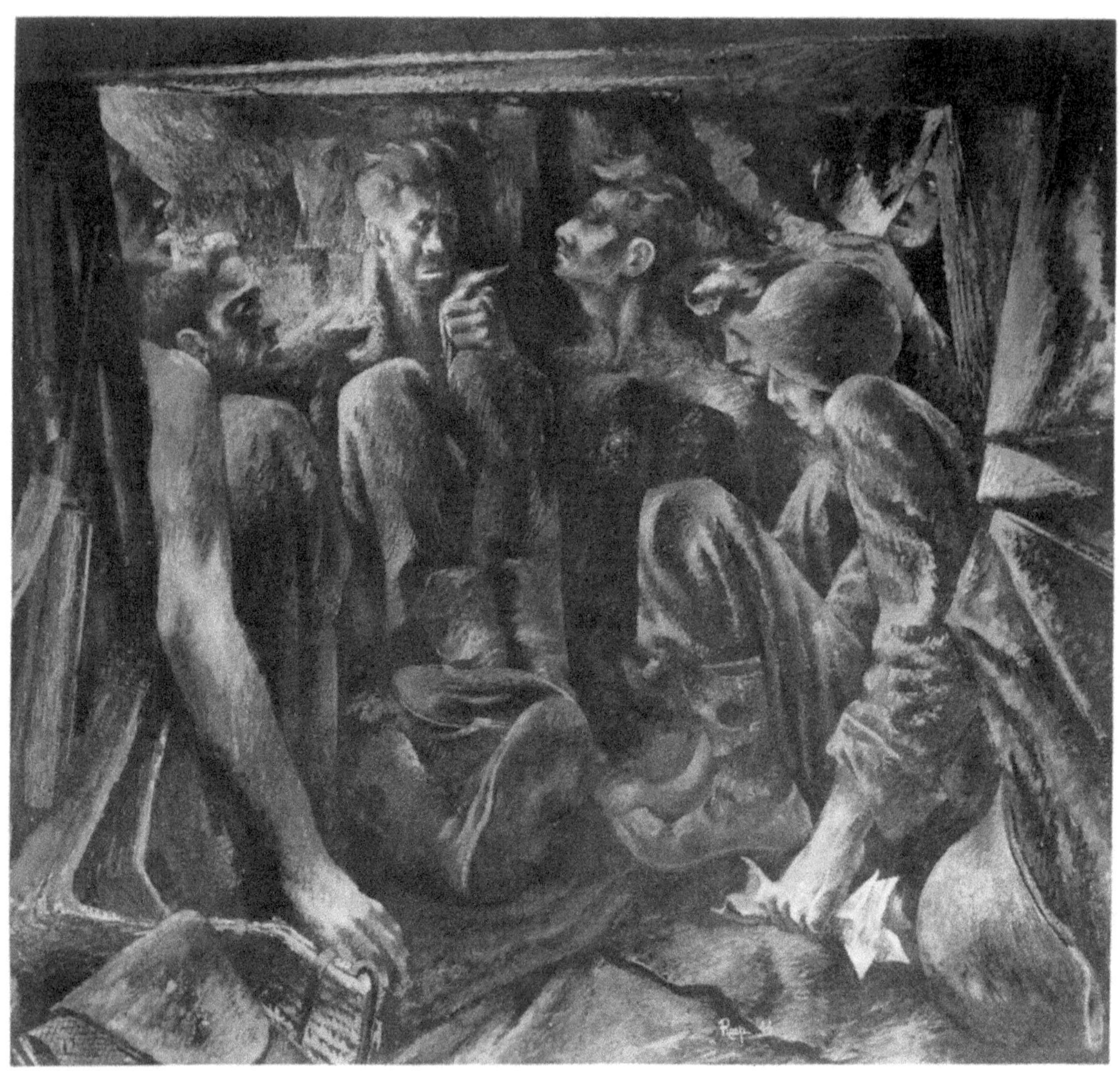

The Dugout
1944. Gouache. 19 x 20½ in.

During the long nights at Anzio, soldiers gathered in the most solidly constructed dugouts. Rails and timbers, hauled from Anzio and Nettuno, often made the best supports for the two to three feet of earth forming the roof. In this fashion, soldiers were well protected from the constant enemy shelling and bombing. However strong, though, dugouts could not withstand direct hits.

When the shells began to land close, soldiers displayed a variety of reactions; contrary to popular belief, most men were frightened. The men I gathered with either played cards, joked, told stories, or sang to the accompaniment of my toy recorder—all this with one ear cocked.

failing, he couldn't function without communications. To be fair, some army officers had a keen understanding of just how far to push a lowly GI, and this particular gentleman, whom I never met, must have been a pretty good egg. The following night we'd simply hook up again.

Some of the men made their own personal receiver sets out of a mere coil of wire, a razor blade, and a telephone receiver similar to mine. I also tried to make one and once miraculously succeeded in getting a faint note or two from my telephone receiver by delicately placing the tip of the wire on the edge of the razor blade, which had been stuck into a piece of wood. But I was and remain ignorant of most scientific advances, notably in the field of electronics, so I soon disposed of the incomprehensible paraphernalia and returned to tying into the generator.

Each day I'd crawl out of my hole, wash and shave out of my helmet, carefully hang my wet towel to dry, and pack my art gear in anticipation of the day's work ahead. I surely didn't have to travel very far for my subject matter. I was living in it—or part of it—and there wasn't anyplace to go anyway. We were packed into the beachhead like sardines, and the front lines were within walking distance; I used a jeep only occasionally to reconnoiter the area speedily and save valuable time. I worked in the fields in plain sight of the Jerries, who enjoyed an unobstructed view of our activities, but to my knowledge I drew enemy artillery fire only once.

Of course, that scared me half out of my wits. But what seemed so incongruous to me as an artist, or visualist, was that once again the sun was brightly shining, the birds twittering, the butterflies fluttering, and the early spring flowers beginning to dot the fields. I was industriously painting a watercolor in an open field, and only the staccato of intermittent artillery fire in the distance reminded me of the war; the gaping shell craters all around me were now familiar landmarks that went unnoticed.

My subject was a tank of the 1st Armored Division, dug well into the ground for added protection and concealed from enemy view by a camouflage net. Since the sun's rays were so intense, I had rigged a canvas shelter-half for shade, erected a makeshift easel behind it, and brought along a small caned chair for comfort. I was totally absorbed in my work, grateful to be in the process of developing a fairly decent if somewhat academic painting from average subject matter.

When the first shell struck, shrapnel whizzed harmlessly over my

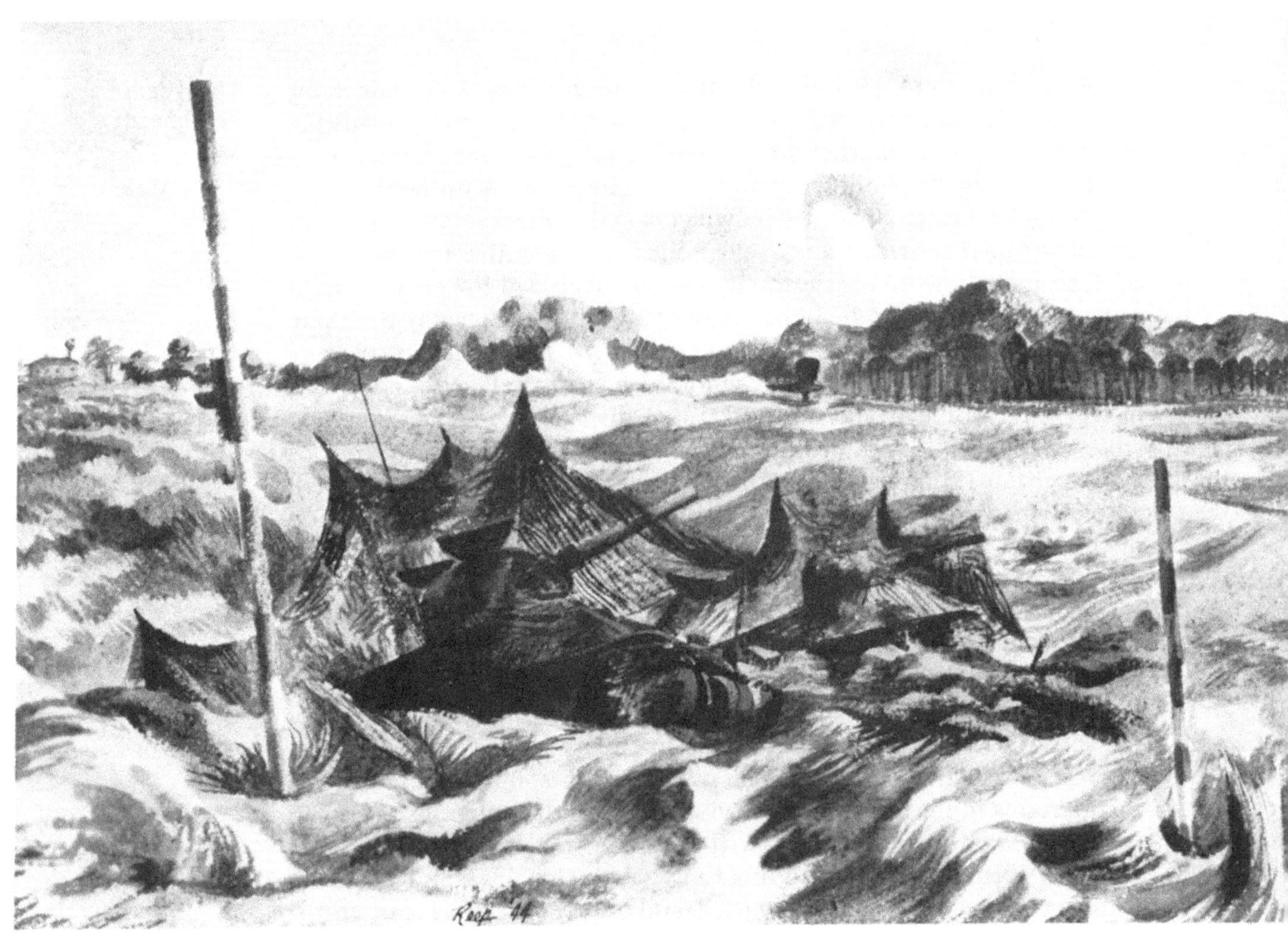

Indirect Fire

1944. Watercolor. 15 x 22 in.

Tanks were used for indirect fire in the Anzio Beachhead fighting. In the distance are the woods that housed the 1st Armored Division and 6th Infantry. Weird patterns from the smoke screens and the ever-present observation plane complete the scene. The painting was nearly finished when the German artillery decided to eliminate me. I took the photograph (p. 85) after I returned to the site; note the toppled chair and equipment strewn about in the grass. But I cannot recall why both helmet and helmet liner, now separated, were lying on the ground—I should have been wearing them.

head, accompanied by a sharp, thunderous noise. I ran like the devil to hurl myself into a nearby drainage ditch, leaving my equipment strewn about. For a solid hour or so I remained there, scared as hell in anticipation of that direct hit—the one you never hear. Random shellfire is not too frightening, but these nuts were zeroing in on me, and my fear was mounting. They must have pounded in seven or eight shells in the attempt to wipe me out. What a complete waste of artillery, I mused; they certainly were a perverse enemy. Eventually, when things quieted down, I returned to finish my painting. I'm sure the Jerries thought me nutty as a fruitcake, but then, the feeling was mutual.

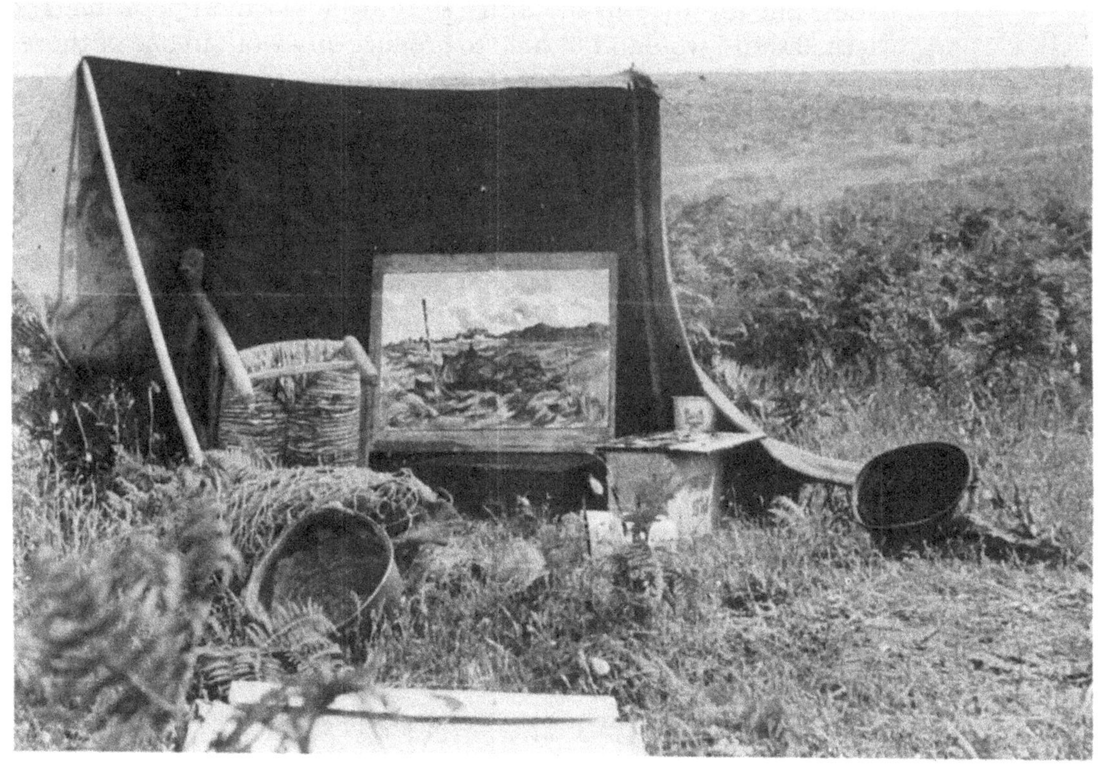

I painted the life underground and the Piper Cubs overhead. These little planes were our eyes, for the few aircraft originally assigned to the beachhead had been damaged by shellfire and stood frozen and motionless like ominous sculpture. My adrenaline was flowing, and I worked diligently from early morning until dusk each day. Most of my work centered on the soldiers in the midst of their daily activities, the *pièce de resistance* being a large pen-and-ink drawing of a score or more soldiers busily washing, getting haircuts, sunning themselves, sitting on the outdoor latrines, or just lazing about. Jeeps, trailers and other artifacts appear amid the leafless trees. (If Hieronymous Bosch had done this picture, it would surely have been a masterpiece; the subject was that abundant.) There wasn't much to do during the daylight hours, and not much more during the night once the fighting had reached a stalemate. Night patrols were active, as usual, but neither side cared to reveal their positions during the day with meaningless activity. One night I was asked if I'd like to go out on a routine patrol in a tank, through enemy lines, but for once in my army life I declined the invitation. I knew darned well I wouldn't be able to produce any work in one of those iron prisons and probably wouldn't be able to see anything either, the view from a tank being what it is.

In the evenings several of us would gather in one of the more spacious dugouts in violation of strict orders, which were never enforced. It was felt that if men congregated, especially at night when the shelling was at its peak, a direct hit could prove disastrous. However, there were other considerations; one of the most significant was that a soldier alone in a small hole in the ground night after night might very well crack up emotionally. So we took our chances and crowded into an area no larger than six feet square, there to tell stories, joke and kid one another, gripe, play cards, and otherwise comfort one another in our misery. I had a toy "Tonette," which is an excuse for the musical instrument called a recorder, and played it on occasion. The small plastic flute had been given to me by the Special Services section, which also supplied baseballs and mitts and other sports equipment. (If I thought myself a trifle silly sitting out in an open field painting a watercolor, consider how ludicrous it was for groups of soldiers to play baseball on the battlefield in clear view of the enemy.)

The simple melodies from the Tonette delighted my companions,

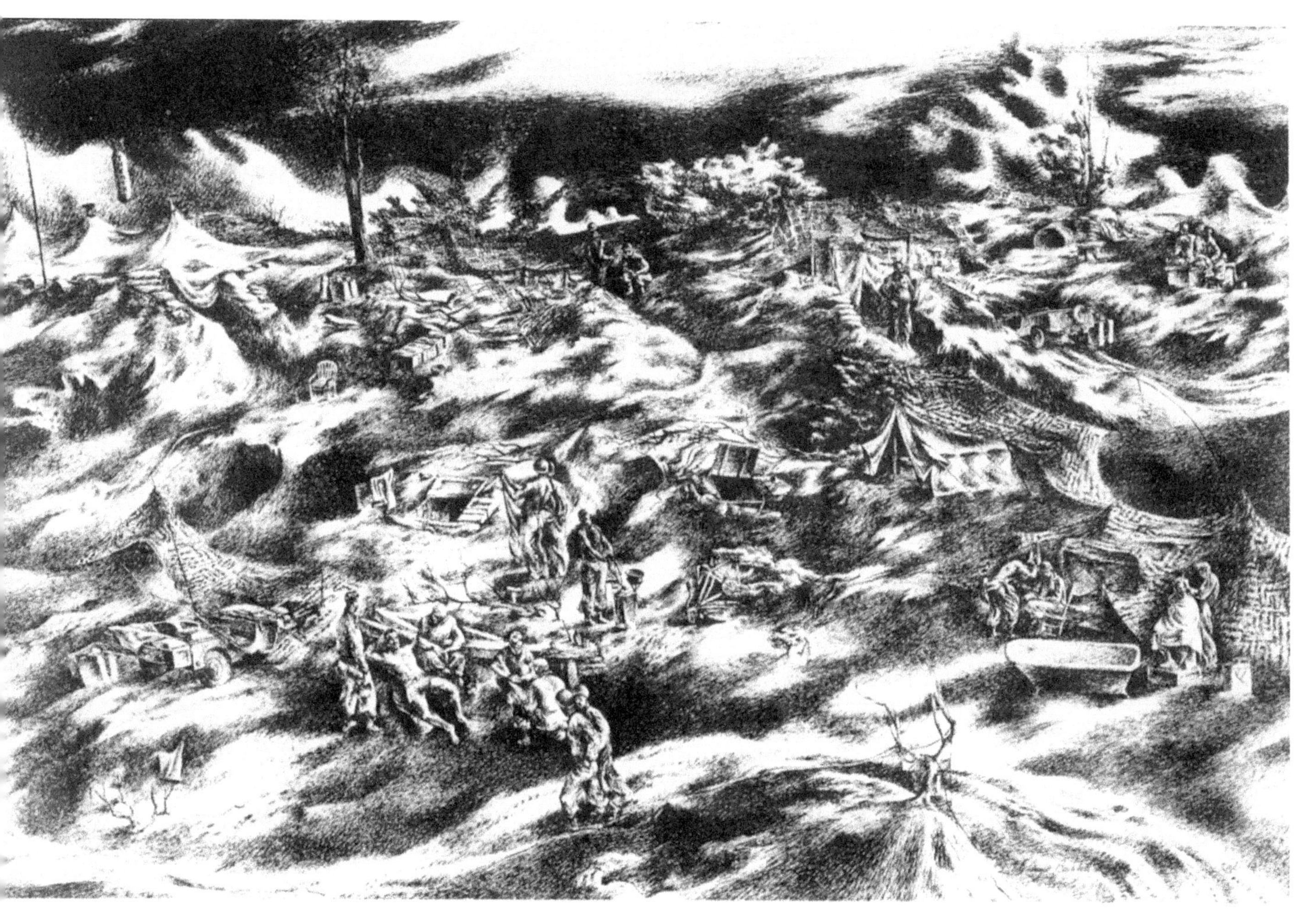

The Anzio Beachhead

1944. Pen and ink. 26½ x 40½ in.

This glimpse into the daytime life on and in underground Anzio shows how the men went about their duties or spent their leisure hours, unmindful of enemy shellfire. It was a unique battlefield; everything was dug into the ground—vehicles, offices, sleeping quarters, and doughnut machines. In the upper left is the theater, dug in and sandbagged, built to replace a movie tent that suffered a direct hit. The dugout below and slightly to the right of the theater, its lid open and a striped towel hanging nearby, was my home for over two and a half months. Anzio has to stand as a tribute to the American spirit, to the ability to carry on and even joke about a very nasty situation. (See details on pp. 88–89.)

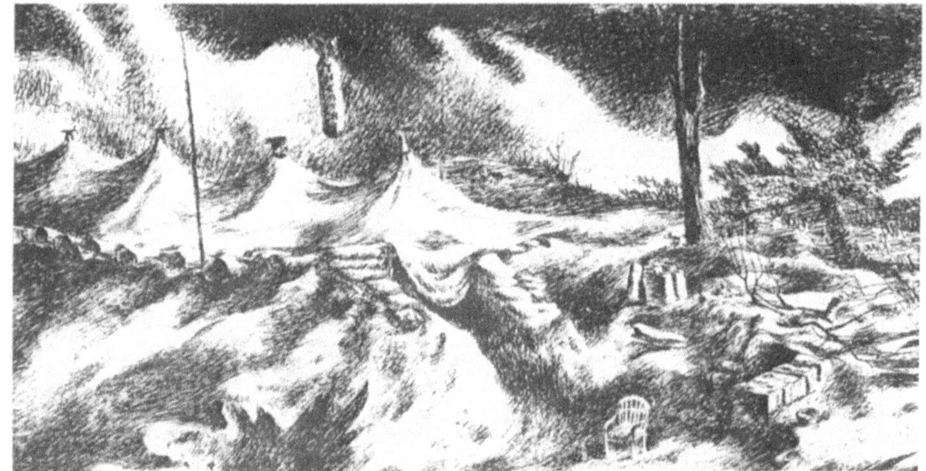

The new theater.

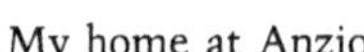

My home at Anzio.

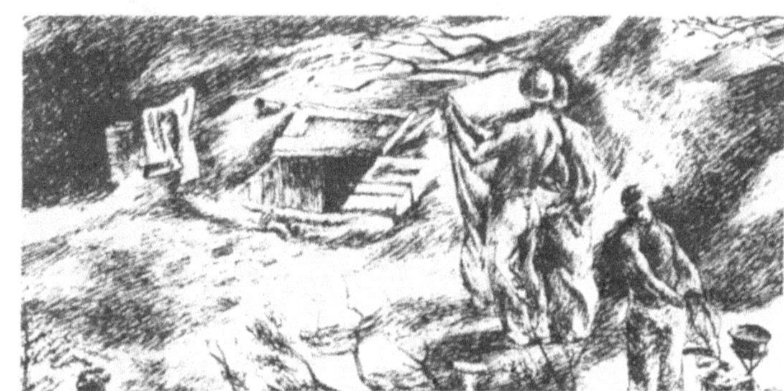

Soldiers sunned themselves, wrote letters, etc.

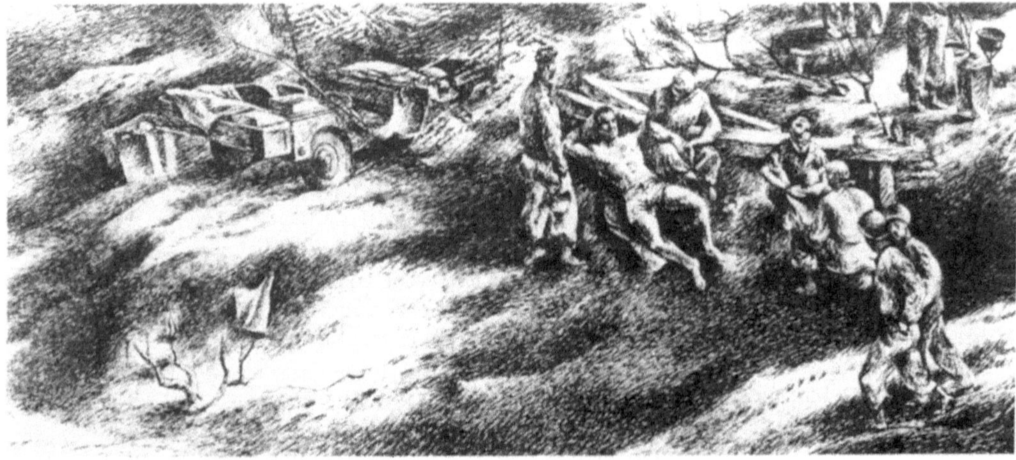

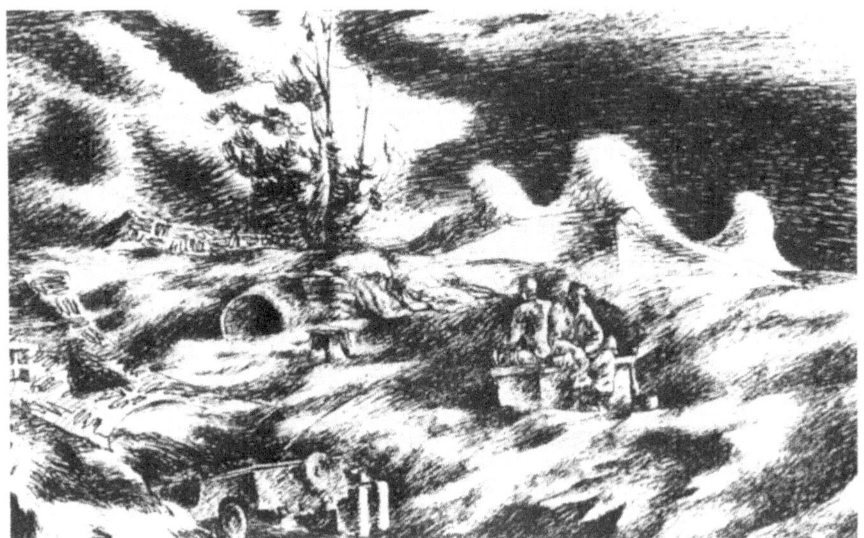

The omnipresent outdoor latrine.

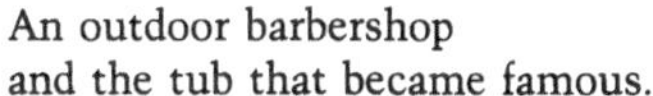

An outdoor barbershop and the tub that became famous.

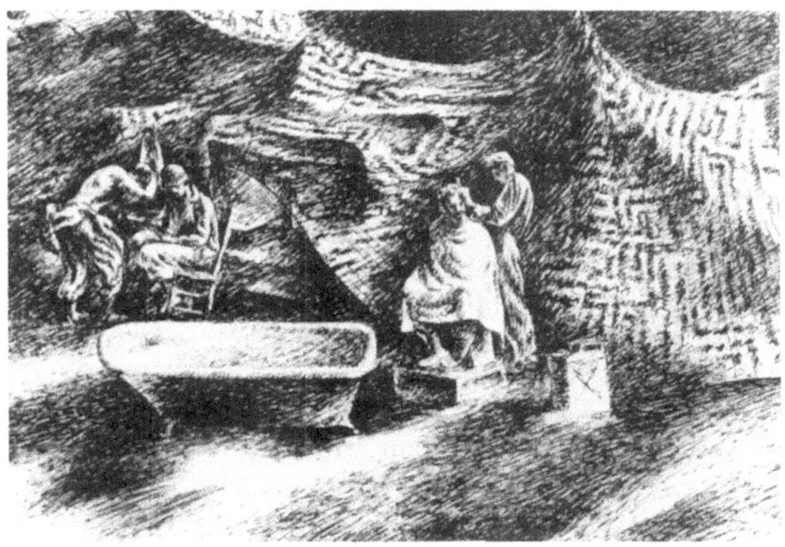

Details of The Anzio Beachhead.

crammed together in the dugout, and carried out into the dark night to cheer some of the men in nearby foxholes. It is remarkable how poignant an otherwise absurd and meaningless popular song can be under such circumstances, even when performed by an amateur musician. I must have played "Lili Marlene" a thousand times during those long nights, and by request. All things are relative: in that dugout, it was my music or none at all, and it turned our thoughts from the constant shelling.

While I was busily sketching a tank commander one day (most of the soldiers were eager and proud to pose for me), an enlisted man approached in typical fashion to ask what I was doing. Even in civilian life (and for the life of me I don't know why this is so), when spectators confront an artist at work, they invariably ask him what he's doing. Maybe they just don't know what to say and are attempting to break the ice politely in making contact with an off-beat, uncommon creature. It once made me furious because any person with reasonably good eyesight could see at a glance what I was up to, but I grew accustomed to the query and in time developed some pretty lighthearted replies. It never ends there, though, for it always turns out that the questioners have a sister or mother who paints and who is *really* good but hasn't pursued art as a career—or that they themselves "never could draw a straight line."

Back to my inquisitive friend: to answer his question, I stated that I was drawing a picture of a tank commander sitting on his tank. "What for?" I told him that this was my job, my assignment, and that I was an army officer and war artist-correspondent attached to the Fifth Army Historical Section but really a member of the First Armored Division. I took pains to explain that while I was documenting the war in pictures, others with whom I worked were writers and historians preparing a history of the Italian campaign. "Yeah,"—there was a long pause—"but what do you really do?"

I believed that I had given him a very complete answer, that I had been patient and understanding and coherent. Clearly, however, he wasn't convinced. I repeated most of my response and hoped he'd go away. My wish was granted for one of his buddies was summoning him to join the important daily card game, where the betting was heavy. He called back to his pal, "Be there in a minute—I'm trying to find out what this guy is doing." He couldn't resist one final comment. "This all you do—really, all day? That's all? Geez, what a racket. They really pay you for this—geez." Assured that I had a cushy job and had it made, he bade me goodbye, but not without reminding me that he would return to see how my drawing turned out. Everybody promises to return to see how your work turns out, but almost nobody does.

The day turned out to be very productive for me. Working in a charcoal pencil on small paper, I executed several good likenesses of the models; that is, I thought I had captured their character as well as the ambiance of the place. It had been a long day, I was pooped, and the sun was now setting. But as I packed up to leave, the character returned and wanted to see the results of the tank commander drawing in particular. I obliged by showing him everything I had done that day, hoping my work would convince him that I was truly a very important, necessary, and useful person. After all, we all need approbation, regardless of the source, and he was one of the rare ones who returned as promised.

"Hey—they're pretty good," he responded, to my delight. (*Pretty good* is as far as most sidewalk critics go, never for a moment concerned about their lack of credentials as judges of color, composition, draughtsmanship, and the like.) And then he spoiled everything by falling back upon his original line. "This all you do? Geez, what a racket. Second Looie—geez, what a breeze—all you do is make pictures."

Anzio was surrounded by the Pontine Marshes. One of the few things that Benito Mussolini, Hitler's Fascist partner, accomplished for the benefit of the Italian populace was to drain the marshes and establish a sophisticated network of irrigation canals to control the flooding. He followed this with the construction of low-cost living accommodations. The "Mussolini Canal," heavily mined by the Germans, now formed the periphery of the Anzio beachhead. At times I would sit on the edge of the minefield to look out over no-man's land and paint, in clear view of enemy territory, which delusively appeared unoccupied. My only problem there was due to a large cow.

On a bright coolish morning I set up my gear to paint alongside an outpost bordering the minefield. Two soldiers perched in their trench were my willing models but disappeared as soon as their watch had ended. Left alone, I worked on, struggling a bit with an only mildly successful work. Artists come to expect a struggle somewhere along the line with every successful painting they produce; conversely, those things that paint easily are often not worth a hoot. I suppose this is because when you face the unknown and wrestle with unfamiliar creative problems, you're in new territory and being challenged.

Looking up from time to time, I was astonished to see a patrol of American soldiers in enemy territory walking slowly toward me in loose single file. As they neared the canal and picked their way through the minefield, which had been clandestinely cleared and marked for the use of just such patrols, I noticed that they were pulling along a huge, reluctant cow. These men were rangers under the leadership of the fabled Colonel William O. Darby, a proud force with an enviable record. As they passed by, casting what I chose to believe were admiring glances at my work, it was obvious that they were weary from their night mission. Their cloth masks—which resembled those worn in snow country during bitter storms—were pushed aside to reveal their blackened faces. They wore no helmets and looked like the tough, grim fighters they were reputed to be. When I asked what they were doing with the cow, they gleefully replied that they intended to slaughter her and eat steak. They went on, pulling and tugging at Bossy.

A few minutes later I became aware of a great clopping behind me. I turned to see what all this commotion was and broke into laughter at the sight of that great beast wildly rushing back to where she belonged. In seconds she was in the minefield only a few feet from where I was at work. Before it occurred to me that she might not be able to negotiate the field safely, there was a thunderous roar smack in front of me; shrapnel whizzed by my head and severed the small plants at my side. I sat dumfounded. I hadn't had the presence of mind or the military experience to anticipate the danger and take cover in the trenches, and now what did it matter? It had happened too fast. Bossy was dead, and I was in shock.

The rangers didn't bother to come after their prize; they were apparently too weary to pursue her. To this day I can vividly recall the entire incident and have the nearly completed painting as a reminder. I dug out some of the chunks of shrapnel that were embedded in the ground at my feet, curious to examine what had missed me, but I need no reminder of the frightening whirr they made as they passed by. The bushes had been severed with such force that their stalks momentarily hung in midair as in an animated film; only after realizing that they had been amputated would they consent to drop. This time I didn't pursue my painting; instead, I packed my gear and left the scene, still shaken. Trudging back to my foxhole residence, I pondered the vagaries of fate: how farcical it would have been had I lost my life at Anzio because of a wretched, frightened cow.

My subject matter continued to center on the soldiers at play or work. My watercolor of one nutty soldier taking a hot bath in a real tub out in a field was shown in the newsreels back home (which in those pre-TV days were an integral, inviting part of every movie theater's fare) with that magnificent lady Eleanor Roosevelt. Though I was never to see the actual newsreel, my family wrote proudly of the event. The same painting was also reproduced in *Newsweek* (16 October 1944) with an item announcing that the army, the Treasury Department, and the movie industry were cooperating in "one of the biggest art-circulating ventures in history": an exhibition of some 125 paintings and drawings by 20 soldiers and civilians was to open at the Roxy Theater in New York, then tour 27 other cities to reach an estimated audience of 25,000,000. The closing line reads "The above sample is 'Soldier's Bath,' a watercolor by Lt. Edward Reep, done in Italy where he was promoted for valor at Anzio with his armored unit."

I felt very good about this turn of events because it seemed to me that few civilians were getting a true picture of what war was all about most of the time. Artists and writers who simply visited the front lines tended to glamorize the battlefield; it wasn't really that way at all.

Nor was the soldier so happily posing stark naked in the bathtub looking (as some suggested) for a "section 8," which if granted meant that he could be sent home for reasons of insanity, battle fatigue, or inability to cope. He had discovered the tub in Nettuno, an elaborate white porcelain model with beautiful clawed feet, and had hauled it back over the dusty roads tied to his jeep. Ingeniously (and this raised some doubts about his insanity, for he surely knew what he was doing), he had punctured a small hole in a five-gallon gasoline can and placed it beneath the tub full of water. As the gasoline dripped onto the ground below, he bravely ignited it to create a continuous flame that kept the water hot as he soaked contentedly. To this day I cannot understand why the gas can didn't explode. I would have been petrified to light the fuel, must less get into the tub, yet I couldn't resist sitting there about ten feet away to record the event. My model, whose name I regret not having learned, was

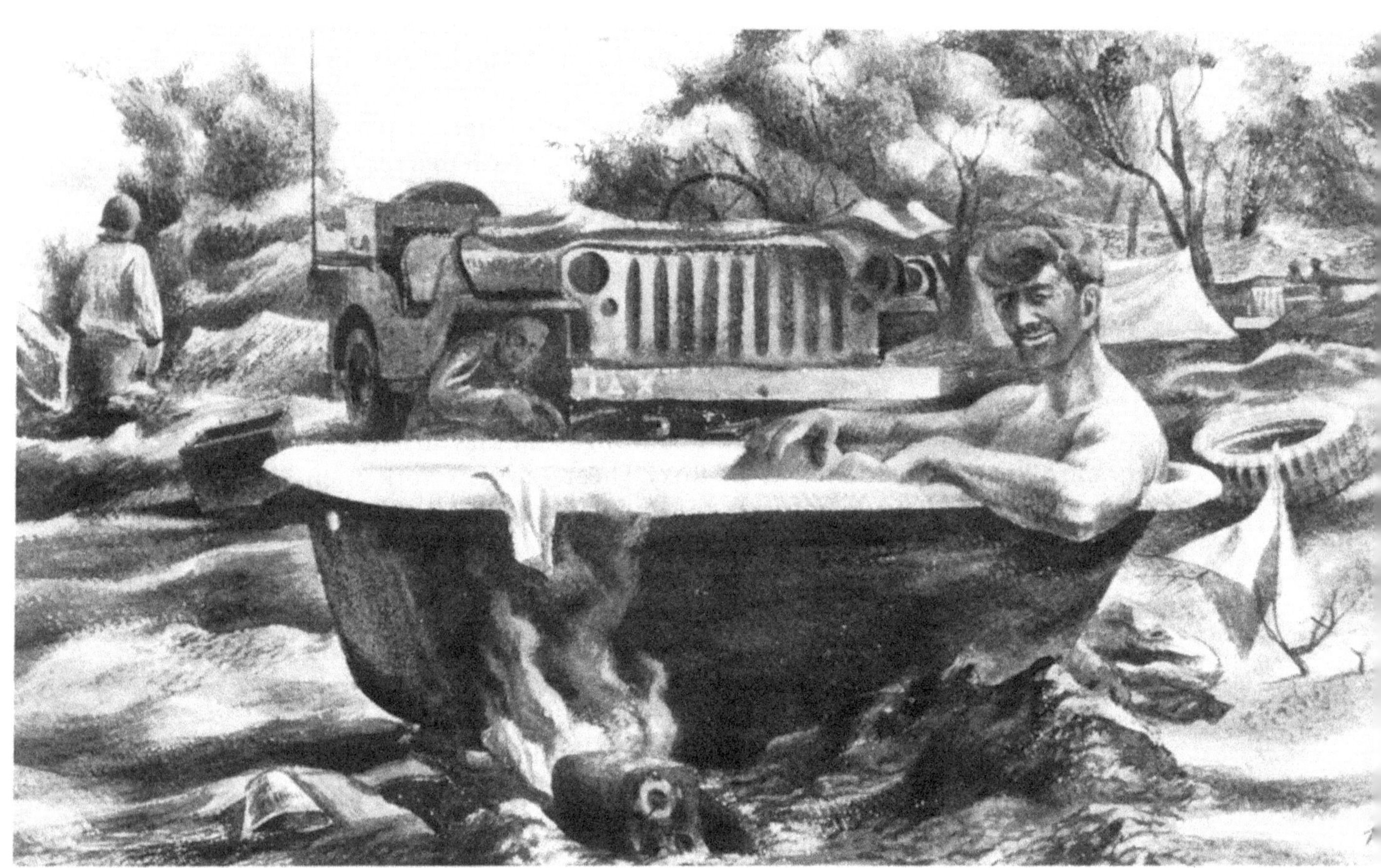

Soldier Bathing
1944. Watercolor. 12½ x 22¾ in.

A soldier of the 1st Armored Division enjoys a hot outdoor bath, largely through his ingenuity and effort; another works on the wheel of his jeep. Although aboveground activity was under constant observation by the Germans in the nearby hills, during the warm spring days it was impossible not to get out and enjoy the sunshine. If shelling commenced, everyone scurried like burrowing animals seeking their holes. Note the huge camouflage net strung amid the trees to conceal our vehicles or materiel.

a damn sight smarter than he led others to believe, and I daresay he was the only soldier at Anzio to luxuriate in an open-air "hot tub." That microcosm of GI ingenuity reassured me that the Jerries were fighting a losing battle, and that they had sadly underestimated American resourcefulness.

A movie was shown each night in a mammoth tent about 30 feet from my foxhole. One night when Bing Crosby was starring in *Going My Way,* which I had seen, I decided to stay home in my dirt hole and write letters to my family. Stark naked and dripping with perspiration—it was a warm night and the dugout lacked ventilation—I was halfway along with a short V-mail note to my mother when a German 155mm shell exploded between my foxhole and the theater. The noise was deafening, much louder than any I had ever heard before, and my ears felt as if they were bursting (the ringing in them remained for days). Screams of agony and pain ensued; woeful cries for help from the dazed and wounded, and I knew that the theater had been hit. As I tried to pull myself together and get out there to aid the injured, a second shell struck. That did me in; I lost my courage and froze. I stayed in the hole all night, a total wreck. Dirt had fallen down through the rafters and turned to mud on my wet body; the pitiful cries of the wounded tortured me, but there was no way that I would be of service—I was scared gutless. Worse yet, I deemed myself a coward.

By the time I meekly ventured outside the following morning, the area was being cleaned up. Where the theater tent had stood a day earlier, stacks of clothing and equipment were piled, bordering fresh shell craters that came almost to the edge of my debris-covered foxhole door. I walked slowly to the field hospital to report the incessant ringing in my ears but was released after an examination revealed no blood or concussion. I was still in a state of mild shock and felt so bad about my behavior that I pondered returning to the rear area Historical Section back of the main battle lines. But if I were to leave, I concluded, I might not summon the courage to continue working at the front, so I dealt with the situation in another way. Instinctively, I knew that my days as a combat artist were hanging in the balance. I decided to paint—immediately, right then and there at that tragic spot. Seventeen men, including the projectionist and his assistant, had been killed by those shells, and a score of others lay injured.

Gathering my equipment, I painted there for the remainder of the day. The work, in watercolor and casein, depicted dazed soldiers stripped to the waist and emotionless, gathering up the remnants of clothing and equipment of the fallen men and stacking it in neat piles. A small tree, now brutally stripped of its bark and foliage, reached upward into a bleak sky, heavy and colorless. The clouds formed a vague monsterlike image with gaping jaws and elongated clawed hands—not obvious at first glance but strangely insistent. I fought against being melodramatic or too pictorial, and as a result the painting remains in my judgment as one of my most potent statements of the war.

At day's end, emotionally spent but encouraged by the success of my painting, I decided to move up closer to the front, to the parameter marked by the Mussolini canal, and bunk with friends in a more spacious dugout. I disliked giving up the old quarters that had served me so well and probably saved my life, but I knew deep in my soul that I couldn't stay there any longer. Moving on was the only way I could deal with the overwhelming fear that had possessed me for the first time. (It never occurred to me till just now that I was an officer bunking with enlisted men, and I really don't think anybody gave a damn. It only added meaning to my observation that in battle, rank is meaningless.) Meanwhile, a new movie theater replaced the old, this time buried half into the earth by army bulldozers, with great walls of sandbags piled high on all sides. Only the tent portion necessary to conceal the light of the projector during evening performances, rose into the air, suggesting that even the army brass had learned a lesson.

Not everything was grim at Anzio; from time to time humorous incidents seasoned our daily routines. At one point I hitched a ride back to the caves where Mark Clark was headquartered and courteously requested a jeep from the motor pool. My credentials allowed for this, so—grudgingly, as expected—I was told to go see if there was anything available. The only vehicle not in use was the general's personal jeep, but since he was neither on the beachhead nor expected soon, motor pool people surprisingly checked it out to me—along with a driver, which I considered a waste of manpower. We set off to visit a regimental headquarters where I had some business to attend to, and from there we would search for new painting sites. It was a pleasant day for a drive, but as we rolled along in leisurely fashion I seemed to be receiving inordinate

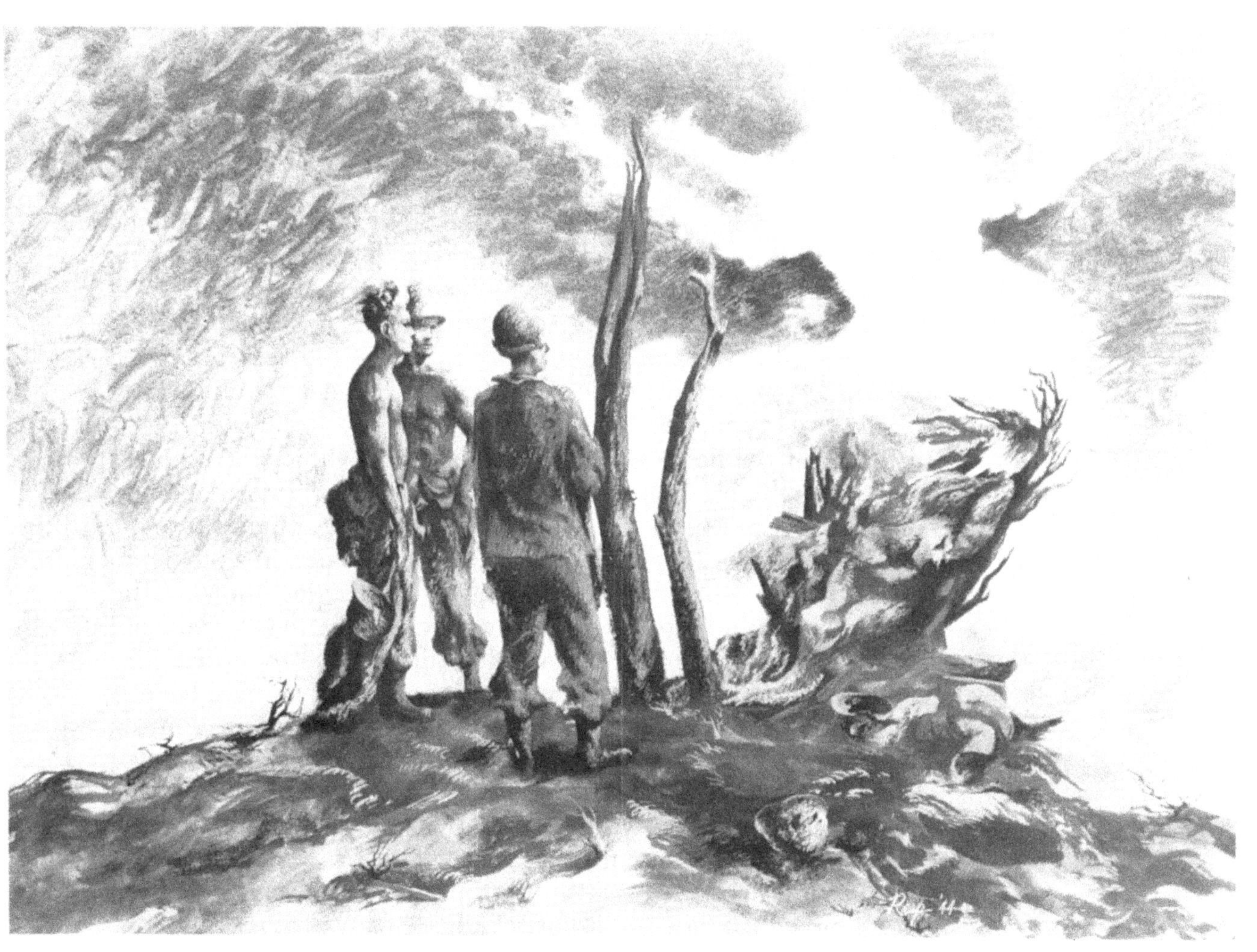

The Morning After

1944. Watercolor and casein. 15½ x 21¼ in.

Soldiers stack the uniforms and equipment of men killed in the shelling of the movie tent. All that remain of the theater are the trunks of three trees and debris. Even underground we would not have been protected from a direct hit, and we were all very conscious of being sitting ducks. Confronted with the issue of courage or cowardice, I knew that, without positive measures, my career as a war artist would be over.

attention from soldiers everywhere: they were highballing me right and left, standing at strict attention, smiling and apparently pleased just to get a glimpse of me. I recall a couple of real clowns, who'd been conspicuously sitting on an outdoor john, jumping up to salute with one hand while holding up their pants with the other. What in hell was going on?

Arriving at regimental headquarters, I was astonished to find the entire complement of regimental brass lined up to greet me. They stood at rigid attention, neatly attired and beaming hopefully. As we drew closer, however, the pleasant expressions slowly turned to hostile stares of disbelief. A chicken colonel approached and angrily bellowed, "Who in the hell do you think you are?" There was no salute to return but I saluted anyway, and leaping out of the jeep to stand at attention, I offered my name, rank, and serial number. It did little good.

"Well, what the hell are you doing riding in a three-star general's jeep?" He was irate, mean and displayed little patience with me—and I can't say that I blamed him. "Sir," I volunteered, "they assigned it to me back at the catacombs car pool, Sir." I had learned, when in a pickle, to hang "sirs" about my sentences like bookends. "Well," he fumed, "why don't you cover up the stars?" The stars were on the little insignia plate on the front where a license plate would ordinarily be mounted. The colonel hadn't really asked me a question; it was the opening salvo of a scathing reprimand and prolonged dressing down before an amused audience, but my head was swimming at the time, and I cannot recall many of the details.

No disciplinary action was taken against me, and again I had escaped a fate worse than death, or so it seemed at the time. My driver, that same responsible man who was shepherding me about and knew his business to a tee, had failed to secure the little canvas cover that concealed the stars when the general wasn't aboard; to the delight of everyone, I was catching the flak for his negligence. The regimental delegation had undoubtedly got wind of the jeep on its way and ordered everyone to clean up the headquarters and *look smart* when the old man arrived. The soldiers out in the field had been dutifully saluting the jeep with respect for a commanding officer who would bravely appear among them, but any who got a close look must surely have believed that I was the youngest three-star general in American military annals.

Not until we finally broke out of Anzio in May 1944 did I have an opportunity to vindicate myself for my reprehensible conduct, bordering on pure cowardice, when the theater was struck. It wasn't much compared to the countless heroic deeds of the real fighting men, but it helped restore my self-esteem and confidence. We were set to break out of the beachhead and chase the enemy northward, for getting to Rome had become an obsession with Winston Churchill and Franklin D. Roosevelt.

In order to accomplish the breakout rapidly and with minimum casualties, the surrounding minefield along the Mussolini canal had to be successfully negotiated, and to do this, an unusual device known as "the snake" was being assembled. As an artist-correspondent, I was privileged to be invited to a demonstration of how the snake would function, as were reporters and photographers representing presses throughout the free world, where much was made of the preparation. I suppose one could regard the affair as pure public relations.

The snake was a 400-foot-long metal container formed in tubular sections designed to hold hundreds of pounds of TNT, and it did indeed resemble a monstrous snake with a contraption at the leading end that rose into the air like the head of a cobra. Skillfully conceived and engineered, it would be pushed into and beyond the farthest border of a minefield by one of our tanks; once in place, it would be detonated. Recalling my brief training as an engineer, I knew that *induced* detonation would be relied upon, which meant that the explosion would not only set off the mines directly beneath the snake but those in adjacent areas too, thus providing a safe, wide crossing for our men and machines.

On 20 May 1944, a confidential communiqué was issued by Major General L. K. Truscott:

> TO: The Officers and Men of the Allied Beachhead Forces:
>
> For more than four months you have occupied the most dangerous and important post of any Allied force. You have stopped and defeated more than ten divisions which Hitler had ordered to drive us into the sea. You have contained on your front divisions which the enemy sorely needed elsewhere. You have neglected no opportunity to harass and injure the enemy. Arduous conditions you have accepted willingly and cheerfully, and you have not failed to improve in discipline and training and in condition. You have set a standard that has won the admiration and respect of our United Nations. For your services during these trying days, I congratulate you.

> Now, after four months, we attack. Our comrades of the Fifth and Eighth Armies—Britons, Poles, French, Americans, Italians—have achieved a great victory on the southern front. They are driving the enemy to the north. They have set the trap—it is for us to spring that trap and complete the destruction of the right wing of the German Tenth Army.
>
> I need not tell you that the battle will be hard and difficult. But we are superior in strength. Our pilots control the skies under which we fight. Our equipment, our weapons, are the best the world has ever seen. Our plans have been carefully prepared and in great detail. Every officer and man knows the part he is to play. No preparation has been neglected. You are free men, against whom no slaves of a tyrant nation can ever stand.
>
> Our comrades in the south are fighting their way toward us. The eyes of the world will be upon us. Be alert—vicious—destroy the hated enemy. Victory will be ours.

During the early morning of May 23, the day for the big push, I attached myself to a reconnaissance company, eager to get involved in the action. The captain in command was a smallish fellow who was on his last legs as far as combat duty was concerned, so battle weary that he should never have been allowed to lead men at this point. As a consequence he was removed from his command shortly after the initial assault and assigned to head up a Special Services section, a position tailor-made for a man who had formerly played big-league baseball. I'm making a point of this because it has a direct bearing upon the events of the day.

We were deployed along the banks of a small stream, awaiting final orders to attack. I had just bathed in the cold, shallow water and, not knowing when we would next be able to eat, opened a can of C-rations, the food we ate at every meal when in the field, morning, noon, and night. I had long since tired of the stuff, most of it tasted the same, whether it was labeled spaghetti, hash, whatever. Only the beans had been tolerable for some time—whenever a fresh carton was opened I sought out the beans and stashed them away—but on this day even the beans nauseated me. Standing in the stream while opening the can of beans with my trusty little GI can opener, I stared down into the mass of those slimy little things and almost sickened. I turned the can over, letting the contents pour into the water, and that was the last time I ever attempted to eat C-rations. From that day forward until the cessation of hostilities, whenever I was in a zone of combat I foraged my meals from the farmhouses nearby.

Now, however, I was dressed and itching to go when suddenly the roar of the exploding snakes resounded throughout the beachhead. They worked to perfection in providing the urgent means of escape, but also alerted the enemy, who responded at once with thunderous artillery fire. One of our men standing out in the open field was hit; he was about 100 yards from me, and I ran like mad to his aid. The captain saw me take off and screamed, "Get back, Reep, you damn fool." He was probably right; he wanted me to take cover and let the aid men minister to the wounded soldier, but there was no stopping me. The hell with that, I muttered, pretended I didn't hear, and kept on, insubordinate or not. When I arrived at the man's side, I could plainly see that his right leg had been virtually severed from his body and was just hanging by a hunk of flesh. What could I do for him? I had an ampullette of morphine inside my helmet and was just about at the point of figuring out where to inject it into him when an aid man arrived and took over. He administered the morphine and tended to the man as best he could, and ordered me to go get the stretcher. Together we lifted the wounded man onto his jeep, and I got in beside him to make certain he didn't fall off as we headed for the field hospital.

The dusty roads were crammed with army vehicles of every description, moving chaotically at breakneck speed. Tanks lumbered into view, menacing, noisy, and determined. We were held up at an intersection by a long line of these hulking brutes; despairing for our victim, I leaped out and tried to halt the tanks, but it was merely a gesture; the tank drivers had their orders. The view from a tank is confined to what can be seen through a slit in the armor. In addition, there were thick clouds of dust everywhere, and I damn near got run over. I returned to the jeep, where we waited until the intersection cleared and then proceeded to the hospital.

With one hand I held the wounded man to prevent him from rolling off of the stretcher, and to comfort him I kept my other hand on his forehead. All at once he turned ice cold and his eyes closed. I shouted to the driver that he was dead. Our "casualty" opened his eyes and looked up at me. "Like hell I am," he replied.

We delivered him to the surgical unit at the field station, which was little more than a few hastily erected tents. The doctors worked rapidly, attending to the mounting number of wounded, so we waited there just long enough to make certain that our man was ministered to. In a split second the doctor assured us that he would survive but that his leg would have to be amputated. Months later word arrived that he was home in Minnesota, his war over, and was doing just fine. He wanted to thank the two men who had aided him for their assistance. I felt a lot better about myself after that.

Returning to my company, I was assigned to a half-track, which is precisely what it sounds like—half armored car and half tank, with treads on the rear and wheels up front—, presumably to man the two 50-caliber machine guns that were mounted in the back. Our immediate objective was the town of Lanuvio, and then Genzano a bit further on. Both were in clear sight and being relentlessly pummeled by our aircraft. Tremendous clouds of white smoke billowed above and about the buildings, and the fields were dotted with foot soldiers and all types of vehicles moving steadily forward in shoulder high grass. We'd inch ahead, then stop, then repeat the routine. I was alone in the cavernous rear compartment of the half-track, fully aware that there were two machine guns at my disposal, but I saw no enemy to fire at. Angry, terrifying shells were exploding in the air overhead, creating puffs of black smoke and raining down shrapnel. It was my first encounter with "airbursts," and since there was no way to gain protection from them short of crawling under the vehicle, I decided instead to sketch. So there I was, right in the middle of a battle with nothing to do but draw, my studio the back end of a half-track. It afforded very little protection, since it had no heavy cannon—only the machine guns.

One problem with sketching in that metal prison was the constant bouncing as we drove over the rough terrain. Consequently, I worked mainly when we came to a halt, and to give you an idea of how long it took to get through the fields, I completed two rather complex pen-and-ink drawings during the ride. One dealt with the bombing of the towns nestled in the foothills before us, revealing troops plodding through the high grass amid assorted vehicles. The other caught the angry black fingers of the airbursts exploding above. I was so excited that all fear had vanished. The adrenaline was pumping again, and I knew that I was doing my job as well as I could.

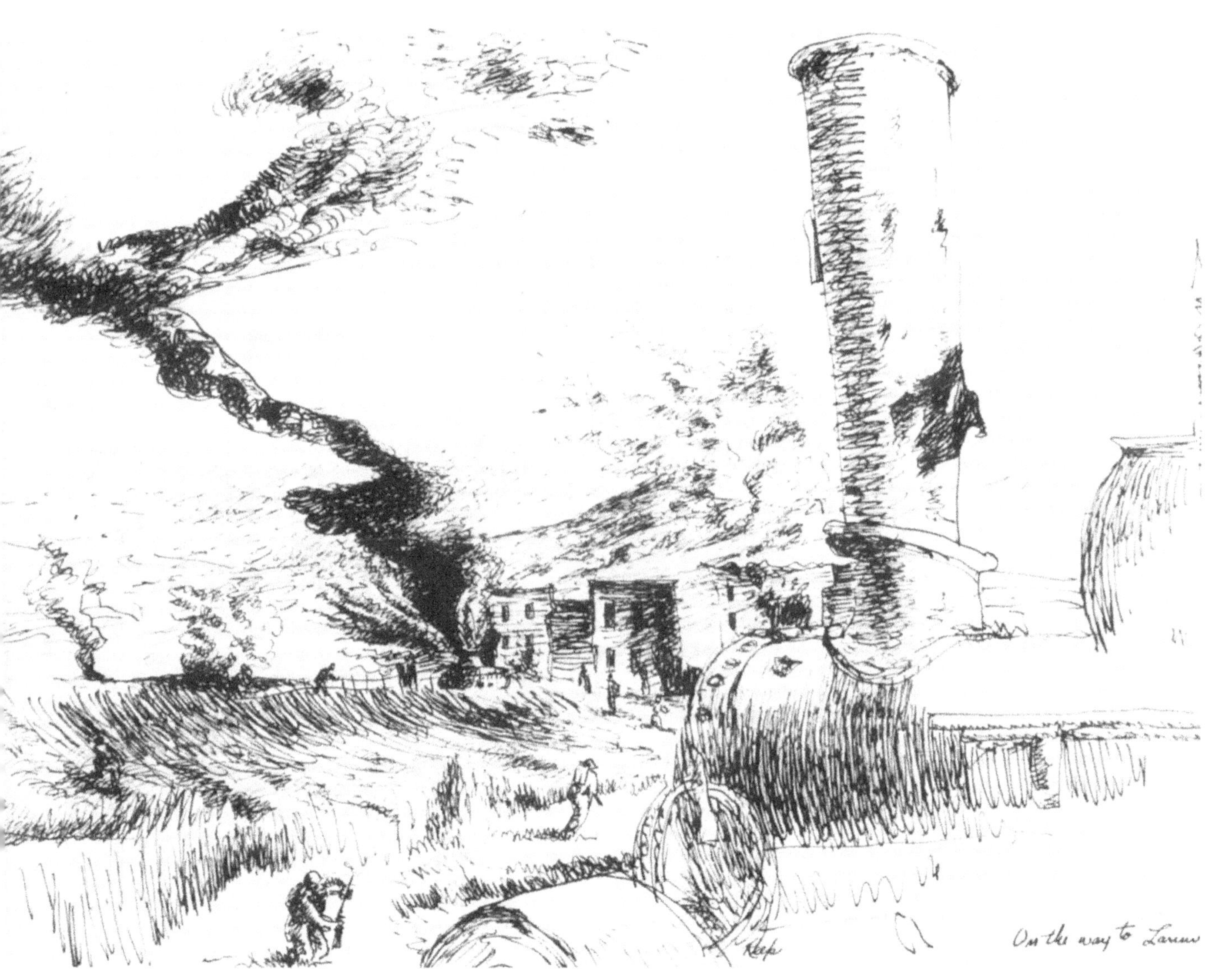

On the Way to Lanuvio

1944. Pen and ink. 12 x 18 in.

Our tanks assault an enemy stronghold as 34th Division infantrymen close in; one tank has already been set on fire. This was my first experience as a soldier on the attack, and while I had two 50-caliber machine guns in the back of the half-track ready to fire, I didn't see even one Jerry. I saw a lot of their artillery fire, which was very intense at times.

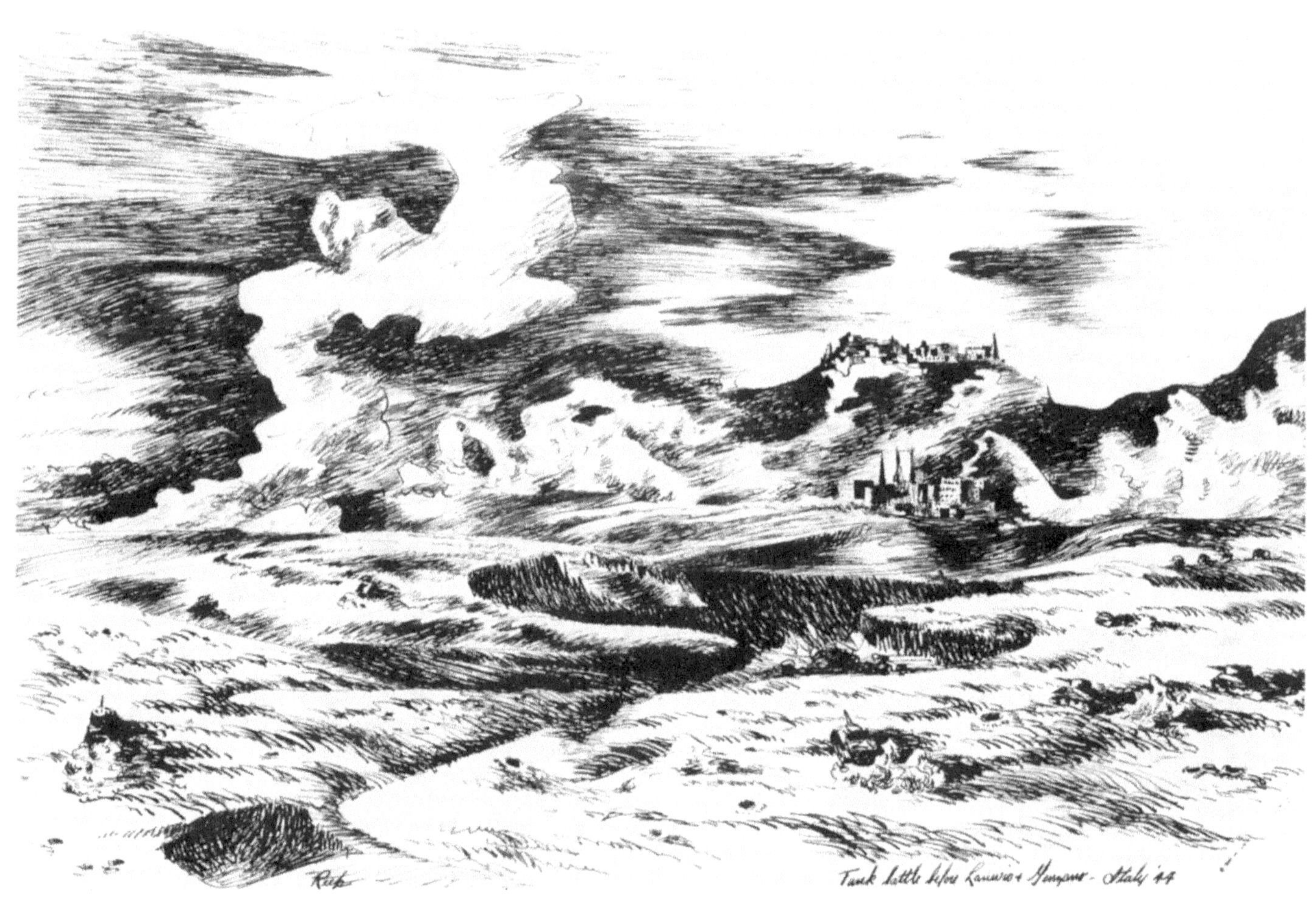

Massing for the Attack

1944. Pen and ink. 12 x 18 in.

Tanks are in position now, and both Lanuvio and Genzano are under fire. Our aircraft are bombing both towns and hillside approaches, causing dramatic columns of white smoke to rise high into the sky. Despite this softening attack, plans were ultimately altered, and our main thrust went to the left in the direction of Campoleone.

Railroad to Campoleone

1944. Pen and ink. 12 x 18 in.

Infantry and tanks begin an early morning attack on the way to Campoleone. German airbursts and artillery fire were heavy, but we soon captured the high ground to the rear. The airbursts were frightening, sending shrapnel down to ping away at our steel half-tracks and tanks.

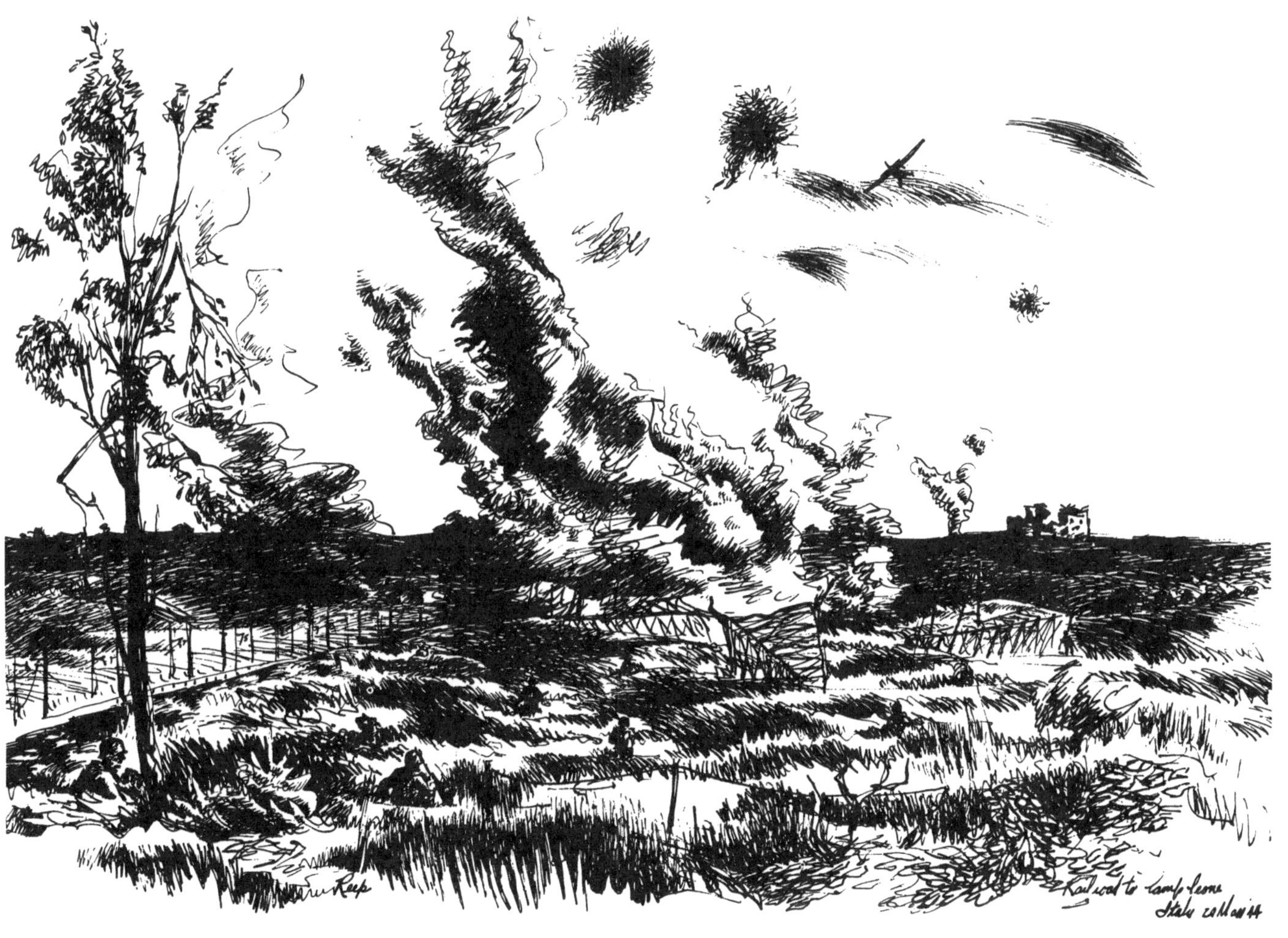

We came to a village and rested. The infantrymen were exhausted, sitting about or leaning hard against the numerous walls of the devastated buildings. It was here that I first understood what a tired soldier did. He collapsed. The invented paintings of war by artists who recreated their work from research or their wild imaginations began to seem invalid to me. There were no dramatics present at this moment, no shouts or cries—all was calm, and we were grateful that we had come this far without overwhelming casualties. We were indeed on our way to Rome.

When I eventually returned to the Historical Section, after 23 months as a second lieutenant, I was awarded a battlefield promotion to the rank of first lieutenant.

CHAPTER NINE

Rome, Rest, and the Arno

Churchill and Roosevelt were not alone in their desire to see the Allies in Rome; the military, from the lowest dogface to the top brass, were captivated by the dream. As the capital and heart of one of the three Axis nations, Rome would provide a prize beyond belief, a morale booster for the fighting men and the folks at home. For all we knew, it might be years before the same could be said for the conquest of Berlin and Tokyo, the remaining Axis capitals.

It had taken less than two weeks for the push to reach Rome on 4 June 1944, and a bit more than three weeks to crush the Gustav Line defenses, continue through a secondary and less well-known series of portable steel pillboxes and other fortifications in the Liri Valley, known as the Adolf Hitler Line, and pursue the regrouping Germans. The next great enemy defense would be the Gothic Line, high in the Apennine Mountains 20 or 30 miles north of the Arno River, and there both armies would spend the long, bitter cold winter. The enemy realized that this new line of defense, nearly 175 miles north of Rome, would allow them time to reorganize and at the same time serve their revised purpose in Italy, which was unknown to the Allies at the time but revealed after the war in an enemy document: "This war will not be decided in this theater. To relieve our forces in the west the missions of our armies in Italy are to keep strong forces of the enemy occupied, to weaken his armies, and to inflict heavy losses in men and equipment" (cited in Chester G. Starr, *From Salerno to the Alps*, p. 211).

The Historical Section moved forward following the rapid advance, so when I returned from the fighting, it was to Cecina, a small city in Tuscany on the Ligurian Sea just south of Leghorn. There I could finish my work, relax, and join tantalizing sightseeing trips to Rome. In one of his rare visits, Von Ripper checked in at the Historical Section, and we decided to return to Rome together. Rip had friends all over the European continent, particularly in the major cities, and Rome was no exception. They were people in high office, royalty, artists, writers, and scholars. Upon our arrival he contacted some of his prewar companions, and we were promptly invited to dinner.

In an elegant room of what appeared to be some nobleman's townhouse apartment, we chatted and sipped wine prior to feasting. I was introduced to counts and their countesses, a prince or two, and some influential businessmen and high officials. The immense table was lavishly set with fine linen, crystal, china, and silver, plus flowers and candles—everything of the finest quality except the food. Even for these privileged persons, commodities were scarce, but I must confess that our relatively spartan cuisine that evening tasted better in that sumptuous atmosphere.

Our dinner conversation centered on the war. Of prime concern was the fate of Italy and its monarchy, and naturally the destiny of those present, who had been the upper crust or Roman aristocracy. No one knew how the Allies would react to the old system, in particular to the monarchy. The dictatorship of Mussolini, or for that matter the resumption of any dictatorship, would be inconceivable—but what about the nobility? Where would these people fit into a system based upon democratic principles? Further, what would become of their titles and holdings? The discussions were animated.

I was thoroughly bored, however. I have never enjoyed myself in the company of snobs, and I had pegged this bunch for a vintage collection. My solid American background had been tempered to distrust and even despise *any* titled nobility as bloodsuckers living soft lives off of the sweat of their chattels. I envisioned this crowd engaging in one orgy after another, all the while contemptuously looking down their Roman noses at the common horde; I assumed that their blood lines had been weakened by inbreeding, leaving the lot subject to such diseases as hemophilia; I had called up all the stories my parents had told me about the rotten side of royalty in the "old country" from which they had emigrated, plus a few thousand attitudes from American revolutionary history. I had these people stereotyped in the same way that they viewed

Chicago as a city of gangsters with machine guns, and the Wild West as filled with cowboys and Indians.

We conversed in English most of the evening, since their command of English was far superior to my Italian. We smiled politely at one another at all times and upon occasion even laughed. It was all very civilized. Once we finished dining, our aristocratic hosts and their guests openly bummed cigarettes from Rip and me, as the only tobacco available to the Italians was downright foul.

When the discussions became monotonously unbearable and waned to small talk, it was time to depart. I was so disenchanted throughout the evening that I scarcely recall the conversation—with one exception. When I suggested that their present King Umberto might shortly be deposed, a mild protest followed. "But Tenente, you don't understand—we love our little King."

The next day, quite by accident I bumped into George Krikorian, my former art director boss at the Psychological Warfare Branch in Algiers. Krik, a devout Catholic, had arranged for an audience with Pope Pius XII and asked if I might be interested in joining him. I eagerly accepted, probably out of deep curiosity; not being a member of the Catholic church myself, I would be able to remain detached from the mystifying spiritual implications and to view the proceedings dispassionately and objectively.

We formed a relatively small group, numbering eight Americans, and I suppose this is what is meant as a private audience; no one less than a head of state could possibly have conferred with the pope one on one. There were others in the large room where we would be greeted, but they were not privileged to rim the platform and personally meet this powerful religious leader. In short order, the pontiff, stately, ascetic, and resplendent in his wondrous regalia, was ushered into the room. His entourage surrounded him, obviously trained to allow a precise amount of leeway as he cast sweeping gestures of blessings to the appreciative congregation. The pope walked slowly but directly to the low platform about which the eight of us stood. With consummate gracefulness, His Eminence stepped up and onto the platform but did not immediately acknowledge our presence.

After a few more general papal blessings to the audience, he gazed downward at his immediate circle of admirers and then moved from one to the other, offering his great emerald ring to our lips. For devout Catholics, the kissing of the pope's ring represented an incomparable and deeply moving experience. Krik was in tears.

When it was my turn to kiss the ring I looked squarely into the pope's eyes as he looked into mine, and at once we understood each other, for he had faced non-Catholics before. His hand descended toward my face, paused but a split second, and continued upward in an immaculate arc; it was utterly graceful and done with ease. His movements were so coordinated that no one could have been sure whether or not the ring had been offered or refused, for his arm was already moving downward to the next person. Obviously, he had performed the act thousands of times. It was flawless.

Our group was accorded a leisurely tour of the Vatican, the highlight being the Sistine Chapel brimming with Michelangelo's inspiring frescoes. Elegantly attired Swiss guards dotted the corridors, motionless and silent. I was transported and departed emotionally spent.

The stay in Cecina couldn't have come at a more propitious time, for it allowed me to complete much unfinished work. I mounted a solo exhibition of my paintings in a huge army tent, and it was very well attended. In the days to follow I'd go out to sketch, mainly in pen and ink, but not to the front lines as had been my custom. On one such day with little else to do, I wandered along aimlessly searching for something to draw. It would have been a grand day for a picnic, or even artillery practice.

I spotted some soldiers atop an ancient Roman tower and wondered what they were up to, so I asked permission to climb up with them. They were young artillery officers and enlisted men in the process of training newly arrived replacements in the art of plotting targets and directing fire. The officers in charge of the practice session already had their scopes in place and communications established. By the time I clambered up the rough stone tower, the courses for firing at selected targets were being plotted. I was impressed by their knowledge and skills in the use of extremely sophisticated instruments.

The artillery shells to be used in this exercise were dummies and relatively harmless, although a direct hit might prove dangerous. The shells would explode with enough force to expel smoke instead of shrapnel, and the resultant giant puffs of white smoke would easily identify the various landing sites.

This activity, so unusual in such a glorious setting, seemed worthy of a sketch, so I stripped to the waist and got to work. What a relief from the relentless pressure omnipresent in the dangerous areas where I had been working, and what a magnificent panorama to view. In centuries past, chains of these stone towers had been used by the Romans for observation and communication purposes. Touring Spain years later, I was fascinated by similar towers on hilltops and could envision crude messages being signaled for hundreds of miles in a matter of minutes.

The result was one of my better drawings. The men were extremely active and interested in their lessons; they took the practice seriously and were therefore good models. They used powerful scopes and binoculars, and had colorful maps spread out over folding tables. All this elaborate equipment provided an attractive means of identifying the activity.

Communication between the spotters in the tower and the gunners in place with their cannons was by field telephone. There was some delay, and because of this a good deal of chatter ensued, which I thought typical. In truth I was pleased with the turn of events because it gave me a bit more time to study my subject and refine my careful pen-and-ink drawing. It was almost completed when the plotting ceased and the officer in charge called for clearance to fire away at the target. I stopped work and expectantly watched with the others.

The roar from the big guns resounded through the valley. They were not far from us, but their various locations were carefully hidden, as the camouflaging of the gun emplacements was also a vital part of the exercise. Everything went as planned—with one exception: none of us could spot where the shells were landing. We heard the blasts and the subsequent thump of explosions, but where in the world were the white puffs of smoke? Could the shells have been defective? More fire was called for—and still more. Nothing!

In a few minutes a call came through from, of all places, the colonels' mess. "What the hell's going on? Where the hell are you? Who's in charge of this damn snafu?" I could read these and other delicate comments in the expressions on the men's faces. All firing ceased at once.

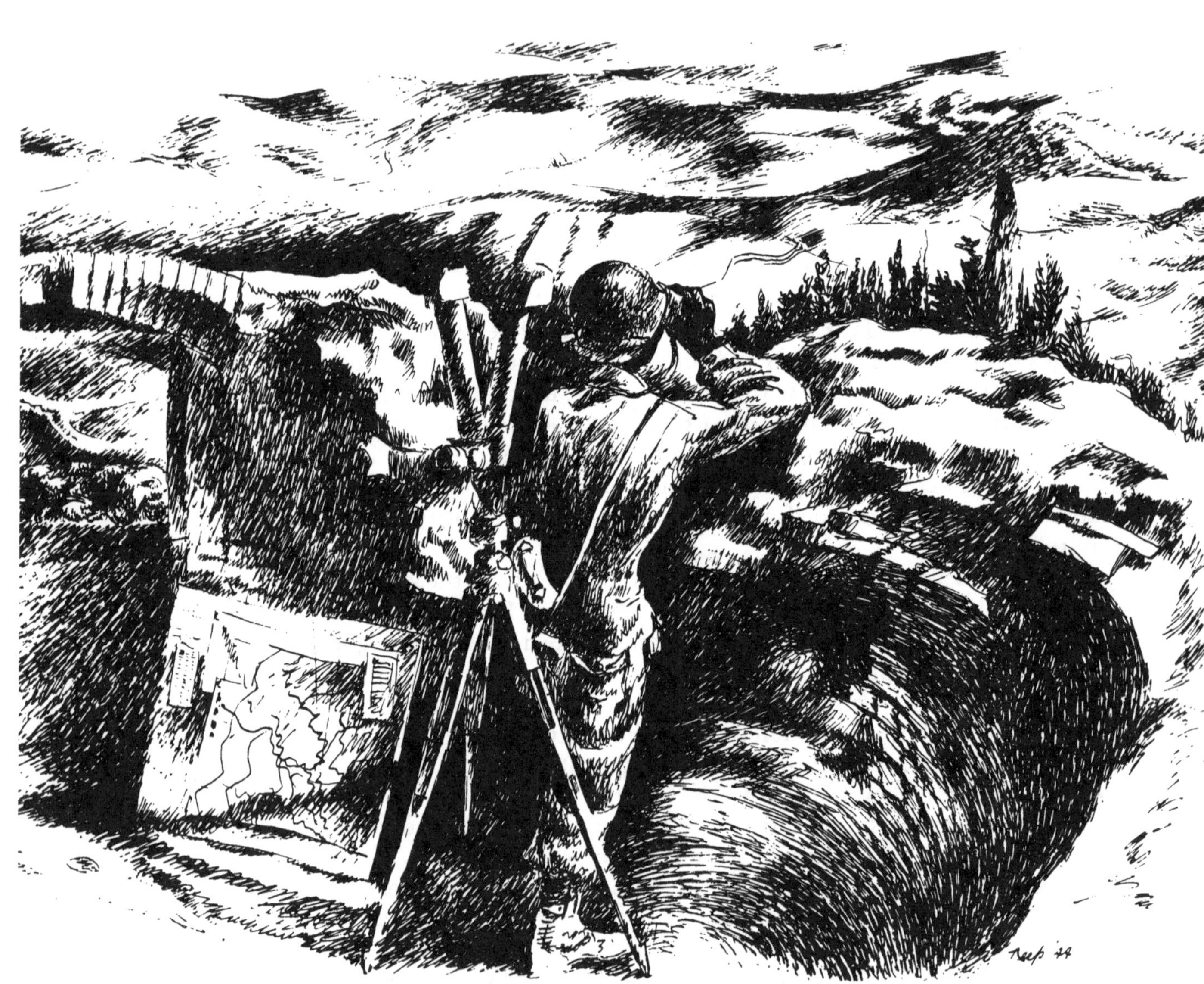

Observation Post (Practice)

1944. Pen and ink. 12 x 18 in.

Standing atop an ancient Roman tower, an observer directs the practice fire of his tanks and checks its accuracy. White smoke in the upper right denotes the landing area or target—an American officers' mess, as it happened. I thought the plotting error made here was inexcusable, but a friend with acute knowledge of such things commented, "Another fine tale of an upside-down map." Apparently this had happened before.

In a diametrically opposite direction, or precisely 180 degrees in line and to the rear, the army brass had been breakfasting al fresco on a sunny veranda. The plotting officer in our tower had made his computations with great care, and the firing was carried out efficiently. Unfortunately, however, he had done his exacting work on a map that was upside down, or that had north where south should have been. The shells were exploding miles back of our position, virtually on top of the field officers enjoying a leisurely morning repast. I got the hell out of there—fast.

By mid-July our troops had moved forward more than 150 miles, taken Leghorn and Pisa, and established a new front on the south bank of the Arno River. The Germans were no longer falling back but had reinforced their troops and were putting up stiffer resistance. The Arno was a fine place to stop. The broad river made an excellent buffer zone, and the beautiful shoreline homes offered our men lush accommodations. Our troops were exhausted from the three months of continuous fighting and needed a rest; additionally, they had outrun their supply lines. I returned to the new front with renewed vigor, roaming the banks of the river for subject matter and staying overnight with various units that were doing little more than observing or holding the line. I dropped in rather casually on one group of men who were manning an observation post for our artillery, told them what I was doing, and stayed on a couple of days.

The observation post was a beautiful riverside residence that commanded an expansive view of the flowing water and the dwellings on the opposite bank. Affluent persons had lived there—that was supremely evident—and the house appeared to have been abandoned hastily, because it was still completely furnished. Like the residents of many homes tucked away on river fronts or in other remote areas, the owners had never dreamed that *their* property would lie in the path of the fighting.

We lived in high style while carrying out our missions. I painted, and the soldiers took turns at their scopes, otherwise relaxing for the most part. I found the place attractive as subject matter for my paintings; the incongruity of fighting a war out of a tastefully furnished dwelling appealed to my pictorial sense, and I certainly had never been a part of anything like this before. It was unreal. We sat about in fine chairs, some overstuffed, and we dined off expensive china, drank from real honest-to-goodness *glass* glasses, and spread out our lavish repasts on nothing less

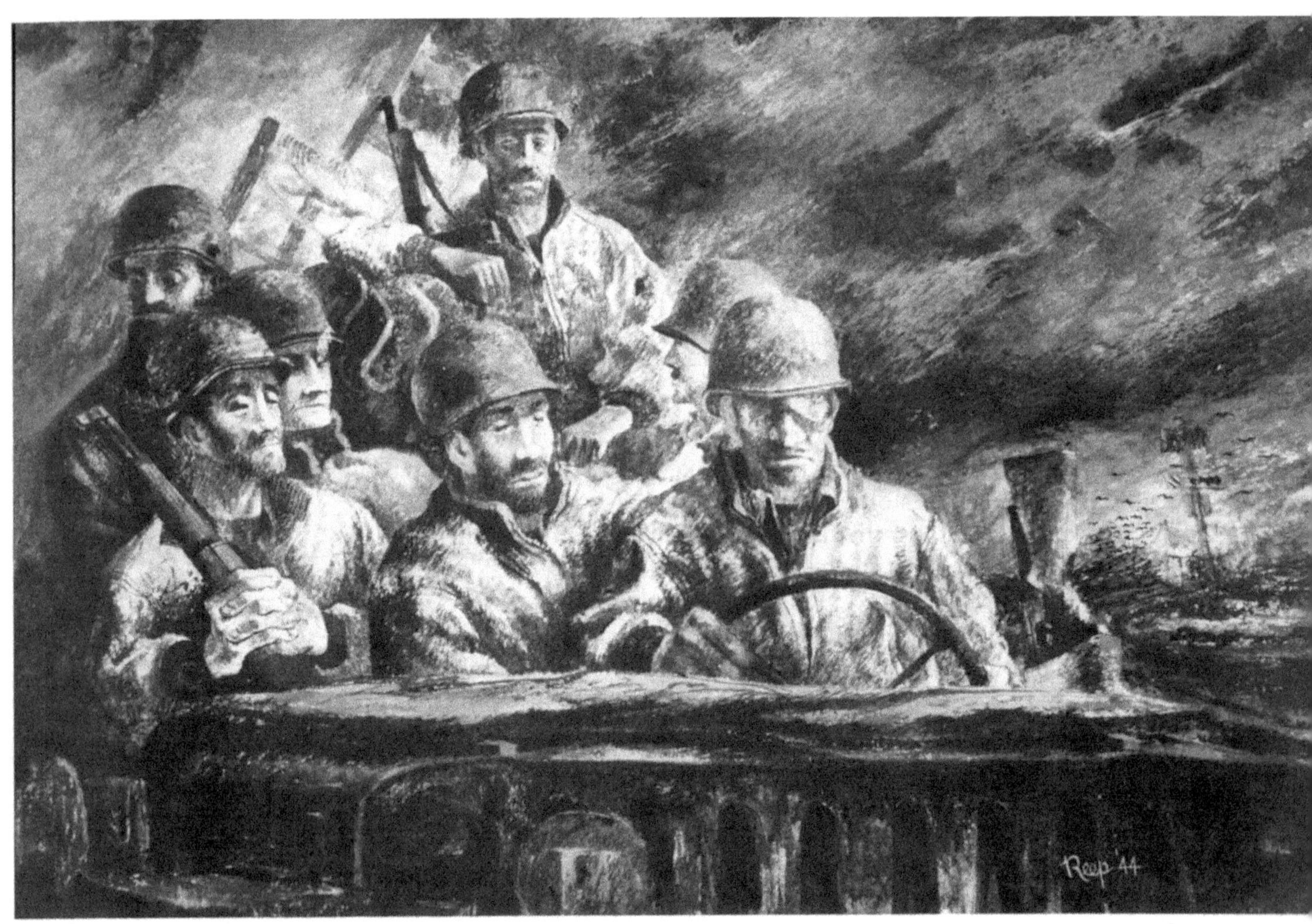

We Move Again

1944. Gouache. 14 x 20 in.

Executed on Anzio, this character study of tired soldiers on the move could apply to the entire Italian campaign. Never knowing what tomorrow held in store for them, always on the alert and ready to go, tired, unshaven men impassively squint their eyes to avoid the dust and move on. Note the caned chair piled onto the rear of the jeep. Such items were important to soldiers and were taken along wherever they went when at all possible.

Observation Post on the Arno

1944. Watercolor. 15 x 21 in.

Overlooking the broad Arno River, this room—once part of a luxurious home—served as a forward observation post for tanks and artillery. When the enemy, situated on the opposite bank, mortared the area, everyone but the somewhat protected observer (note the sandbags surrounding him) retired to the safety and convenience of the wine cellar.

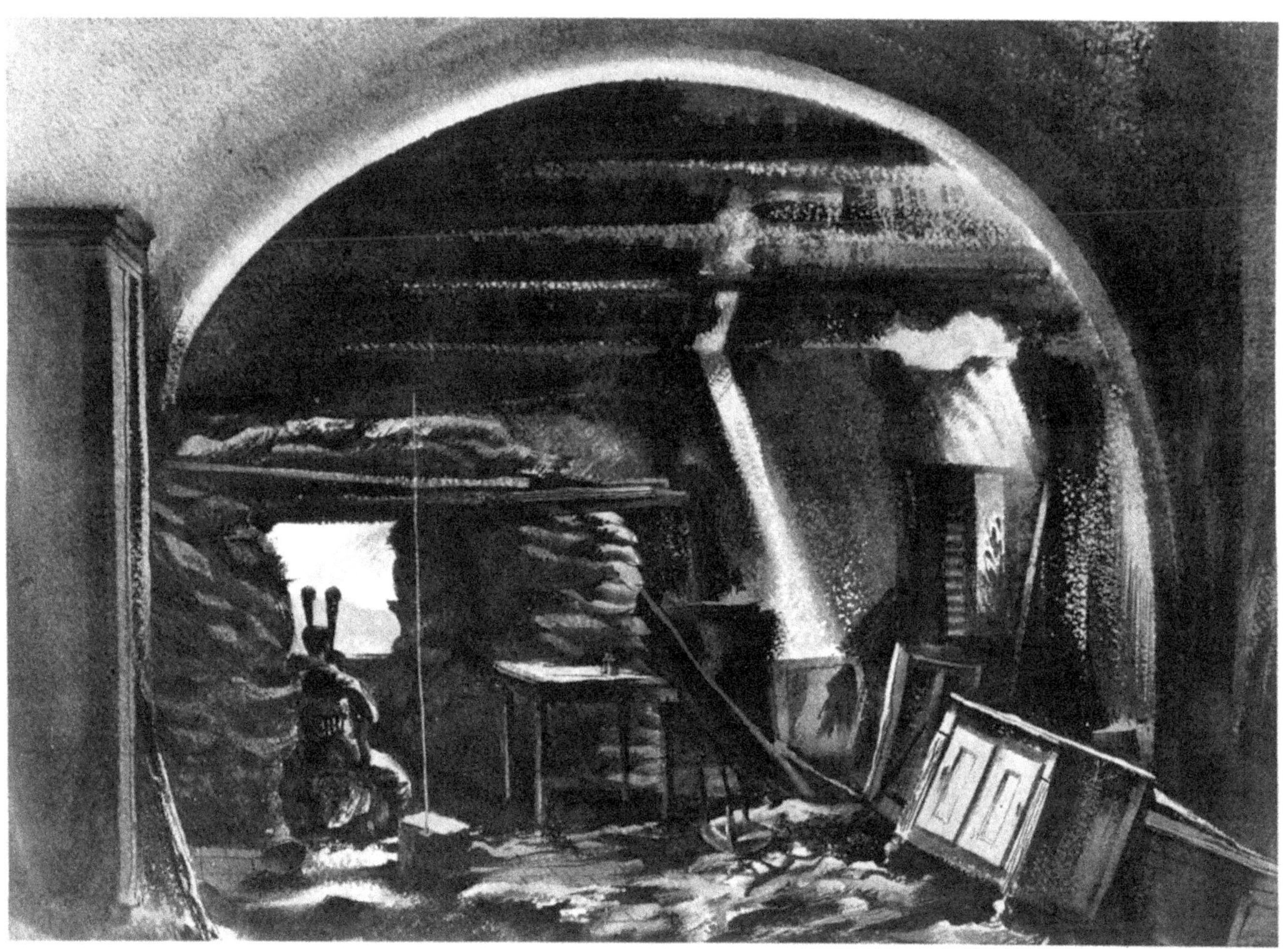

than the best linen. Deep in my heart it made me uncomfortable to use (abuse) these things, because nothing was washed and much of the dinnerware was broken. When we gathered for another meal, we simply went to the china closet and took out a fresh supply.

There were a number of chickens running around the back yard, and naturally we feasted on them. The soldiers had become great cooks; they had been foraging for some time and took pride in preparing delicious meals. I went berserk at one meal because only I savored chicken livers and thus had the lot to myself. I remembered my boyhood when there was one liver to a chicken and we were nine at the table—whoever got that single liver or even a share of it felt fortunate indeed. I don't think that during those Depression days one could order a batch of chicken livers from the local butcher; he knew there was one to a chicken, too. But oh, how tender and sweet my meal of chicken livers was on that evening in the observation post.

The overall responsibility of these artillerymen was to keep a constant eye on the opposite bank of the river, which was occupied by the Germans. There wasn't any small-arms fire to contend with because the river was too wide for such weapons to be effective, and both sides were content to relax and draw a breath. When I'd pause from my work I found it fascinating to man the BC scopes. They were so powerful that you could see a man's eyelid from a quarter of a mile, or so it seemed; I scrutinized everything in sight on the opposite bank. (I'm not certain what the letters BC stood for, but I recall tossing the descriptive name about casually as if I did.)

A church clearly evident across the river held my interest to the extent that I kept returning to it. Once, as I did so, I thought I saw movement toward the rear of the structure and began to look more carefully at the spot, focusing intently on it for longer periods of time. Suddenly I was startled to see a Jerry dart from the main building to a shedlike structure behind the church; then another followed, and still another. Excitedly, I summoned the men about me to inform them that I could see uniformed enemy soldiers at the church, and in minutes they had artillery raining down on the place. Heretofore they had avoided shelling the church because it was deemed off limits, but with visible proof that the Krauts were in the building, they said "the hell with it" and blasted away. Everyone knew that the enemy was using churches and

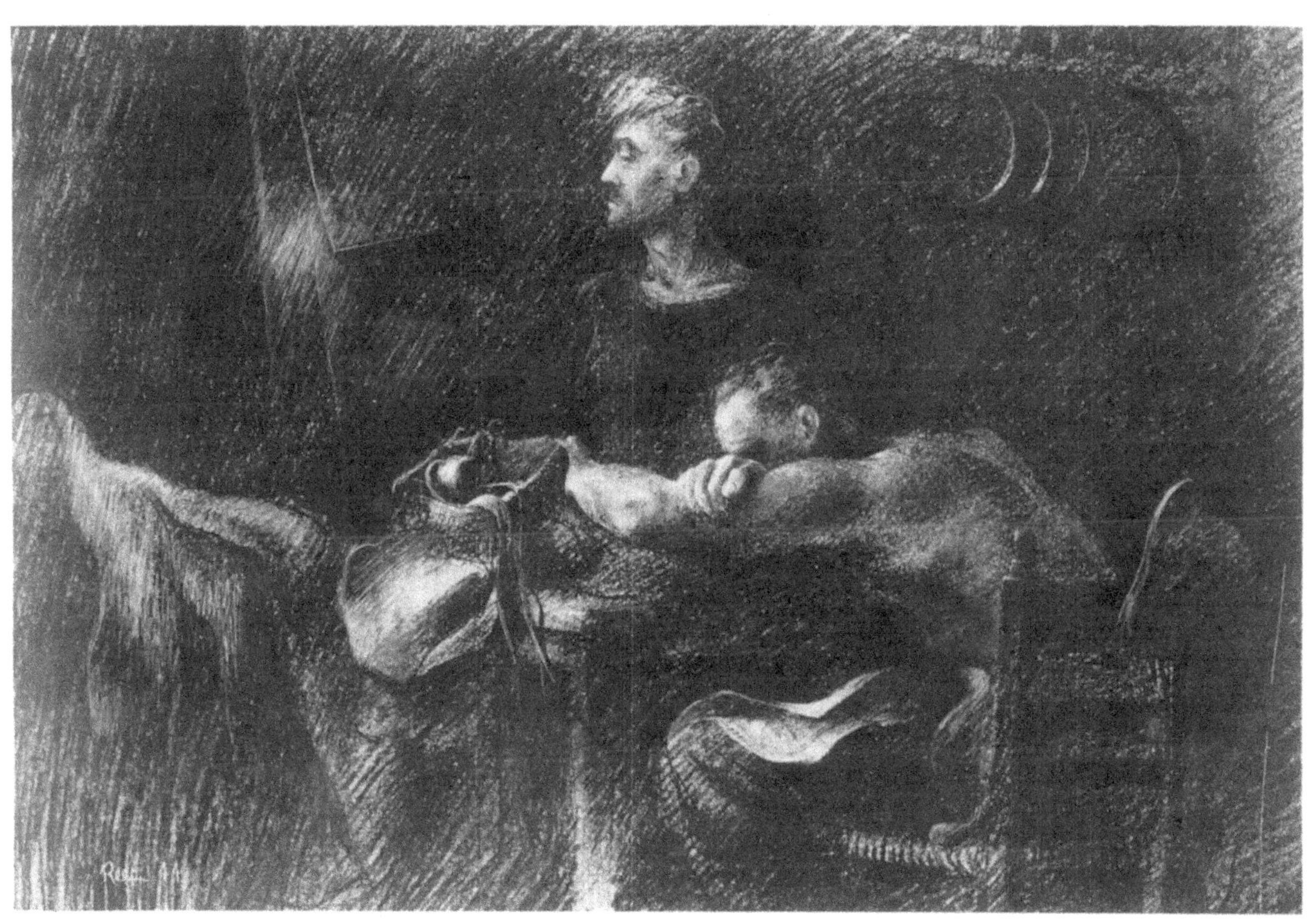

The Fire Direction Center

1944. Sepia and pencil drawing. 12½ x 18½ in.

All night long men remained on duty to direct the fire missions of their tanks. Any abandoned farmhouse that could be blacked out served well as a fire direction center. This drawing of two weary soldiers was done in such a farmhouse on an exceptionally warm night. Note the scythes hanging on the wall to the upper right.

other historical monuments for shelter or for arms and supply storehouses, but proof was rarely available until after we had captured their positions.

We were now curious to see what was going on across the river, so we took turns watching the church take a pasting. Great quantities of smoke and dust made visibility poor, so the experienced soldiers quickly lost interest and wandered off—but not me; this was a new adventure, and I was the guy who had spotted the movement! I doggedly continued to scan the area. In a few moments I saw the Jerries carrying out their wounded on makeshift stretchers that resembled doors. As I followed their path, I noted that they were being taken to a German ambulance, clearly marked with a large red cross. All at once I wasn't so pleased with myself.

In the late afternoon the tranquillity was broken by two very loud explosions emanating from our own back yard. We rushed outside to discover a sight so horrible that I almost became ill. Two nuns from the local church (on our side of the river) had ventured into the fenced yard to pick the fruit ripening on the trees; the sisters gathered food constantly to feed the hungry. But the Jerries had booby-trapped the trees. (If I hadn't been so busy with the events taking place, as well as my painting, I might easily have been a victim myself; certainly, I would have enjoyed a taste of fresh fruit. Later I discovered that the others knew of the booby traps; some wary veterans knew enough to look for that sort of thing right away.) One of the men rushed in to summon an ambulance, while another tended one nun and I the second. There wasn't much either of us could do apart from making our patients as comfortable as possible, so I fashioned a cushion, placed it under my patient's head, and held her hand. Both of the sisters were very much alive; the mines hidden in the ground had wounded their legs and ripped and bloodied the skirts of their habits. Neither woman made a sound, though they must have been in agony.

The sister I was attending to looked at me as if asking for something. She began to speak softly, almost whispering, and I could not understand what she said. Finally she gathered enough strength to reach for her rosary, and, feeling somewhat foolish in my ignorance, I realized she wanted them desperately. I succeeded in getting the beads in her hands, and as she fingered them gently, she looked up at me and smiled. I must confess that I have never seen such a look of serenity in the face of any other human soul, injured or otherwise. The ambulance and first aid men arrived and took them off to the hospital, and I knew in my heart that they would survive.

After leaving the observation post, I fell in with an infantry company down the river a bit. The company was commanded by a captain who had a dog as a companion, and the two were inseparable. The captain was a rough character, hard as nails and well respected for his leadership abilities as well as his courage. His dog was even tougher.

The middle-sized mutt slept next to his master, at his feet on the cot or on the captain's chest or back. Anyone approaching the bedroll on the cot while the man's eyes were closed did so at his own risk, for the dog would snarl fiercely and attack in an instant. We kept our distance. I think he was part bulldog; I *know* he was mean. When the captain drove his jeep, disdaining the services of a driver, his faithful companion rode astride the hood with astonishing skill. The dog had to have been part acrobat, for his sense of balance was unsurpassed. The men would gather to watch this man-dog act whenever possible; it was greatly admired and produced gales of laughter. When the jeep struck an impediment in the road (and the roads were generally unimproved), the pooch would fly high into the air but miraculously land back on the hood on all fours, no more than a foot or two from where he began. The twisting and turning in air, the expressions on the dog's face, and the nonchalance of the captain remain clearly in my mind's eye. The two of them had been in combat together from the inception of the Italian campaign.

Being impressionable and perhaps a bit envious, I adopted a stray mutt of my own that was found wandering the banks of the Arno River, frightened and half starved to death. I promptly named him Arno. The difference between my dog and the captain's was that Arno didn't watch over me at all; I protected him. The little guy was predominantly Airedale, but unlike every Airedale that attacked me when I was a kid, Arno made friends with everyone. His loyalty to me surfaced mainly at mealtime.

Then Arno became very ill. I was distraught because even in so short a time I had become attached to him, innocently entertaining visions of my faithful companion turning into a splendid watchdog not unlike the captain's. Now those dreams lay in jeopardy. I knew virtually nothing about the training or proper care of an animal and was at a loss as to what course to take. An Italian laborer working with the company suggested that Arno might have distemper and could die, and I'd better get him to a *veterinario* as rapidly as possible. There was one just across the river, he said, and he could provide me with a map and directions to get there.

That evening I bundled up Arno and headed for the veterinarian's residence on the outskirts of the little town of Ponte Buggianese. The great bridge situated in the center of the town had been destroyed by heavy shelling and bombing from both armies, so I was forced to drive down the bank of the river and over a temporary bridge in order to reach my destination. When I knocked at the doctor's door, sick pooch in my arms, he seemed inordinately perplexed to greet an American soldier. Examining the sick dog (he had distemper) and recognizing the urgency of the matter, he immediately began scraping Arno's chest until it was bare and bleeding, and followed with a heavy poultice over the tender skin. He guaranteed nothing, adding that there was only a 50-50 chance of the dog's survival and that it would be several days before we would know his fate.

The *dottore*'s name was Carlo Dal Pino. He and his family were very kind to me and I rewarded them with all the rations I had stored in the jeep, thanked them profusely, and departed, leaving the dog in their care and assuring them that I would return.

Arno survived. A few days later, traversing the same route as before on a bright sunny afternoon, I went to fetch my beloved pet. Doctor Dal Pino was proud of his accomplishment, and his entire family stood at his side beaming. We had a little drink that tasted a bit like coffee and attempted conversation in a feeble, embarrassing fashion; then I paid my debt with sincere thanks plus an entire carton of rations that I had liberated for the occasion. The Dal Pinos were very grateful. They were modestly well off, but food was scarce.

I returned with my healthy pooch to the company of infantrymen commanded by the captain with the dog, and continued my painting assignments. Within the week the captain's beloved dog and Arno were both destroyed by shellfire. Dogs, it seems, never learned the lessons of taking cover as did their masters.

Not until later did I discover that in getting Arno to the veterinarian's home I had unwittingly crossed our front line into a sort of no-man's land where patrols of both armies were operating—which explains the look of astonishment on the doctor's face when first we met. By the time I returned for Arno, the Allies had cleared the area and there was little to fear. For several years after the war I sent a CARE package to the Dal Pinos at Christmas.

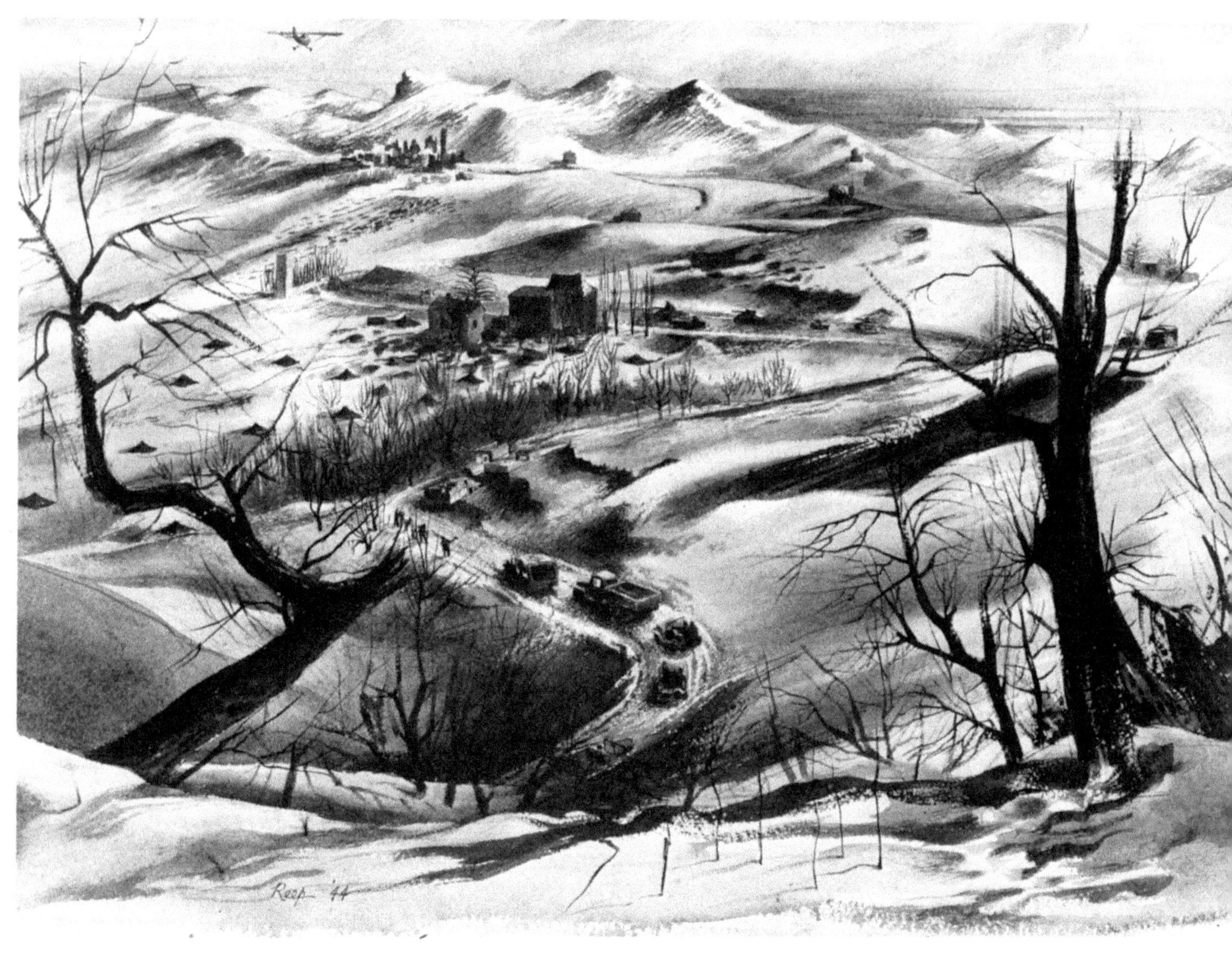

Highway 65 and the Promised Land

1944. Watercolor. 15½ x 22 in.

Highway 65 was the main artery for supplies being brought forward over the Gothic Line into the hills before Bologna. In this panoramic view, as seen from Alto Monghidoro, the highway twists and turns past Loiano, by German-held Mount Adone, and out into the Po Valley. In the distance the Alps rise high over the fertile plains of the valley. Throughout the long winter, cold soldiers came to know this inviting scene as "the promised land."

CHAPTER TEN

The Gothic Line

The enemy forces in Italy had now fallen back to their third and what would prove to be their final line of defense high in the Apennines. The Allied goal, the broad Po Valley to the north, lay before our eyes, beckoning, inviting, but as cold weather came on, there was little that could be accomplished in heavy snow and mud. The Jerries, conscripting Italian civilian labor, had constructed one line of defense behind another to which they could retreat in carrying out their relatively new strategem of keeping the enemy occupied, and it was working. Coupled with the general state of fatigue of our fighting men, the weather would keep the Allies at bay for yet another cruel winter.

I roamed the lines daily searching for pictorially appealing subject matter and was rarely disappointed. The mountainside community of Livergnano, located directly on Highway 65 and in the path of the intense struggle, proved particularly appealing, but it was subjected to enemy artillery barrages 24 hours a day. I didn't know precisely why at the time, but the Fifth Army's history explained it later: "The heaviest fire was concentrated on Livergnano, which the enemy set out to demolish systematically in an effort to block the flow of supplies along Highway 65."

The GIs dubbed the community "Liver and Onions," probably because the phrase bore a lively phonetic resemblance to a name otherwise difficult to pronounce. I likened the nickname to the town's appearance, for it was so badly beaten up that it bore a tactile likeness to a plate of liver and onions. In any event, Livergnano was situated on a ridge in clear view of the enemy, and it became necessary to keep smoke pots going throughout the daylight hours in an attempt at camouflage. Fantastic shrouds of smoke gave the town a ghostly appearance not unlike the delicate phenomenon of aerial perspective prevalent in Oriental art. From an artistic viewpoint I found such subject matter irresistible, though it was like an exotic flower: the rarer the bloom, the more vicious might be the protective thorns. Nevertheless, I was determined to paint in the town.

The gallant soldiers from the 91st and 34th Infantry Divisions who had fought so hard to gain this foothold in the Apennines thought I was loony and didn't hesitate to tell me so. It took just three hours for me to prove that they were 100 percent correct. Early one morning I packed my gear and headed down the road to where the smoke pots were already at work with full force. It was a dramatic scene, and as I passed through the smoke, I felt like part of the activity and was eager to get started. I found a relatively comfortable spot a couple of hundred feet up the little road toward the heart of the town, and set up my makeshift easel squarely in the middle of the street. There was no traffic at the time and most likely wouldn't be during the daylight hours; with the exception of a soldier occasionally darting from one building to another, I had the place to myself.

The street was lined with ravaged buildings often revealing great holes, the result of direct artillery hits that cracked and ripped away the stucco. The roadway was a quagmire, a mixture of mud and snow creating slush so deep that a man could sink in to the knees with each stride. Three Sherman tanks directly in front of me formed distinctive wings to the stagelike setting of the intersection of roads. The tanks were tightly huddled against the protective walls of the buildings and parked at crazy angles, heightening the dynamic nature of the scene. A few trees, typically leafless and barely alive, served as utility poles for the countless temporary lines of communication. Against the spectacular configurations of the billowing white smoke, the criss-crossing wires and their unique supports presented flickering silhouettes: now you saw them, now you didn't.

I worked like mad, for it was an inspiring moment and unlike any other I had experienced. As a rule I attempted to instill excitement and build movement into my work, but this time I was faced with containing or editing the persistent movement and changing patterns caused by the restive smoke. I was limited to the use of pen and ink because the intense

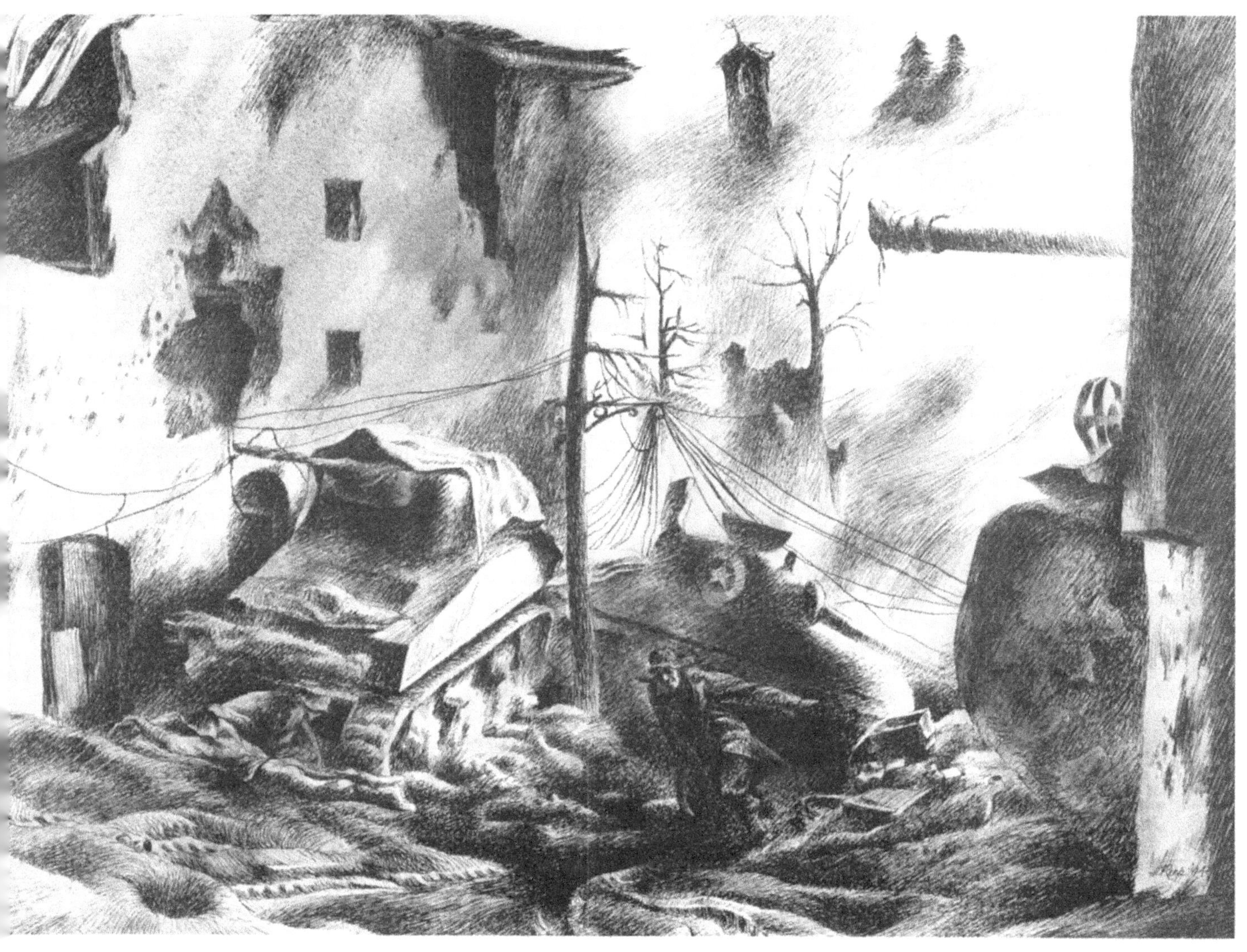

Livergnano—Liver and Onions

1944. Pen and ink and watercolor. 14½ x 22 in.

"Liver and Onions" was the soldiers' name for the shell-torn town of Livergnano, high in the Northern Apennine mountains. Life was barely visible here and soldiers seldom strayed from their dugouts or cellars in the rubble. Straddling a vital road junction on Highway 65, Livergnano was shelled heavily day and night all through the winter stalemate. The town was in full view of the enemy and smoke pots operated continuously during daylight hours. Though sunny days were rare enough all through the Northern Apennines, sunshine did not penetrate here. This pen and ink drawing was done over a field of neutral gray-green watercolor wash.

cold would have frozen watercolor as it was applied to the working surface (that had happened to me before, and I had lost a day's work when the painting melted away). The thick black India ink was not likely to freeze but made my task more tedious and infinitely slower than the broader brush strokes of more spontaneous watercolor.

After about three hours of nonstop work my efforts were brought to a rude halt by a powerful enemy artillery shell that landed not more than 50 feet in front of my crude easel. The violent explosion sent mud and shrapnel flying in all directions. The backside of my working surface was completely coated with the thick pasty mud, but at least it prevented me from being splattered. The roar was deafening; in one instant the world before my eyes was transformed to a brilliant blood-red emptiness. Wham—and it was over.

When I finally regained my composure, I began to fit the pieces of the incident back together. It was apparent that the deep mud had cushioned the blow, thus sparing my life and those of two soldiers who were in the street when the shell struck. Miraculously, not one particle of shrapnel had come close to my person; at least I had not been aware of that dreadful, menacing, familiar whizzing sound that only lets you know it didn't get you on the way by. (The old adage that all soldiers cite is quite true; you never hear the one that hits you.) Moments earlier the two GI's had been sloshing up the street toward me, one carrying a bucket. Now one man lay prone, unharmed but face down in the mud where he had taken cover behind the huge tank to my left. The other soldier had disappeared into a building. Whether or not their instinctive efforts would have averted injury or death, who can say? The mud had spared the lives of the three of us.

I didn't remain on the scene one moment beyond the time necessary to clean most of the debris off my equipment and pack up. High-tailing it to the relative safety of the aid station where I was bunking, I knew that in the comfort of that heated room I could go on with the work while the details remained fresh in my mind. Artistic license now permitted me to fit one of the soldiers in behind the tank, lying in the mud as I remembered, while the other could appear frantically rushing forward, his pail swinging wildly as he sought cover. Artists are purported to have eidetic memories that allow them the vivid but perhaps unreal recall of images, but I experienced no problem in viewing the entire scene and the characters in it in very authentic detail. The final work, now including the soldiers, was undoubtedly enhanced by the near catastrophe.

The aid station, located a few hundred yards down the road from the heart of Livergnano, was manned by the Blue Medics of the 3rd Battalion of the 34th Division. It had formerly been a modest dwelling ingeniously carved out of the side of a solid rock mountain slope. It was admirably suited to its current use, for only a direct hit could inflict any serious injury on the good doctor and his complement of aid men working and bunking there. In fact, shells had exploded around the place and on the road in front with little effect beyond some brutal scarring of the thick facade. I never fully appreciated how charming a residence this had been until many years after the war when an author and fellow soldier, Roy Livengood, sent me a photograph of the restored dwelling.

By coincidence, Bill Mauldin had stayed at the aid station and departed only the day before I arrived; hence I inherited "his" stretcher on which to sleep. The litters were in constant use during the day because of the heavy concentration of fire in the immediate area, but at night when things calmed down a bit, they served as fairly comfortable cots for our bedrolls, better than the dirt floor. Since they sat only a few inches off of the ground, it became a moot question whether you wished the rats to run over the top of you or scurry under the litters and brush your bottomside. The vermin infested the place and found some way to get into the warm room night after night, despite all our efforts to plug every visible hole in the wall.

It was Christmas, and in that drab room filled with litters and shelves of medical supplies hung an olive green army blanket that served as a provisional partition. Pinned to the blanket was a tiny red paper bell, the old-fashioned kind that unfolded into a Christmas ornament. In a rather elaborate pen-and-ink drawing of the doctor treating two wounded men in the middle of the night, I employed a neutral wash of pale green watercolor as a foil for the minute touch of red provided by the paper bell. Someone back in the States had sent the bell to one of the men as a gentle reminder of home, but it had an adverse effect upon me. I became terribly homesick; this was a rotten way to spend the holidays, and I began feeling sorry for myself. Then I thought of the guys down the road crammed into their dank little foxholes.

Wounded men were being brought into the aid station with reg-

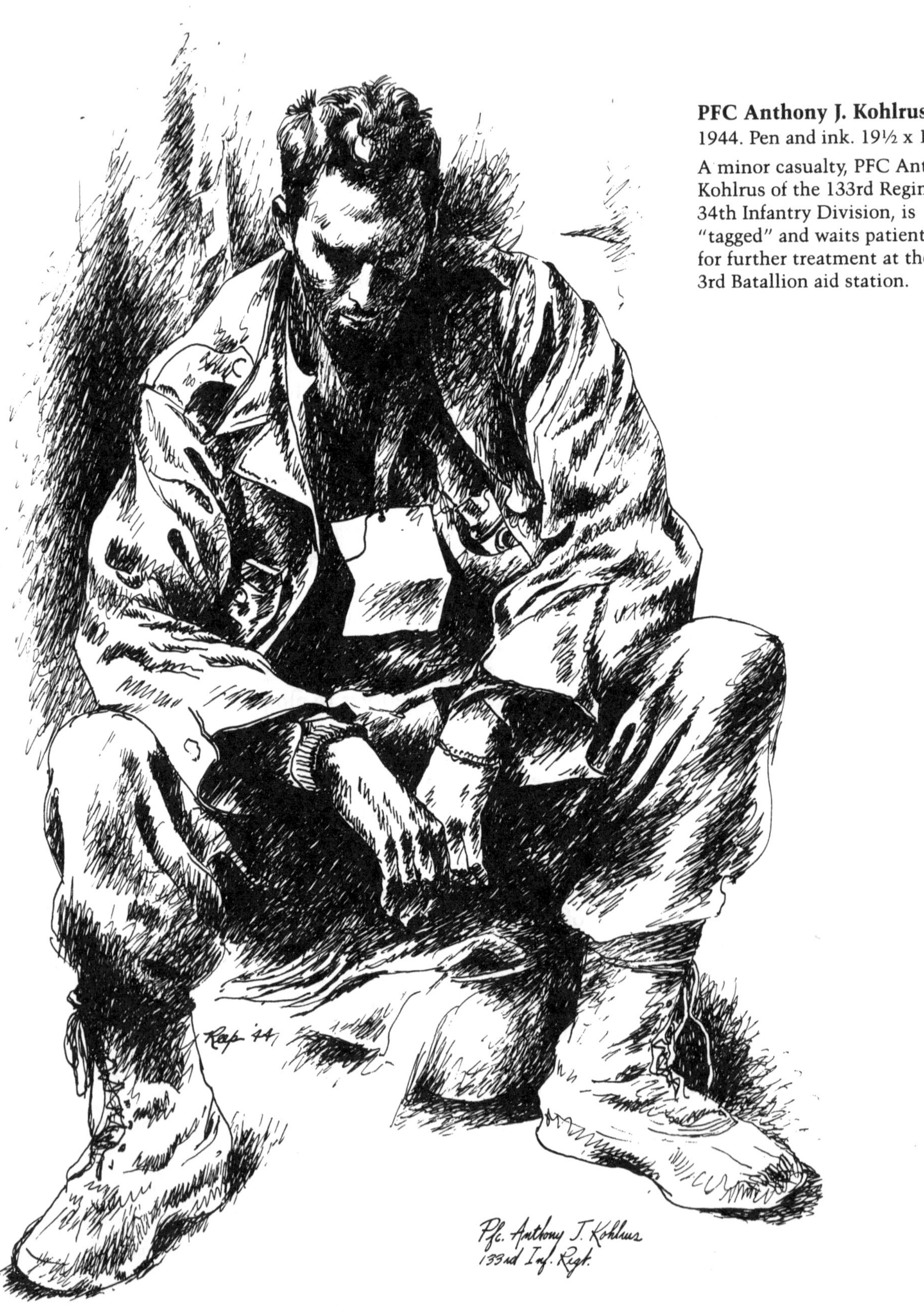

PFC Anthony J. Kohlrus

1944. Pen and ink. 19½ x 14¾ in.

A minor casualty, PFC Anthony Kohlrus of the 133rd Regiment, 34th Infantry Division, is "tagged" and waits patiently for further treatment at the 3rd Batallion aid station.

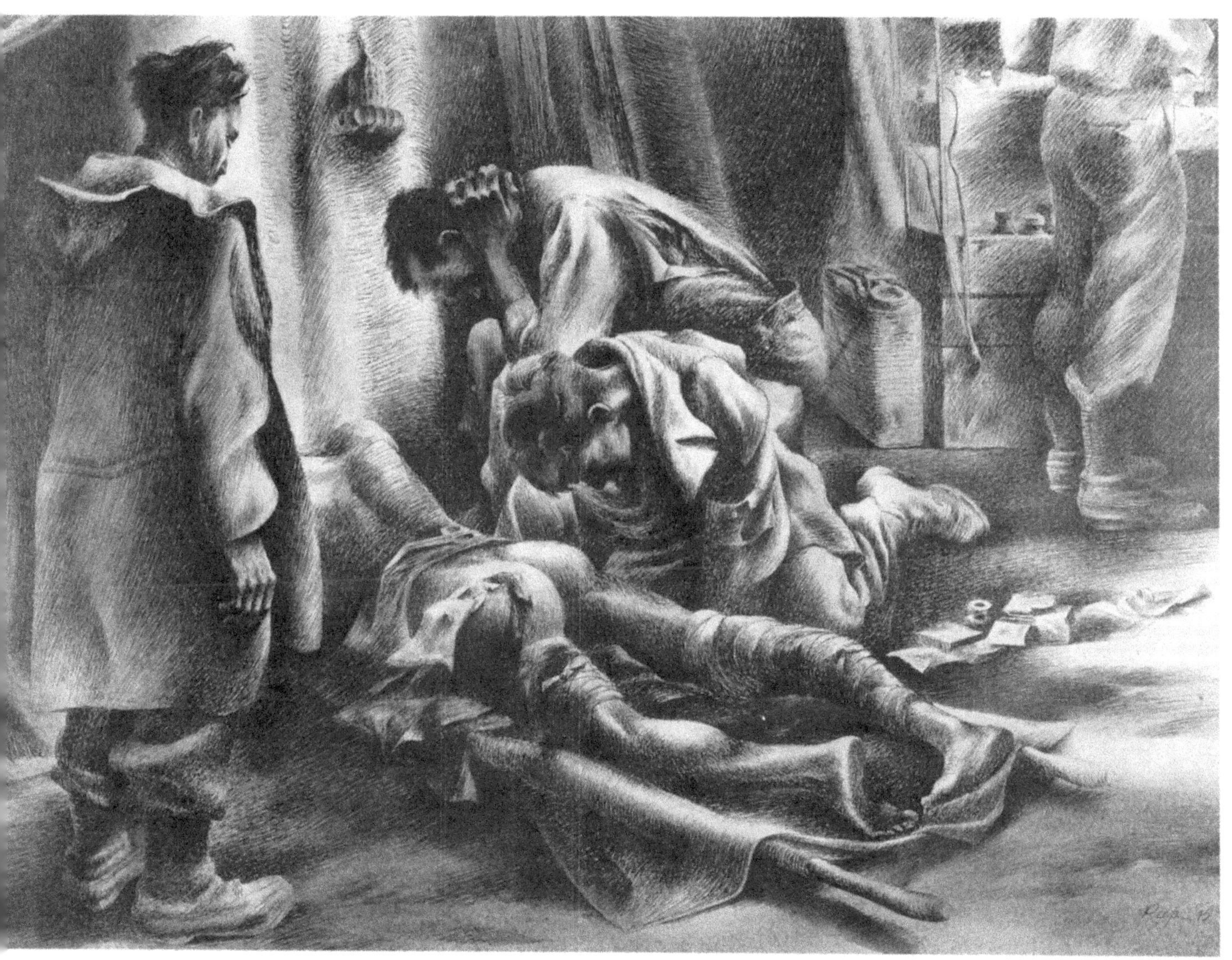

Christmas in an Aid Station

1944-45. Pen and ink and watercolor. 15 x 22 in.

The casualties came in during the holiday season as always. Severe wounds were treated first. These men of the 34th Infantry Division were hit by German mortar shells near Livergnano and received initial treatment at the 3rd Batallion (Blue Medics) aid station. Many soldiers manning foxholes just down the street were injured, treated, and returned to their dank quarters immediately.

This drawing in pen and ink has a cool green wash of watercolor beneath the drawing, in contrast to the small touch of red on the Christmas bell which hangs from the blanket to the rear.

ularity, some for minor emergency treatment; others, more seriously wounded, were prepared for evacuation to the rear hospitals. I remember two cases in particular, one a runt of a kid from the city streets in New York, the other a strapping brute from somewhere in the Midwest. It doesn't matter who came from where; this was the way it was on that night. The point is that the big guy had a small cut that the doctor was able to treat with a band-aid, but the man complained so bitterly that he had to be sent back to a field hospital for further examination. The little character, on the other hand, required considerable stitching up, but when it was over, all he asked for was a couple of aspirin tablets before returning to his foxhole. Brave men, big and small, came from all parts of our nation; it is understandable that some were hurt more than others, physically and emotionally. Neither the doctor nor I discussed it further.

The two pen-and-ink sketches executed while I was staying at the aid station rank as two of the more significant things that I did as a war artist. They both attest to the hardship and peril that the men faced each day and night, whether in battle or on a routine patrol or in merely performing their daily assignments.

Somehow I had the idea in my head that I ought to cover an infantry outfit, possibly an outpost of some sort, so I headed for a regimental headquarters at the front. There I met Gustav Braun, a colonel in command of the 133rd Infantry Regiment of the 34th Division. He was a squat, sturdy sort who had gained a reputation for insisting upon a *tidy* battlefield; he was continuously policing it up. Colonel Braun must have been a forerunner of the environmental ecologists, and I took to him immediately. He was on the verge of becoming a general, obviously because of his superior performance in the command of troops in battle. His outfit had recently seized two key points on the front, Monte Del Galleto and Monte Venere, against stubborn enemy resistance. Now he too found himself at stalemate for the winter.

In the long evenings while I bunked in that crude farmhouse high up in the mountains, we held protracted discussions about everything imaginable. I was flattered by the attention, especially from a man with such heavy responsibilities, the lull in the fighting notwithstanding. I drew the colonel's portrait—by candlelight as there was no generator in his remote mountain headquarters. He was very pleased with the result, and

Colonel Braun

1944. Pen and ink. 15 x 19 in.

One evening, by candlelight, I drew this portrait of Colonel Gustav J. Braun, the commanding officer of the 133rd Infantry Regiment, 34th Division. The colonel, later killed in action and posthumously made a general, was a tough, strict, and efficient, yet compassionate and caring, leader.

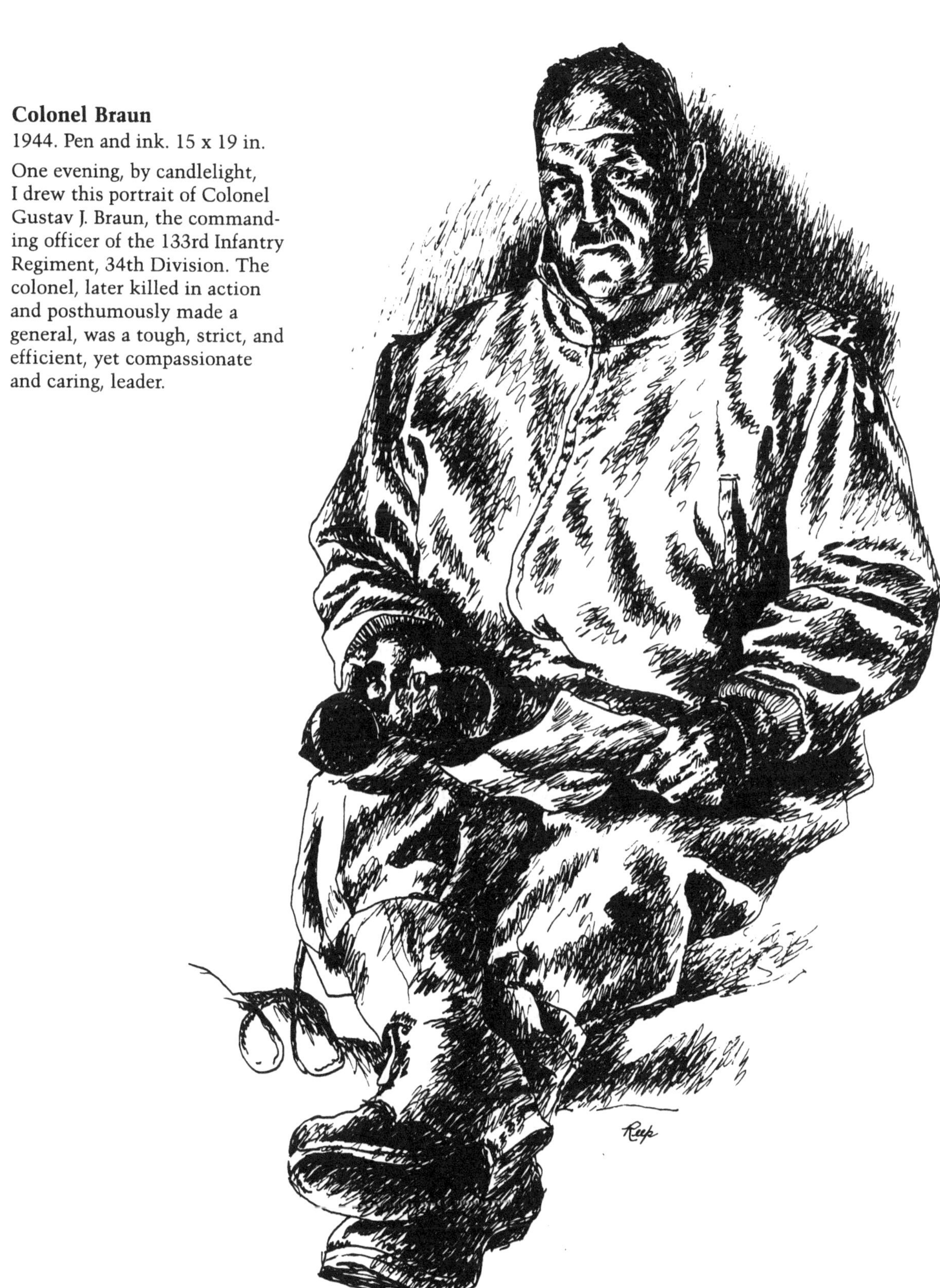

when hostilities ceased I forwarded the sketch to his family as a remembrance of our friendship.

From Braun's HQ, I journeyed to remote outposts with foot soldiers who were toting supplies or moving up to relieve others. One morning, very early, I set off on foot with a group of men moving up to a machine gun position. I had visions of painting there and had lugged along my supplies, which proved to be a grievous mistake. But being quite strong and in reasonably good shape, I gave little thought to the arduous task and the long day ahead. I contemplated hiking up to the outpost to sketch and possibly paint, and returning with another group later in the day. Since all the men in our party did this sort of thing routinely, often daily, what would prevent me from carrying out my mission? Little did I realize that I had overestimated my strength and stamina, or underestimated the difficulty and distance of the march. Over that hilly and muddy terrain it took several hours to reach our destination; as a consequence, when at last we arrived at the outpost, I found that it would prove impossible to do anything but take notes. There was little time for sketching because, I was informed, the return patrol would be heading back to regimental headquarters in an hour or two. I observed, snooped around a great deal, and completed a few minor sketches.

The machine gun position was in a very large home, a mansion perched high atop a mountain promontory overlooking a great valley surrounded by walls of lush tree-covered mountains. The machine guns were dug in and around the perimeter of the estate, commanding excellent points of observation, which was about all that took place there on that particular day. I can't recall a single shot fired, either small arms or artillery.

The major distraction that kept me from producing more sketches was the house itself. Its wealthy Italian residents had gone to great lengths to safeguard their possessions. Throughout the campaign it was not unusual to come upon caches of precious commodities, hidden away in the belief that they would remain undiscovered. In this instance, the owners of the mansion had not only secreted away their finest household possessions behind dummy walls but had moved in valuable stock from their places of business. It was a wasted effort: the men on·duty at the outpost, intensely curious about such things, in their free moments managed to solve one mysterious ploy after another. They discovered rooms that had been so skillfully closed off and concealed that only by knowing the house intimately could a casual observer have detected the clandestine alterations. I first got wind of this prying and snooping by inadvertently bumping into a couple of GI's who were tapping away at the walls, testing for hollow rings. They had already broken through one wall into a sumptuous living space now bursting with crates of furs. The crates were so large that they had to have been built on the spot; they could not have been moved in or out of the existing doors.

I liberated a small karakul lamb's fur to use as a warm seat when working in the snow. I could have taken a few more furs to send home, but I didn't feel right about carrying off anything beyond what might be put to immediate, practical use. The fur I did take brought back memories of a recent experience in the Idice River valley where I drew all day at a snowbound mortar position and suffered a tinge of frostbite on my toes caused by sitting on my feet. I could almost feel the soothing warmth of that gorgeous black fur under my butt the next time out.

None of the other items so ingeniously hidden away impressed me enough to bother with. If material possessions or money had ever been my primary concern, I would never have become an artist. After this damn war was over, I wanted to go home and resume my life by starting on a career. The fact that our term "liberating" was a euphemism for outright theft didn't bother me in the least, for we didn't owe any of the Axis powers a thing; we had a battle to fight, a war to win. I still had an assignment to fulfill—and who really gave a damn? What the Krauts didn't pillage, our men would carry off. Obviously, I had to come to terms with the matter in my own way.

Our long hike back to regimental headquarters was an exhausting journey made more difficult by an earlier rain. It led to one of the most traumatic moments I had ever suffered and nearly cost me my life. The narrow winding trails were deep in mud, making every step arduous. The effort to keep from sliding, falling, or simply getting one boot after another out of that sucking gumbo was taking its toll; I grew wearier and wearier and began to drop behind the others. As our group struggled along, I could see other parties and a couple of mule pack trains moving up on nearby trails, proceeding painfully and pulling their way through the sticky muck. The image was so clearly etched in my mind that it led to possibly the best (by artistic standards) pen-and-ink drawing that I did

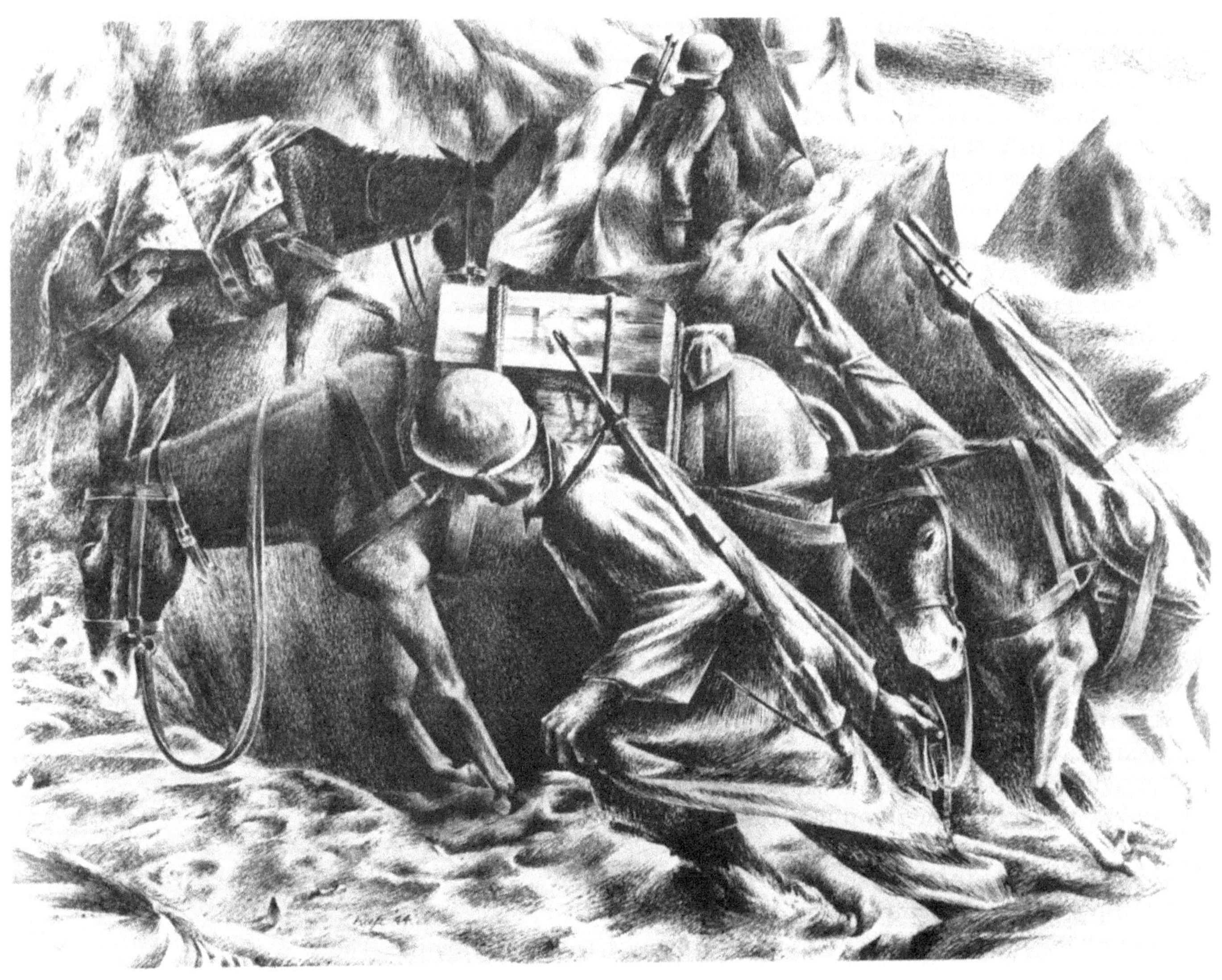

Pack Train in the Northern Apennines
1944. Pen and ink. 19 x 24 in.

Wherever our troops fought or whatever the hardships or obstacles, men and mules brought needed supplies. Over slippery trails at high altitudes, medicine, food, and ammunition were delivered each night by these unsung heroes of the war. At times the mud was so deep and thick that each step became an effort. Both men and beasts are seen here straining to inch their way up a treacherous, winding trail.

in the war. *Pack Train* leaned heavily upon familiar lessons of dynamic symmetry, or thrust and opposition in contest with the earth's gravitational force.

By the time we reached the halfway point, a fellow soldier, tiny in size but tough as nails, sensed my dilemma and asked if he could help by carrying my paint kit, which weighed some seven or eight pounds. I handed it over to him eagerly because I was growing so weary and straining with every step. It was now pitch dark, and I had lagged severely to fall well back of the others, embarrassingly bringing up the rear. Naturally they were all fatigued, as the mud took its toll of everyone, and I could only surmise that it was now a case of every man for himself. Then, about half a mile from our destination, sensing that they were nearing their dry, warm lodgings, the men seemed to pick up their pace to leave me alone and wobbling. Totally spent, I fell face down in the deep mud. The gooey stuff was up to my ears; I couldn't breathe, and although I strained to pull my face upward, it was useless—the suction was too great. I thought, "What a helluva way to die." With one herculean effort I twisted my head to the side and snorted the mud away from my nostrils with the remaining air in my lungs, then lay there in that stuff for what seemed to be an eternity, grateful to be alive and breathing.

After resting sufficiently I pulled my arms up to my face and propped up my head. Then I sat up in the mud and rested some more, wondering where I was. Where was the path to regimental headquarters? I couldn't see a thing ahead of me, it was that dark, and I had no idea of which direction to take even after studying the footprints near me, so I started walking in the direction that I thought I had fallen. Finally I sighted the house and entered, to be greeted with catcalls and laughter, for I was totally covered with mud, head to foot and backside too. The roasting continued for some time, but I was too tired and embarrassed to tell them what had happened. With some effort I got my clothes off, fell into my bunk, and slept through the next morning.

During one of my discussions with Colonel Braun, I told him of a recent flight I had taken in an observation plane, a Piper Cub, high over the field of battle. Some cockeyed American pilot had offered to take me aloft to view the battlefield, and I jumped at the opportunity. At the time there was a pretty fair artillery duel in progress; one enemy shell swooshed by our plane with such velocity that we were bumped off our line of flight by several feet. It scared the daylights out of me, but my nutty pilot got a big charge out of the thing. When we returned from that little sortie, the pilot got carried away with himself and buzzed the airport—if you could dignify that little improvised runway with the name—then swooped upward and came back and buzzed it again. He must have flipped his lid, or possibly assumed that he was entertaining the hell out of me. When finally he decided to land, we were greeted by armed soldiers who promptly arrested the pilot and whisked him away. I walked quietly to my nearby jeep, got in, and drove off as hastily as possible.

As I recited the story to the colonel, talking mostly about the excitement of watching a battle in progress, and avoiding detailed reference to the dizzy pilot, his eyes widened; he poured one question after another at me—for the most part, questions I couldn't answer. Shortly thereafter, I received word that Colonel Braun had been shot down while flying over the battlefield in a Piper Cub, and that he had been posthumously promoted to the rank of brigadier general.

By November 1944, our armies had settled in for the second long winter. Earlier we had concentrated upon rebuilding our forces, repairing roads and equipment, bringing up reinforcements and training troops, and generally building and restoring morale. Rest centers were now more plentiful and elaborate, particularly in Rome; there soldiers could visit the fabled ruins and other points of interest, sleep in real beds, bathe in real tubs of hot water, and partake of city life if only briefly. At the same time plans were being prepared for what would prove to be our final attack in Italy, but given the bitter cold and rough terrain, this would not occur until spring.

I drove daily from unit to unit in search of new and different material. Since the fighting was light, I could be highly selective; hence I spent a good deal of time simply driving about, exchanging stories with the soldiers from every conceivable outfit, sharing chow, and bunking with them for a night or two.

One evening I was bivouacked with infantrymen in a heavily wooded area. The pitch-black night cautioned us against any artificial illumination; a flashlight or candles might reveal our position. As I lay snug in my bedroll, which had been painstakingly spread over a thick bed of forest leaves, only the soft rumble of distant artillery fire interrupted

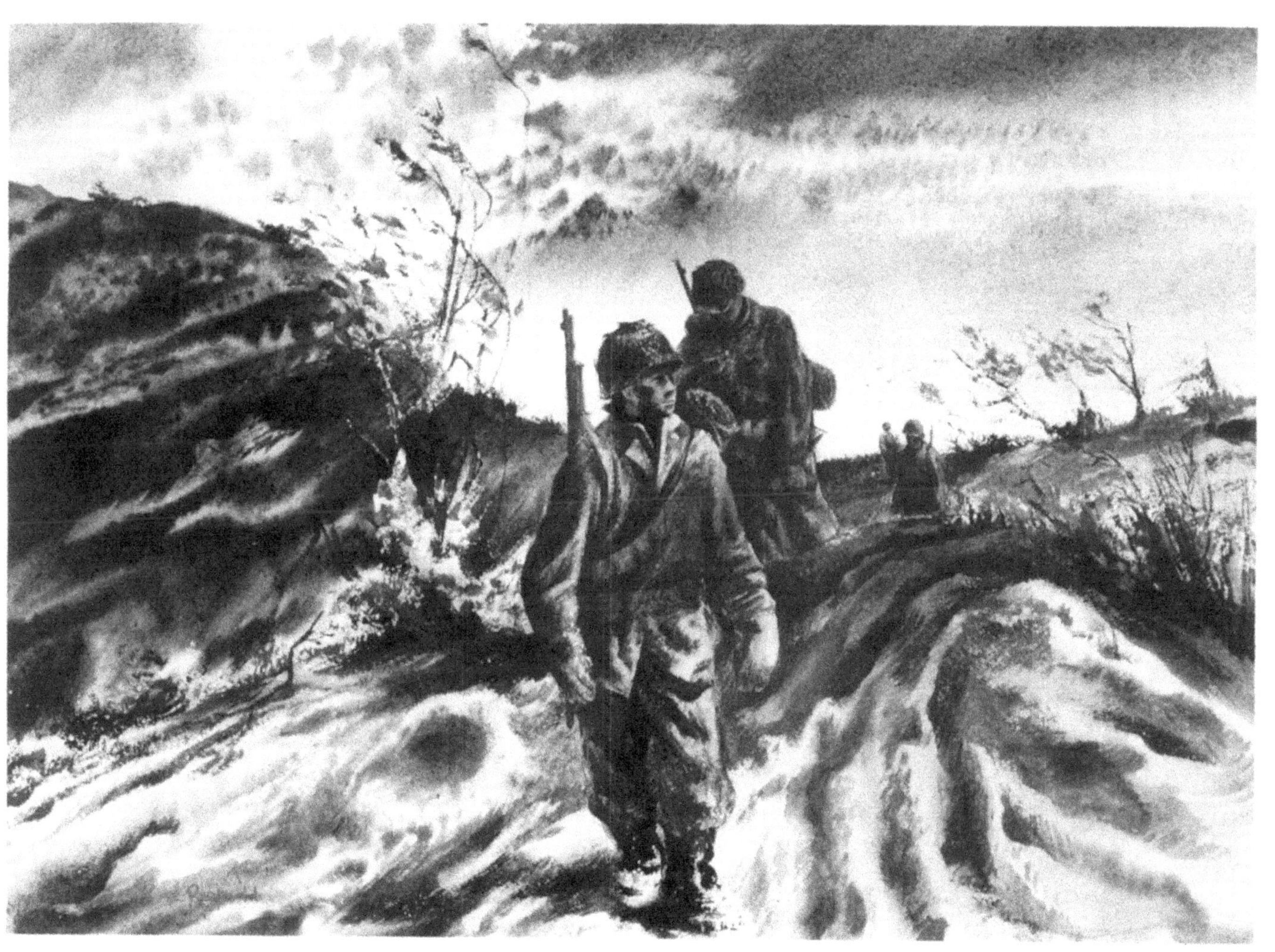

Patrol—First Snow
1944. Watercolor. 16 x 22 in.

A patrol of the 133rd Infantry Regiment, 34th Division, moves through the sluggish first snow high in the mountains before Bologna. These courageous men, many still in their teens, were both rugged and determined.

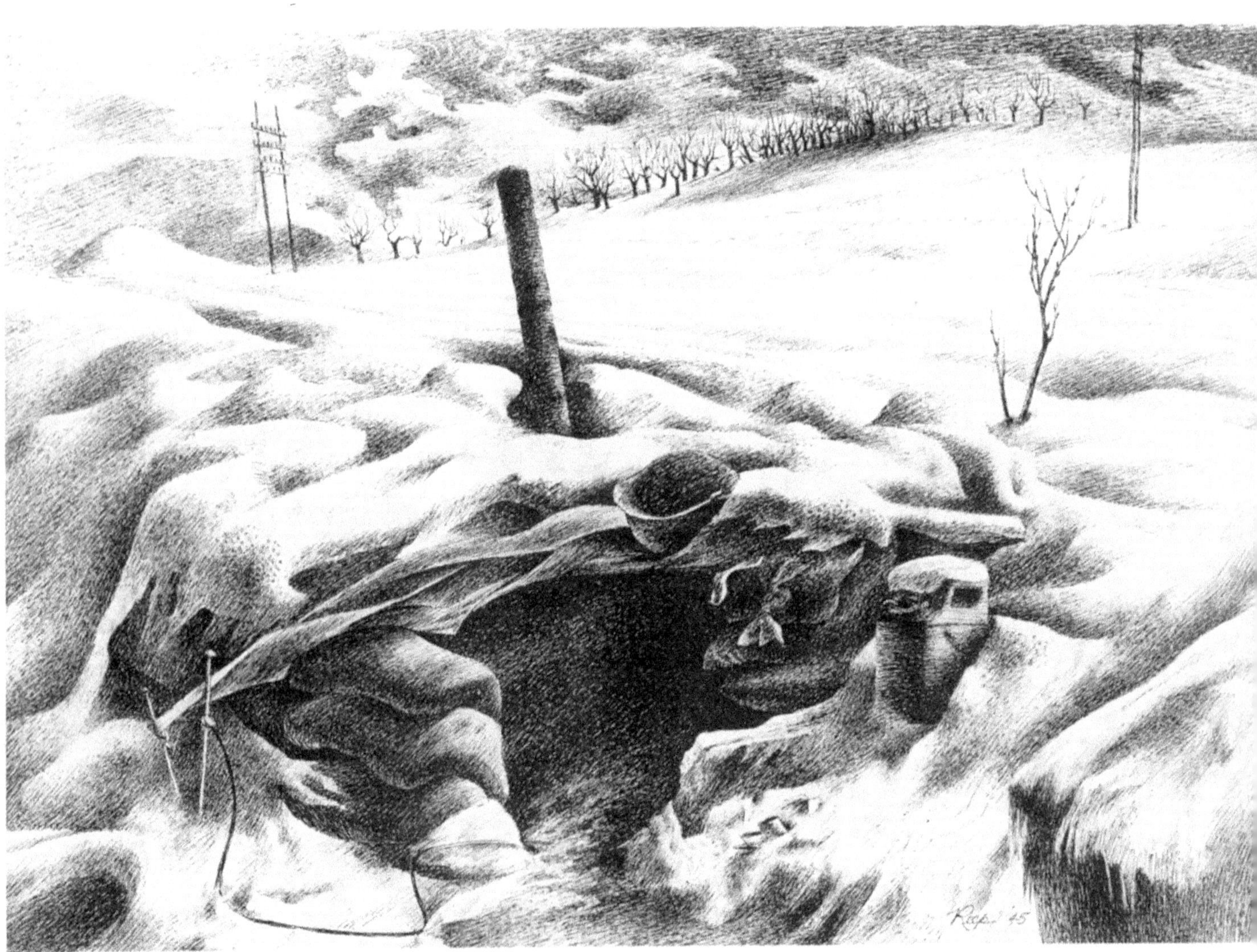

Dugout in the Snow

1945. Pen and ink. 13½ x 20¾ in.

During the second winter's stalemate, this dugout was one of my luxurious dwellings. High in the Apennine mountains before Bologna, I lived here briefly in order to document soldiers struggling to carry out their missions through the long winter months. Dugouts such as these offered protection both from enemy shellfire and from the elements.

Noting the smokestack recalls a woeful experience. I had painted in the snow for several hours and returned to my dugout home, cold and tired. Leaning my painting against the dirt wall near the improvised woodstove, I started a fire and then curled up to read Maugham's *Of Human Bondage*. An hour or so later when I looked up, my painting was gone. The watercolor had frozen in the bitter outdoors, then melted away beside the heater. For the remainder of the winter, I confined my efforts to pen-and-ink drawings.

an otherwise blissful serenity. A night such as this was a welcome relief for one and all. I peered upward through the black silhouettes of the tall trees surveying the numberless cool-white stars blinking back to me, and my thoughts turned homeward to my wife, whom I longed for, and my family and friends.

Then, almost asleep, I heard the faint, unmistakable hum of an airplane engine, which grew louder as it approached. In an instant all about me was bathed in a terrifying light, as if the sun had ushered in the day in a split second. The plane overhead had dropped three flares, simultaneously disgorging thousands of propaganda leaflets. As my eyes adjusted to the shock of the blinding light, I detected the myriad specks of paper fluttering gently to earth. It was my first experience with flares, and for the moment I was frightened and confused. The phenomenon defies description, especially when it happens so unexpectedly. My first reaction was to take cover—find a ravine or maybe huddle close to a large tree trunk—for surely bombs would soon be on their way. But there was only the one plane; its mission accomplished, it had departed.

We scurried about gathering up piles of enemy "junk mail" until the last flare had burned itself out; when that happened we were in darkness so relatively overwhelming that there was little to do but grope our way back to our bedrolls. In the morning there would be ample opportunity to resume our search.

No one there really gave a damn about the propaganda, and few would even bother to read the text. It was the pictures that were of interest. There were nude cuties to scrutinize, guaranteed to produce an avalanche of salty wisecracks and keep the gang in good humor for hours on end. We all played "trading cards," that universal American pastime, each working toward a complete set of safe-conduct passes and other assorted Nazi baloney.

Another strange experience at this time was perhaps not quite so startling but a good bit more frightening. Some Jerries had been flushed out of a cave where they had been holed up, comfortably riding out the stalemate; that was apparent by the manner in which they had built their beds of straw and neatly stored their food supplies. I came upon the scene soon afterward and poked around, considering doing a drawing of the caves. The forms were interesting enough, but the setting lacked color, and I had decided that it was unworthy of a painting.

Hearing an airplane overhead, I turned in time to see that it was diving right at me, or so I believed; when the pilot opened fire, every round was directed right between my eyes. To this day, whenever I see a movie or news report of helpless refugees or soldiers being strafed, I shudder in remembered fright for those poor souls.

But what made matters worse on that awful day was that the strafing was done by one of *our* planes. We could easily recognize that it was an American P-38 fighter—a reassuring sight, at first; in fact, some of the men had been aware of the plane's presence for much of the morning and thought little of it. Then it dived, opening up with a deafening roar of rapid machine gun fire in concert with the intimidating whine of the fleet aircraft.

The cave immediately to my rear quite possibly served as an echo chamber, amplifying the noise to an unbearable level. It all happened too fast for me to take cover. I remember only that I ducked as the fighter plane zoomed by at low altitude and was gone in an instant. I'll never know whether the fire was intended for me and the other American soldiers in the immediate vicinity, or the vehicles passing by on the road at the top of the bank above the cave. If the motor traffic had been the pilot's primary target, I reasoned, wouldn't he have flown a path parallel with the road, not at right angles to it? Fortunately, it made little difference; no one was injured, nor was there any damage to the vehicles. Then we were informed that this sort of thing was becoming quite common; there were Germans piloting our captured aircraft for just such sneak attacks.

My original desire and deepest obsession persisted: to paint *at the front*. In my continuing innocence, I supposed that once stationed there, with assurance from the fighting men holding the line that "this is it—you go no further," I would be privy to something rare, dangerous, exciting, richly pictorial, and worthy of an elaborate masterpiece. Nothing was further from the truth.

The war in Italy—the only war I knew—involved a long, slow, sometimes torturous movement northward up the rugged spine of the Italian peninsula. Two consecutive winter stalemates had left men marking time with little to do. Thus, apart from Anzio, where the beachhead itself was a front line, I had customarily worked as close to the front as possible yet found no way to portray that circumstance graphically in my work—with one exception.

One of my favorite paintings from the standpoint of color, structure, and pictorial vitality was executed in late November 1944 while I was at last practically sitting on the borderline between the two opposing armies. It depicts several white ribbons drawn across a little road wending its way through the heart of a long narrow valley. The ribbons, or tapes, were tied to iron railings guarding both sides of a small bridge that spanned a culvert and drainage canal. The rails, little more than oversized pipes, were now grotesquely distorted, mutely attesting to the fierce struggle that had been waged over this tiny but strategic landmark. At this juncture both armies had recognized that they were hopelessly deadlocked, prompting our forces to string the ribbons as a warning not to proceed beyond that point—and they meant *precisely that point.*

There were personnel mines everywhere, buried, half exposed, or just strewn on the road; they were little wooden boxes cleverly hinged so that when a person stepped on one, the lid would sever the pin and detonate the mine. The minute craters clearly visible demonstrated their effectiveness. Our soldiers had undoubtedly cleared the area by setting them off harmlessly—at least that was my assumption—so, proceeding with extreme caution, I set about collecting several deactivated boxes to take back to my friends as grim souvenirs. These wicked little devices weren't intended to kill, only to maim. A soldier stepping directly on the mine would be wounded in the legs, groin, or—worse yet—in his vital organs.

I decided that this was exactly what I wanted to paint. At last I could emphatically state that here was a rendition of the true front line. It possessed everything I had been searching for short of a sign reading "Front Line—No-Man's-Land Ahead." I set to work diligently, excited and inspired, and the painting progressed far better than I had expected. The subject matter was to my liking, reminding me of my love for still-life painting in art school. This indeed was a still life, or as the French entitle such works, *nature mort*—dead life. When I had reached the point where I could leave the location and do the rest of the work back at the Historical Section, to ensure success I made numerous sketches, took several photographs, packed my gear, and departed. My jeep was parked some distance away on the shoulder of the road. (I had learned earlier to keep such an inviting target out of enemy observation if possible, and to work far enough from it to avoid injury if spotters did zero-in on my

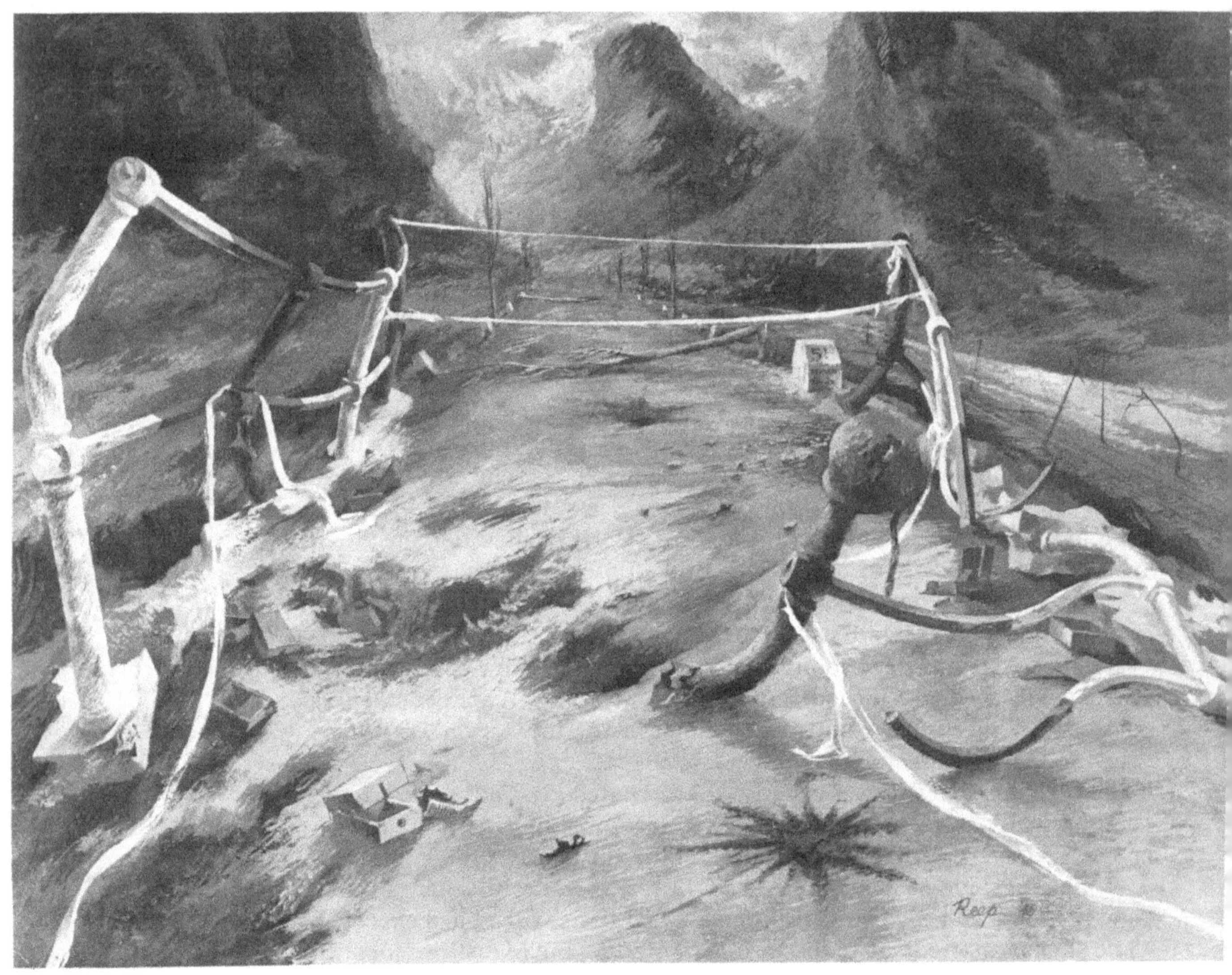

No Man's Road to Bologna

1944-45. Gouache. 19 x 24 in.

On Highway 64, a few kilometers before Vergato, our troops terminated the use of this road. To the right and running parallel to Highway 64 was an Italian railroad and beyond it the Reno River. German artillery and mortars were zeroed in all along this passage to Bologna; the slightest movement of men or machines drew enemy fire.

The color of this painting, begun in November 1944 and completed early in 1945, is particularly pleasing to me; its vivid oranges, yellows, reds, and browns are accented by the stark black and white painted pipes demarking the culvert and small bridge.

sitting duck, as they had in Pisa.) Nearing the jeep, I discovered a farmhouse and barn a short distance off the road and decided to investigate the site. The afternoon was young, my work had gone well, and I felt terrific. Perhaps there were more elaborate souvenirs to be found.

Approaching the barn first, with its great door opened wide, I was startled to see directly before me a fully uniformed German soldier lying dead, his neck twisted awkwardly to the side. It was a gruesome sight, especially so for someone who didn't often encounter this sort of thing. I wondered why he had been left there. Studying him with care, I noted that the buckle of his black leather belt with that misapplied motto *Gott Mit Uns* plainly visible, was still in place. ("God with us"—what an ironic attempt by the brutal Nazis to enlist the Lord on their side.)

Since the belt and buckle were coveted prizes of war and almost everybody wanted one, I determined to strip the dead man of the belt and possibly his helmet, too, as grisly as the task would be. Mustering my courage, I reached for the belt.

Suddenly there were two piercing screams from the farmhouse. "Achtung! achtung!" rang the shrill voice of a peasant lady, who was now scurrying toward me. As I turned to confront her, she was waving her arms frantically, on her face an expression of unmistakable terror. "*Minen, minen,*" she sobbed. The body had been booby-trapped, which explained why it had been left there. I retreated in horror. I had gone about as far forward as possible, and our burial units hadn't yet combed and cleared the area. The distraught *signora* knew of the trap, possibly had seen the Jerry bastards rig it, but was helpless to do much about the matter beyond warning me off.

As I drove back to headquarters reflecting upon my foolhardiness, I puzzled, when would I learn my lesson? The magnitude of my stupidity frightened the devil out of me, and I vowed not to seek souvenirs again, no matter how great the prize and temptation.

The snow lay deep in the valleys that I now sought out in my quest for fresh material. At winter's end, or possibly a mite before, we would be on the attack, and there wouldn't be time to paint in as considered or leisurely a manner. The Idice River valley especially attracted me, for everywhere I looked were little red things poking up from the massive blanket of white snow, pristine and glistening. At the urging of a junior officer in the 34th Division, I visited the headquarters of the commanding general, Charles L. Bolte, first to discuss the possibility of working there and, with any luck, to gain some assistance and advice. The general was very receptive, and after I drew his portrait (the result was dismal; Bolte was a terrible model, fidgeting and moving about constantly) he paved the way for me to work in some very rewarding areas.

I went next to the far end of the valley, where on a small ridge the mortarmen were dug in, both guns and men. Their targets were uniquely designated by long stakes stuck in the snow to the front of the mortars; on the tops of the stakes hung C-ration cans turned upside down to keep the stakes free of snow. When fire was called for on a set target, the appropriate tin can was removed and the mortar repositioned. It was an ingenious way to cope with the elements. I sat in the snow to the front of the gun emplacement as I drew, looking back through the stakes, past the men, and down into the long valley split by the wandering, frozen Idice River. Unbelievably, there were some small trees with leaves—something one rarely sees on a battlefield—and the delicate foliage cupped the pure white snow to enhance the scene further. I was by now drawing far better than at any previous time in my brief career and completed a very good work.

As for those little red dots sprinkled throughout the valley, General Bolte called them his "salvage roses." Everything had been stored on the ground prior to the advent of the heavy snow, in anticipation of which tall stakes had been driven into the ground and topped with inverted tin cans painted bright red. When the troops needed food or ammunition, they merely went to the general territory where the supplies had been buried, found the proper stake, and dug away the snow.

Another interesting feature, one new to me even though I had already endured one winter in combat, was the manner in which the artillery cannon were placed and camouflaged. They were set inside tents with their muzzles protruding upward and out of the door flaps, and both tents and guns were painted solid white. The artillerymen kept fires going throughout the cold days and nights in the tents to prevent both themselves and the guns from freezing. I painted in gouache, a mixture of watercolor and opaque white tempera, and attempted to capture the unusual setting; the result was more important as a historical document than as an art piece. It would be my final painting before the last great assault and the incredible, frantic race to the Alps.

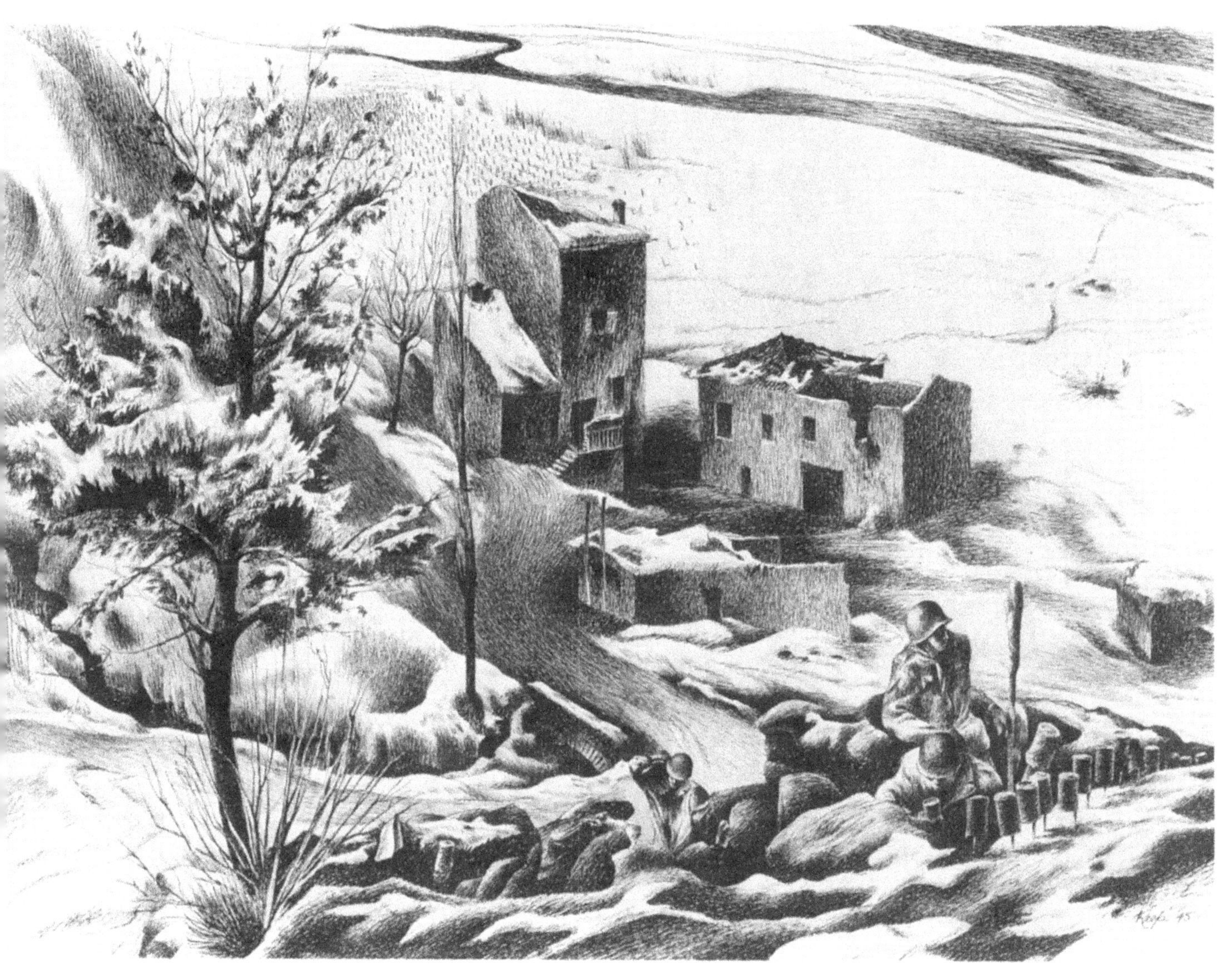

Mortarmen in the Idice River Valley
1945. Pen and ink. 14½ x 22½ in.

After many months of stalemate, soldiers all along the line improved their living quarters and positions. These mortarmen of the 34th Infantry Division cling to the reverse slope of a hill on the east wall of the valley in order to secure both cover and concealment; in this manner they are able to work only a few yards behind the riflemen, even though supplies and ammunition must be packed up the steep slopes. A soldier can be seen toting ammo on his shoulder, while his companions man the position.

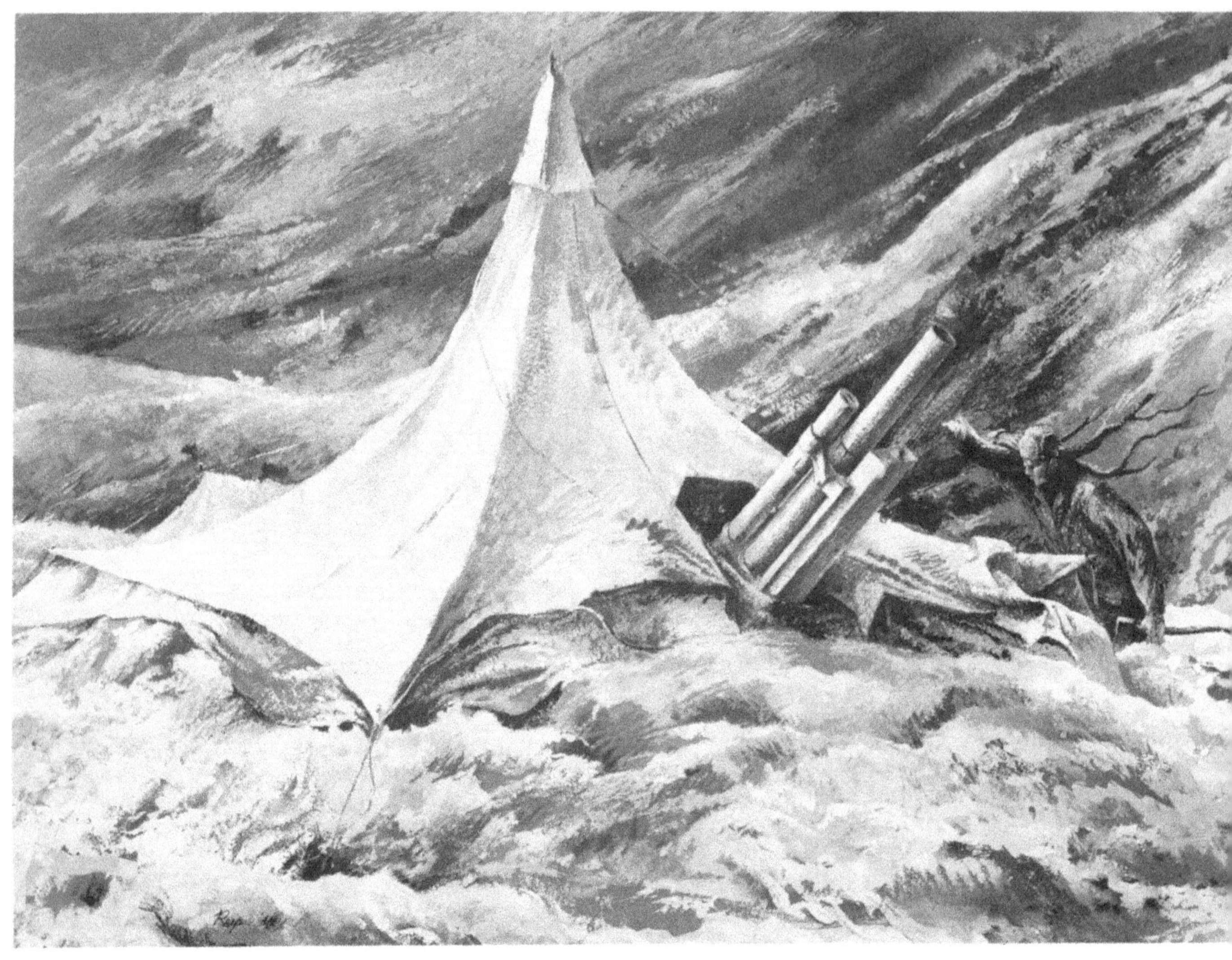

Salvage Roses

1945. Gouache. 15 x 20½ in.

At first, artillerymen lived in tents near their howitzers; then, because of heavy counterbattery, they dug in. When the rains increased, the tents were placed over the weapons, allowing them to be fired out of the tent doors. Soon after, snow began to fall regularly, and both tents and howitzers were painted white. Ammunition, kitchen supplies, and nearly all other equipment were marked by long poles driven into the ground with red cans attached to the tops—General Bolte's "salvage roses." Though they are difficult to discern in black and white reproduction, touches of fiery red sprinkle the mid-horizon at about the level of the soldier toting wood.

CHAPTER ELEVEN

The Enemy Is Routed

Radulovic and I raced into Bologna on the heels of our infantry and tanks. It was early in the morning of 21 April 1945, scarcely a week since the long-awaited offensive had begun, the fuse ignited by troops of the 10th Mountain Division. We did not yet know that the drive would culminate in the surrender of all German forces in Italy or that the fighting would soon be at an end for most of us. The infantrymen I had worked among throughout most of the winter, specifically the 133d Regiment of General Bolte's 34th Division, rode atop the tanks of the 752d Tank Battalion, which now led the way against only modest opposition. Savo and I barreled along with them with no idea of what we were getting into, flushed with the excitement of being in on the fall of a great city; it was a first for us. Despite the light resistance, there was still sniping in the streets, which cautioned us to be wary as we moved about.

We spent the first few hours helping flush out what was left of the enemy and some diehard Italian Fascists. With pistol drawn—an almost ridiculous ploy for me because I couldn't hit the side of a barn with that antiquated weapon—I took cover behind the giant stone columns supporting buildings on one side of the street, to scan the windows of the structures across the way. Most of the shots were coming from the high windows, and while I didn't spot a single sniper, the sporadic firing resounding in the nearby streets gave notice that there was still some last-ditch resistance scattered here and there. By afternoon it had all but ceased. Slowly and quietly, civilians and soldiers made their way out into the streets to inspect the great piles of weapons taken from the Fascist and Nazi soldiers. The partisans had done their work early, successfully taking care of most of the collaborators whom they knew and detested

Tanks Ready to Roll

1945. Pen and ink. 19 x 24 in.

Light tanks of "Fox" company, 81st Cavalry Reconnaissance Squadron, 1st Armored Division, have been alerted and are ready to move at a moment's notice from the forward slopes south of Vergato. Using their tanks for protection, the men have just "feasted" on hard chocolate and cans of C-rations. Some of these tanks and their crew members were casualties in the last big push, but the majority found themselves north of Milan on V-E Day. The entire squadron had been in the line for 93 days when the attack began and more than 105 days when the Italian campaign came to an end.

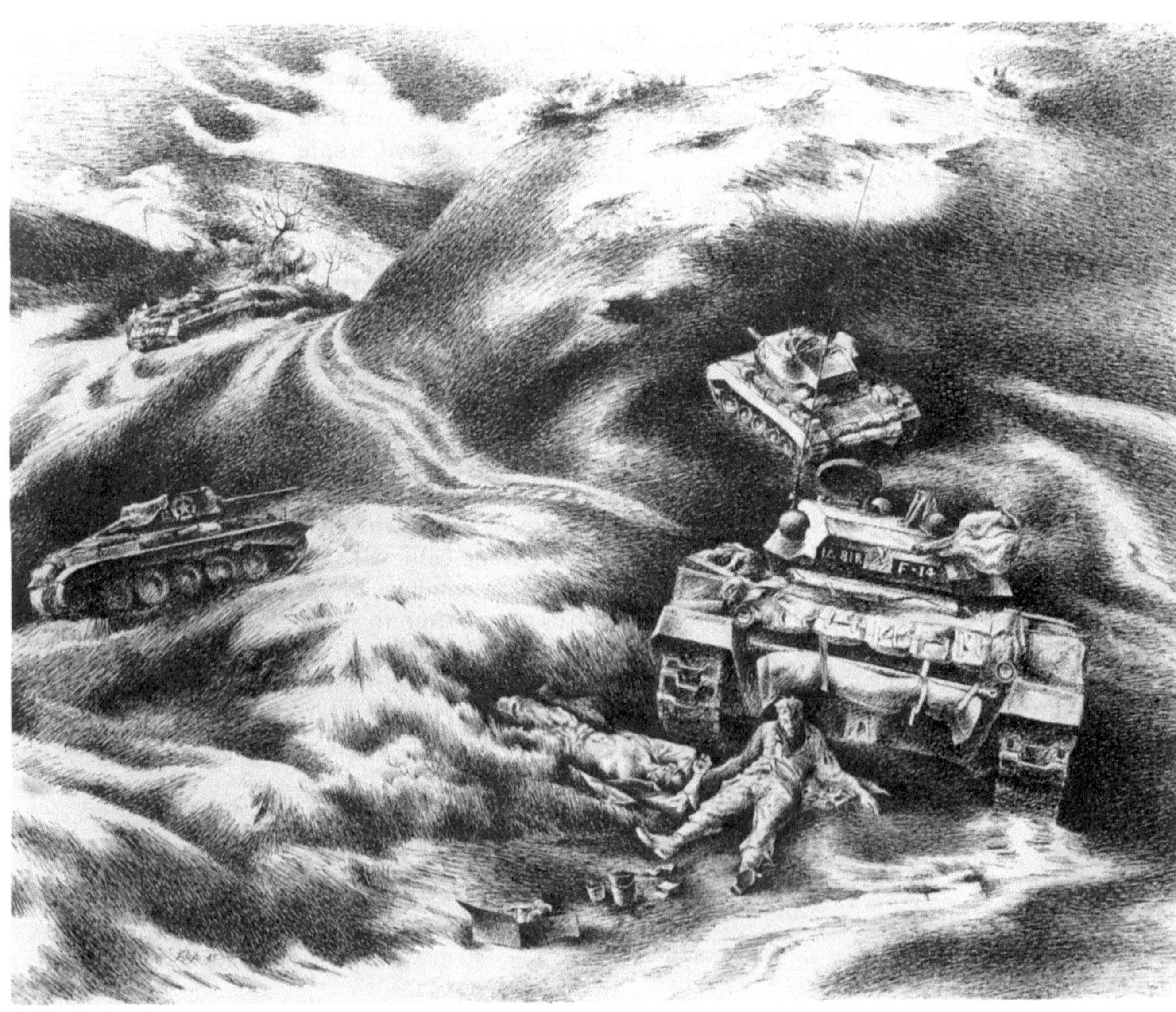

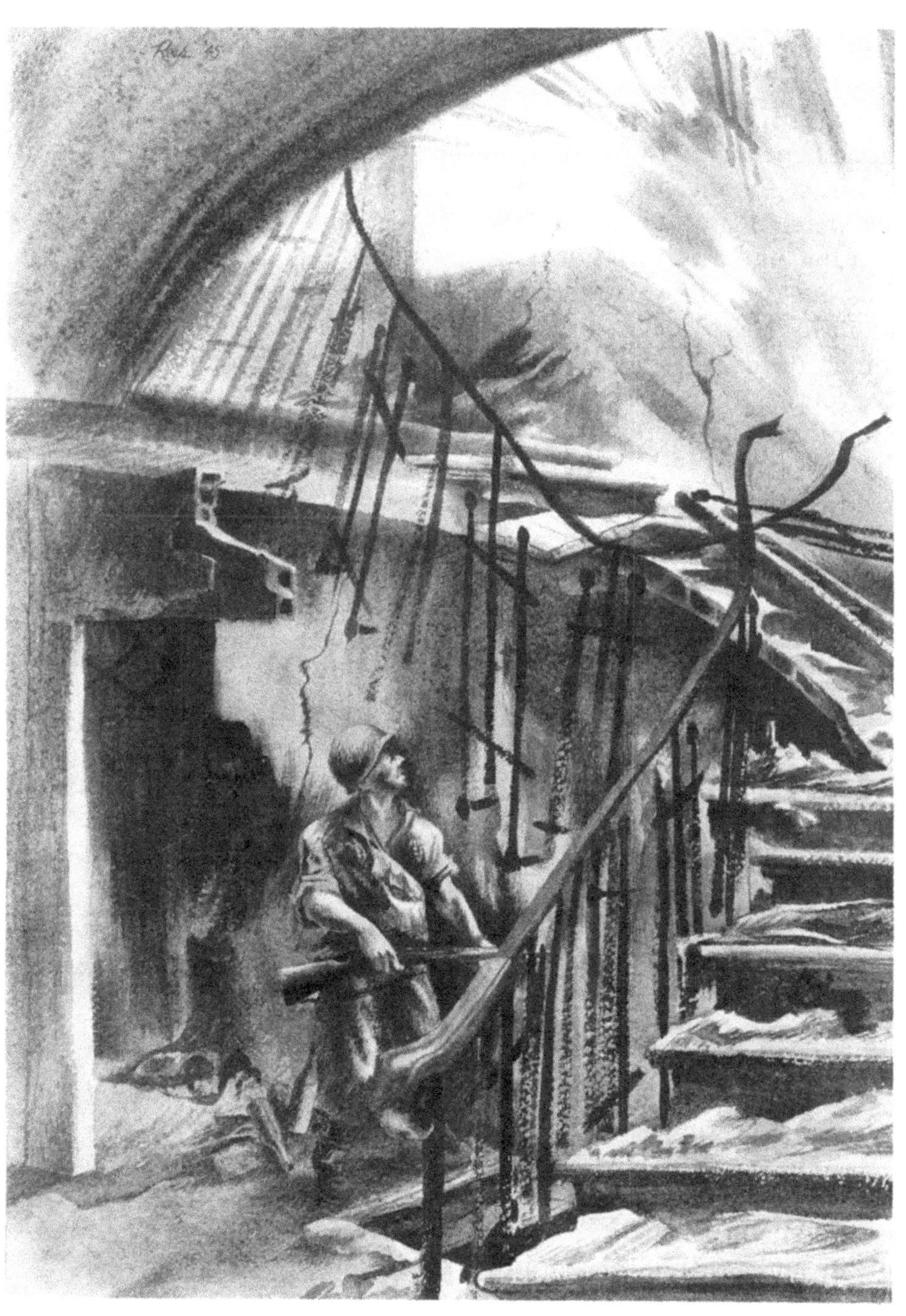

Sniper's Den

1945. Watercolor. 15 x 22 in.

The interior of this building in Vergato was used as a German stronghold. When under attack, the German soldiers would retire to such cellars, where even hand grenades could not follow the winding stairs down to them. Holes were fashioned in all walls to allow passage from one room to another without going outside. All winter long the Jerries lived like caged animals in these small fortresses, always under the direct observation of Allied troops. When the last big push in Italy began, fanatical German resistance in Vergato held up the attack along Highway 64 for days. In this painting an American soldier of the 81st Cavalry Reconnaissance Squadron moves cautiously about searching for remaining defenders.

vehemently. By day's end Savo and I had our choice of every imaginable German and Italian weapon, and as many as we wished. I selected several P-38 pistols—at last I could replace my wobbly Colt 45—and Savo took a couple of the machine pistols aptly referred to as "burp guns."

The apprehension of the civilians had kept them subdued and strangely silent at first but now they were in a more festive mood, and celebrations were in order. Bands of joyous partisans paraded about, waving, shouting, and uttering victorious slogans all incomprehensible to both of us but providing colorful subject matter for future work. I wanted to familiarize myself with these vital, courageous people, so I officially joined a small group of partisans whose leader turned out to be an attractive young girl named Maria. She must have been no older than 14, of medium height and build with lovely blonde hair flowing down over her shoulders. Maria was fully armed with two ammunition belts slung across her chest and over her shoulders. She resembled one of Emiliano Zapata's female warriors during the Mexican revolution earlier in the century. Her little partisan band had just corralled a high-ranking Bolognese collaborator, a true *fascista* who had made life miserable for the general populace for years; presumably, they were marching the terrified man off to his execution. I noted that he clutched at his throat constantly while he was being hauled and prodded forward. Whether this gesture held some signifigance for Italians, I don't know. I mention it because later, in a sketch depicting Maria and her coterie, I attempted to record that gesture, whatever it signified.

Young Maria had lost both of her parents to the Fascists or Germans, and she was determined to avenge this and other long-endured injustices. Now that the Americans had liberated her city, her band had exposed themselves to the public and were not to be trifled with; they meant business. The other members obviously had personal scores to settle, too, for the country had survived 23 long years of humiliation and deprivation under the dictatorship of Benito Mussolini. Whether all of their stories were true or understandably embellished made little difference to me; I was so impressed with them that I decided to become an official member of their organization as a tangible gesture of support for their cause. A card was issued in my name, their first and only American soldier member, and I treasure it to this day. I was now *numero quindici,* number fifteen, and a part of the Comitato Liberazione Nationale unit.

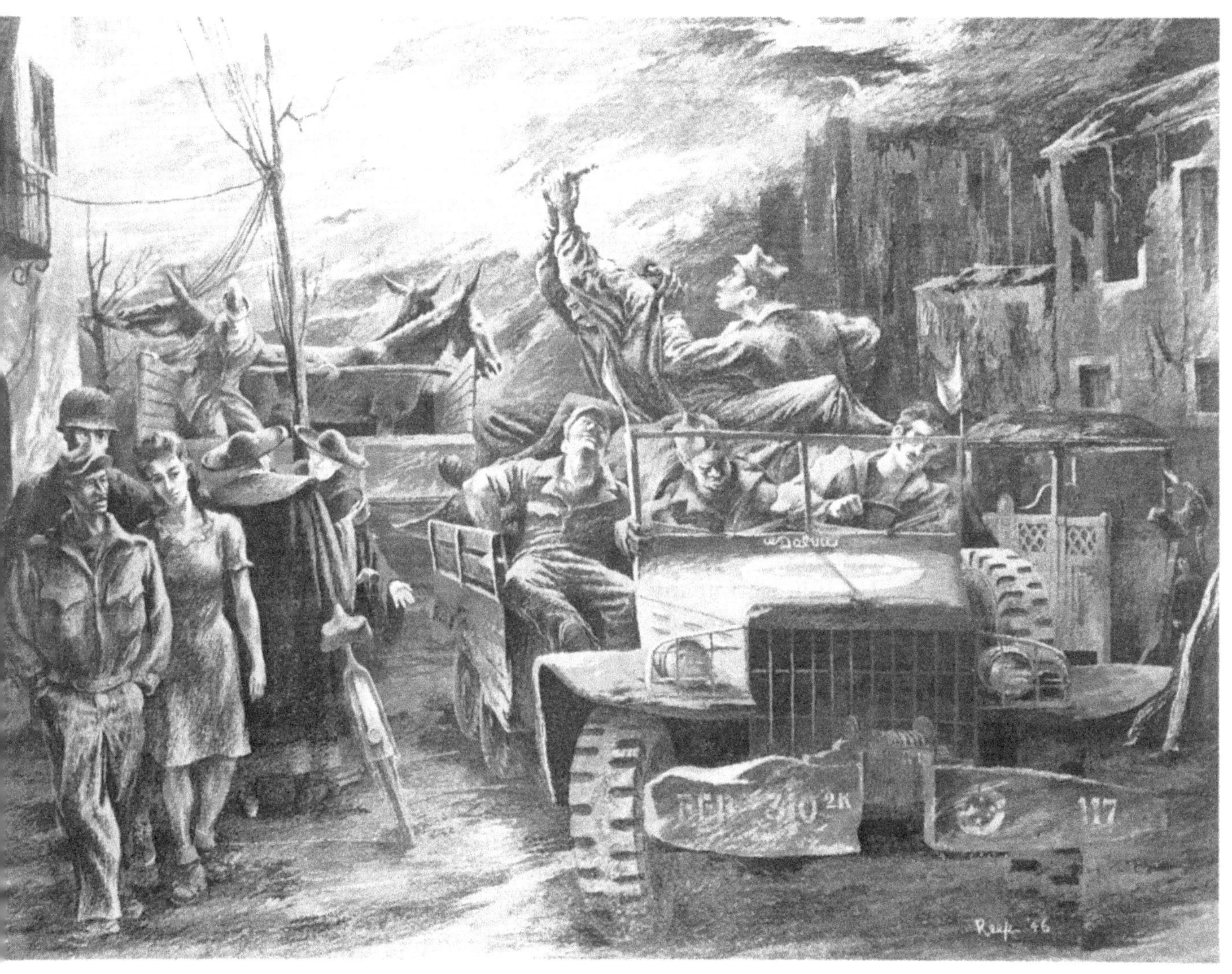

The Cobra Smokes
1946. Gouache. 20 x 26 in.
Collection of William H. Lamson

Brazilian troops frolic while heading down the main street of a war-ravaged town in northern Italy. Drawn from numerous sketches and my vivid recollection of the chaotic events of the war's last weeks. A Brazilian soldier walks toward us, followed by an American GI and his Italian girl friend (in GI boots). Behind them, two priests carry on an animated conversation. The mules loaded onto the truck will be transported to the front by Italian Alpine troops. Meanwhile, children are at play on the public pissoir to the right.

The card was used for identification and called a "Tessera di Riconosciménto," a pass of recognition that would allow me to move freely among the populace. It was dutifully signed by a Professor A. Benedetti, who, coincidentally enough, resided in the little town of Ponte Buggianese, where I had taken my dog Arno to the veterinarian. The card bore an official stamp of the party, showing a star within a circle. Maria's group also presented me with a handsome armband made of silk in the colors of the Italian flag, along with, of all things, a spanking new P-38 pistol in a rich black leather holster with a star carved into the cover flap. To this day I remain proud of that brief association with those brave people.

I left the partisans as they were marching their captive away. Later I discovered that they did not execute him as planned; instead, they put him to work in the fields along with fellow collaborators. I surmised that forcing these former bigwigs to carry out peasants' chores would humiliate and disgrace them; at the same time it was a practical punishment, since the necessary farming would be attended to.

I didn't accompany the group to the fields because time was precious on that glorious day, and I didn't want to miss any of the festivities in the central portion of the city. I'd completed a few rather simple sketches of the partisans and later would do a complex drawing of the entire band marching their captive along. Unfortunately, I failed to capture the expression on Maria's face and in frustration cut it out of the drawing surface with a knife, vowing to begin again one day. But I never have gone back to it. Everything happened so fast that anything of value had to be in the form of spontaneous work executed on the spot in concert with the action.

In the town square of Bologna, where the city jail is located, a collaborator had just been slain beneath the iron-barred windows of the jail, his fresh blood still visible on the brick wall below. Within minutes an Italian flag was hung on the wall, above and to the left of the bloodstain, the tricolored red, white, and green presenting a startling panache of color against the ancient, dull brown bricks. The House of Savoy emblem had been ripped away from the white central panel of the flag; pinned in its place was a stiff black ribbon of mourning. This became a dual gesture: it signified the end of the monarchy and Fascism, and it became a memorial to those who had given their lives in the long struggle for liberation. A derelict green table was then thrust against the bedecked wall, and placed upon it were little mementos, mostly photographs and flowers commemorating the loved ones who had perished; more photos were pinned to the flag. The images of those who had seen service in the Italian army were adorned with delicate multicolored ribbons of red, green, and white. Lastly, an ornate filigree cross of black wrought metal was placed toward the front of the table to become the crowning touch in completing the impromptu shrine. Today, in Bologna, a permanent shrine stands on that sacred ground.

When I returned to America and began working under the sponsorship of the John Simon Guggenheim Foundation, the most important painting of a full year's effort was based upon the little shrine in Bologna. It was depicted faithfully, just as I have attempted to describe it to you. The painting stands as a microcosm of the tragedy, futility, and heroism of war; it now hangs in Washington, D.C., as a part of the permanent collection of the National Museum of American Art.

Events were unfolding so rapidly that Savo and I hardly knew where to turn. In our desperation to stay with the action, even to engage in it, we hooked up with a reconnaissance company. Although I was officially assigned to Reconnaissance Company A of the 1st Armored Division, I knew nothing at all of their duties. Together, Savo and I found out in no uncertain terms.

Within a few hours an order arrived to send out a party posthaste with the purpose of making contact with the enemy. We reasoned that this must be one of the duties a "recon" company performs, so we went along for the ride, not at all sure what to expect. Then our objective was made more explicit: we were ordered to draw enemy fire. It seems that some of our units had lost contact with one another and with the enemy, too, and this condition had to be rectified. As ridiculous as it may sound, we asked to accompany the small scouting party, tagging along in my jeep. So, sandwiched between two armored half-tracks, Savo and I found ourselves rolling merrily along a countryside road, serpentining through lush farmlands, passing quaint farmhouses nestled in the low hills and valleys of no-man's-land—inviting Jerry to take a potshot at us.

And the invitation was accepted. In the late afternoon we drew all kinds of enemy fire: bullets whizzed overhead and mortars began plopping in on the road in front of us. The lead vehicle halted, and the lieutenant in command raced for cover, beckoning the others to follow.

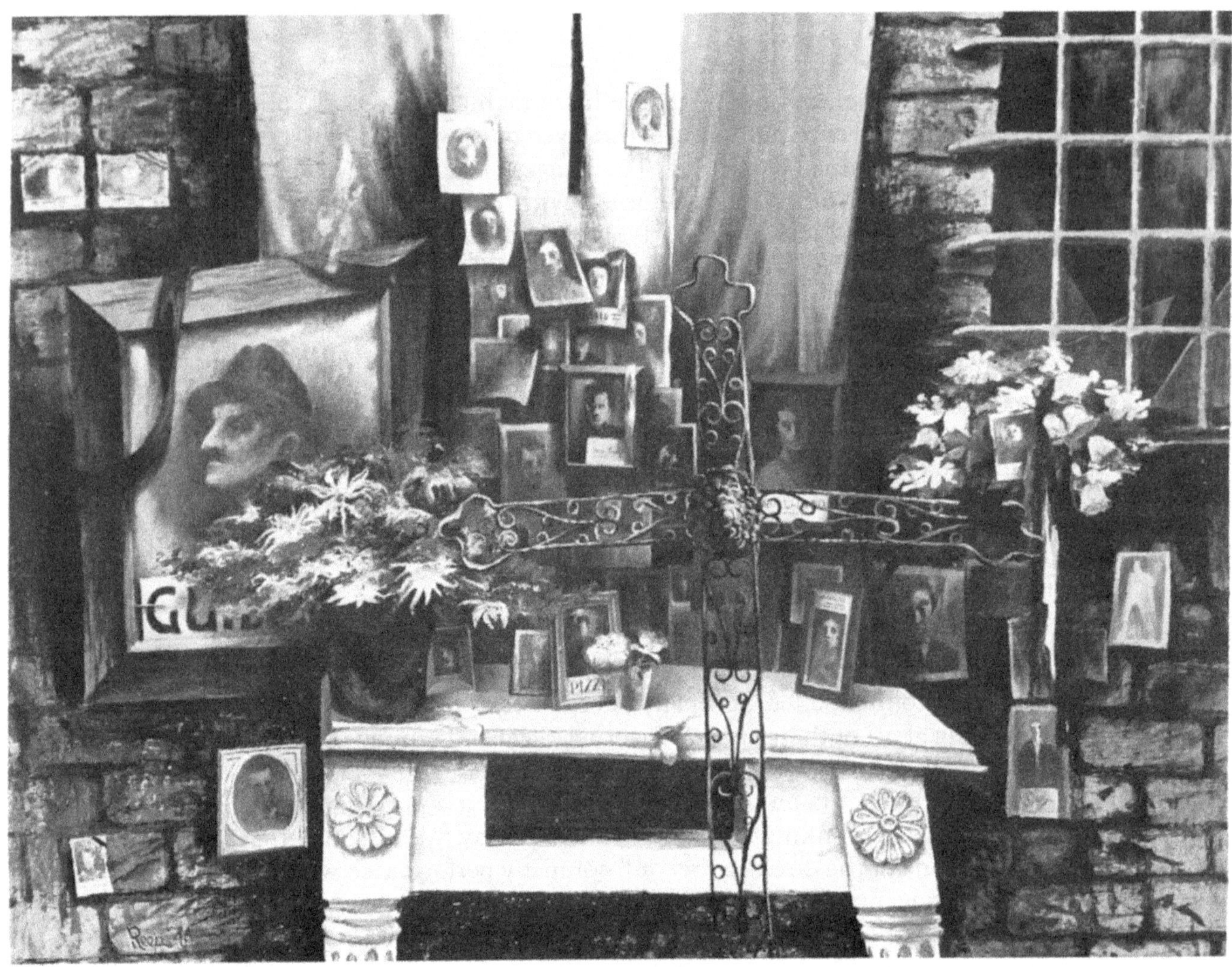

The Shrine
1946. Oil on canvas. 30 x 36 in.
Collection of National Museum of American Art, Washington, D.C.

The Shrine was executed after the war from notes and sketches made during the hectic moments when we captured Bologna. The hastily erected shrine depicted is now a permanent and more elaborate national monument in that city. The painting relies heavily upon the contrast of transparent color glazes against impasto (thick) paint. After initially priming the canvas, I covered it with a green ground that would peer through the multitude of brownish-red bricks. Painting on the field of battle had to be quick and spontaneous; it was rarely studied. Equipment was always portable and never comfortably complete. In my postwar studio I was able to exercise care and patience, select the appropriate medium, and—of greater importance—reflect deeply upon significant issues.

The shells were now falling on the road *behind* our three-car convoy, indicating that the Jerries were getting a fix on us and zeroing in. We were, in the parlance of the artillery, being bracketed; the next barrage wasn't likely to miss. Savo and I followed as rapidly as we could; a formal invitation to get the hell out of there wasn't necessary. As we scurried to keep pace, I glanced back at the eerie trio of deserted vehicles and prayed that my beloved jeep would not be destroyed and meet the same fate as the *Patsy I* had suffered in Pisa. I pictured it in shambles. But our first concern was for our safety, and before we knew it we were tumbling into a large dank cellar beneath a nearby farmhouse, one man atop another.

The spacious underground room turned out to be a glorious storehouse of goodies for the inquisitive soldiers to examine. Of greater importance, it provided us with excellent protection from the heaviest of artillery fire, for nothing short of a direct hit would have been able to penetrate the sturdy upper floors. Later that evening, as we cautiously returned to our vehicles—standing as we left them and inexplicably unharmed—we noted that dozens of mortar shells had landed about the yard surrounding our refuge, exploding harmlessly in the soft earth. The lieutenant in command had immediately radioed headquarters to apprise them of our position and situation, and I can only assume that our artillery picked up the source of enemy fire and silenced it, for the shelling of our position eventually subsided. At this juncture our mission was declared successful.

In the interim, however, the soldiers in our party took the event in stride; for them it was merely another day's work, a routine mission. I, on the other hand, first sweated out my jeep but soon began to fret about our safety and ponder what our next move would be. How long would we stay in this cellar? How truly protected were we, and where would we go from here? I had absorbed one profound lesson early, the hard way, by being critical of a young officer's strategy. At that time Savo had taken me aside and reminded me that it was easy to second-guess but not quite so simple to do everything right under extreme pressure or stress. So this time I cautioned myself not to meddle with the business at hand or criticize the leader. These brave soldiers, every single one of them a civilian draftee not long before, were doing one helluva job, and they didn't need an anguished, frightened, or just plain nervous artist to worry over.

If Savo shared my concern, he kept it to himself, but his misery would have been short-lived anyway, because *vino* was discovered. The soldiers, snooping around the side yard of the farmhouse, uncovered huge—I mean gargantuan—glass containers of red wine that had been buried in shallow holes in the earth. Each bottle contained at least ten gallons of the precious stuff, and before long all of us were beginning to relax. Savo, beaming with contentment and at peace with the world, might well have invited the enemy in for a drink.

I continued to prowl about, expectantly surveying the cellar for something ususual, perhaps of artistic value. The residents had fled in haste, piling things up haphazardly, yet carefully concealing the more valuable possessions behind bulky furniture. It was a small gesture on their part, predictably doomed to failure, but in their frustration and confusion what else could they have done? At any rate, my search was soon rewarded. There, in a small corner of darkness, was an accordion.

Put a musical instrument of any sort in my hands, and I am in heaven. I see it as a challenge; I'll try for hours on end to fathom the thing and produce some sort of sound. I labored at that accordion, and (feeling no pain, thanks to the *vino*) was soon familiar enough with the contraption to pick out some simple strains of popular melodies. This ingenious instrument allowed the player to depress a tiny magic button in order to squeeze out an immaculate chord. In less than an hour I was in command of the seven or eight chords with which I was familiar, and the rest was easy. Only a rhythmic squeezing of the bellows needed to be perfected, and given my modest standards, that didn't take long. I had become the master of another musical instrument, once again playing it poorly with little hope for improvement, but I can assure any detractors that my efforts entertained the half-bombed men and kept me occupied all that late afternoon and into the early evening. The men joined in singing and whooping it up—the concert was a success. My formula was foolproof: "Perform only when fully assured that no other person in the audience can play that instrument—or better yet, *any* instrument." Naturally, I liberated that wondrous accordion from its dismal cellar and took it back to headquarters.

Soon after that adventure Savo and I got into a truly humiliating situation. Some excited *paesanos* confronted the two of us, gesticulating wildly, trying their best to make us understand that there were German soldiers on a nearby hilltop, to all intents and purposes trying to surrender. Our informants were civilians, not partisans, and their chief concern was to get every Kraut out of the way so that the fighting would cease in their area and they could return to a normal life. Other soldiers nearby paid little attention to the rumors. The locals constantly brought them all sorts of information, most of it meaningless and irksome. Savo and I, however, listened intently and decided to investigate the matter, for here was an opportunity to confront the enemy alone. Sure enough, when we reached the indicated spot, we could plainly detect small white cloths being waved frantically in front of very thick bushes at the crest of the hill. Only the hands of the enemy were visible.

Savo was pumped up. He had listened to my tales from the front for so long that once he was with me, he was far more eager than I realized to get involved in something dramatic and dangerous. We solemnly agreed that it was our duty to do something about these Jerries, who were obviously terrorizing the natives. As artists possessed of vivid imaginations, we saw this as a first. And although we were not seasoned fighting men, we were sure that capturing enemy soldiers who were attempting to surrender was well within our abilities.

Because I was the ranking officer—the *sole* officer—in our two-man fighting brigade, it was only proper that I develop the strategy. The plan was clear: I would fearlessly lead the way up the hill in the tradition of all great commanders, Savo would follow, covering my advance. At close range, we would force the enemy to come forward and surrender. The mission would require courage and adroit leadership, and I made certain that my loyal and trusted sergeant was fully briefed and had committed the game plan to memory.

I started up the hill by dashing toward a great tree to lean hard against its huge protective trunk. With carbine ready, I peered around the trunk and up the hill at our objective, then I looked back at Savo to reassure myself that he was alert and in the proper position. Satisfied that our initial move was successful, I scrambled farther up the hill to another tree. Savo followed, doing his thing with enthusiasm and consummate skill. So far so good. Having worked my way halfway up the slope, I knew the time had come for extraordinary precaution in order to prevent vile treachery on the part of the enemy. Dropping to the ground and lying prone, I placed the small carbine rifle across my forearms and crawled forward in the approved way that we had practiced so diligently in basic training and again at Officer Candidate School. If fired upon, I was prepared to roll around, twisting my body rapidly in the low growth of hillside weeds, just like the cowboys in the westerns. All the while, I kept glancing back to make certain that I was still being covered.

It was time to flush out the enemy; before firing, I would call out for them to come forward with hands over their heads. Unfortunately, I couldn't figure out how to say anything appropriate in either Italian or German. Then, as if reading my mind, the awesome enemy emerged and stood before us. They were ours—three little Italian girls scared half out of their wits. I felt absolutely foolish. The next hour was spent sitting under a lovely pergola on the summit of that hill, drinking *vino* with our charming prisoners of war.

Late in the afternoon of that same day, partisans began bringing back corroborative reports of an enemy column, perhaps a company in size, approaching in a nearby valley. They were a few miles away, marching on foot and fully armed. It appeared that they intended to take positions on the front lines in an attempt to stem the Allied advance. For all we knew they might have been fresh reinforcements. Despite the fact that the war in Italy was winding down and that the Jerries were dispirited and losing their incentive to fight as they fell back, it was necessary to run down the rumors. It seemed likely that the reports were true because several partisan observers claimed to have spotted the column from separate vantage points high in the hills forming the long valley.

A young lieutenant took it upon himself to investigate the matter, and prepared a plan of attack should a confrontation ensue. He was in command of an intimidating-looking tank with a stubby 75mm cannon mounted on the front, a howitzer designed to lob powerful shells at enemy targets. The tank would play the key role in his stratagem, supported by two small squads of only six men each, including the eager Radulovic and me. As the only other officer in the party, I was placed in charge of one of the squads with Savo at my side; the second would be led by a combat-proven sergeant. Savo and I were unknown commodities, even to ourselves, and the wary lieutenant had taken precautions in case we did not deliver.

The tank would set up at the head of the valley in position to fire at the approaching column, dead in line. The sergeant's squad would cover one side of the valley, and mine the other. The reports were soon confirmed, and the facts were precisely as the partisans insisted: the column was very real, the men marching in single file. They were about a mile away and moving toward us. I was ordered to take my party out on the right flank and assume the position as outlined. When the leader of the German troops came within rifle range, I was to open fire; this would serve as a signal for the tank to commence firing and for the sergeant's squad on the opposite hill to join in. The two squads would then work their way downhill and capture the lot. The lieutenant, noting the peculiar angle of our attack from high on a hilltop, had already rolled his tank backward onto a huge log that would automatically depress the muzzle of the cannon sufficiently to fire directly at the column. This combination of tactics, he concluded, would lead the enemy to assume that a sizable force was attacking, and they would capitulate easily.

Our leader knew exactly what he was doing; his plan proved superb in every respect. When the howitzer's shells whistled in, I could tell at once that the Krauts were panic-stricken as they scrambled for cover. They had no heavy weaponry or vehicles and had placed themselves at our mercy. So the plan was predictable, even if the participants were not.

Retrospectively, I think the lieutenant must have assumed that Savo and I had some previous battle experience and knew what we were doing. Of course, he was wrong. We had a helluva lot of desire and enthusiasm, and that was the extent of our qualifications. As gentle and retiring as Savo was, though, I had no idea that he could become a holy terror in combat. I would soon learn.

As the column approached and I took careful aim at its leader, fully intent upon wiping him out, I goofed. Nervous as hell and suffused with mixed emotions, I slowly squeezed the trigger to the full extent, only to hear a dull click. I'd neglected to release the safety. Savo didn't wait for the shot; hearing the click was all he needed to spring into action and begin firing away like a madman—harmlessly, hopelessly out of range with a pistol. Then the howitzer opened up with a deafening roar.

In my eagerness I had made yet another gross error, for we had ventured so far out on the promontory of the right flank that we were virtually in the path of the howitzer's trajectory! Luckily, the fire from the tank was extremely accurate, and the shells hurtled menacingly but harmlessly over our heads. I released the safety on my carbine so that it might be of some use, and together Savo and I barreled down the hill at far too great a pace, but Savo had gone berserk and was leading the way. An American of Yugoslavian descent whose ancestral land had been overrun and ravaged by the hated Nazis, he was hell-bent on retaliation, right here and now. I recall stumbling down that hill in an attempt to keep pace with Savo, simultaneously keeping a wary eye on the little dwellings scattered about. For all I knew they could have been occupied by German soldiers who might attempt to pick us off. I seriously doubt if Savo even saw the houses or weighed the potential consequences, and for what all this is worth, I'm not knowledgeable enough in military tactics to know who is the better soldier—the overly cautious or the foolhardy.

It had little bearing on the outcome because we quickly confronted the Jerries making their way up a small winding path to our hillside. All had abandoned their weapons, their hands were high overhead or on their helmets. They were a dazed, confused, and disheveled bunch of "supermen," and our "massive" ambush had done its work. Neither Savo nor I had any discussion with the prisoners, but it must have come as a distinct surprise to them that their captors were a mere handful of men.

We made certain that they possessed no concealed weapons and herded them onto a nearby road. As we did so, a German officer approached, and I spied a pair of coveted German army binoculars dangling about his neck. With pistol in one hand, I reached out with the other to seize the prize. The officer flinched and pumping adrenalin made my movements erratic; the combination was such that I pulled up hard and accidentally struck his nose so hard with the binoculars that blood gushed forth. I think I broke the poor devil's nose.

Several of the Jerries had been wounded, and a couple of others lay dead. If there had been even token reistance, it had occurred down in the valley and involved the sergeant's squad. None of my squad went back down to check on the extent of the bloodshed; we had our hands full getting our prisoners together and in line on the road. With the tank lumbering along behind, more of a symbol than a threat in guarding the throng, we marched them back to a large, high-walled schoolyard for safekeeping. Protecting prisoners in this fashion was the only decent thing to do, as the onlooking partisans were understandably itching to get their hands on the despised Germans.

Savo and I felt considerably better about ourselves after that, especially in view of our fiasco earlier in the day.

CHAPTER TWELVE

Milan, Mussolini, and Victory

When the Allied armies broke from the Apennine Mountains to flood across the Po Valley, Savo and I—recognizing the futility of trying to record the rapidly changing scene—had no idea of what to do or where to go. The Germans were reported to be confused and helpless; they offered little in the way of resistance, and many were individually and collectively attempting to surrender and save their hides. We had long been stalemated by the stubborn German defenses and frustrated by the heavy mud and slush of the bitter cold winter, yet always in clear view of our objectives. Now the attack was accelerating to breakneck speed as we raced across the broad plains of the Po heading for the Alps. Savo and I loaded our jeep and joined an advance column roaring down the broad highway to Milan, in great anticipation of new adventures ahead.

As always, I did the driving; Savo rode shotgun with a Jerry burp gun across his lap. The strange convoy was flying down the highway as fast as the military vehicles could go, possibly 40 to 50 miles an hour, and encountering no resistance whatsoever. At one point we stopped to capture three woebegone and frightened enemy soldiers with hands raised high over their heads in surrender. Savo covered me as I hopped out of the jeep and searched them for weapons. Finding none, I took a long knife and a German army issue wristwatch from their possession; then, as articulately as possible for someone who spoke no German, I attempted to convey to them that other troops would soon be along and that they could surrender at that time. We left them standing by the roadside more perplexed than before, got back into the jeep, and tore off.

We could see Milan ahead and to the left of the highway, and Savo had been doing some heavy thinking. "Tenente, the hell with this column," he roared. "Let's go into the city." Milan, a great industrial and cultural mecca, was the jewel city of northern Italy, and Savo must have instinctively known that something exciting would be taking place there. I turned and headed for the tall buildings on the near horizon. It later proved to be our most meaningful decision of the war.

On the outskirts of Milan an amazing sight came into view: on our left stood a towering, round office building with guns bristling from every window. Just then we were stopped by two armed partisans, waving deliriously and smiling from ear to ear, their white teeth shining in contrast to deeply tanned skin and scraggly, black beards that made them appear fierce and rugged. Tears of happiness rolled down their cheeks as they joyously shouted, "Americani! Americani!" What a marvelous day; they had been waiting for us for so long and then watched, perplexed and riddled with disappointment, as the main columns sped by. They had fabricated two large, crude paper replicas of the American flag in anticipation of our arrival, and assuming that Savo and I were very important persons on an official mission, they set about affixing the stiff flags to the front of our jeep. Then, making it clear to us that danger lurked ahead in the form of enemy snipers hidden throughout the city, they leaped onto the front fenders of the jeep to offer protection on our drive in.

We were told that the circular skyscraper was occupied by a German army, from the commanding general on down to the lowest private. Whether or not an entire army could fit into that building is insignificant; the Germans had commandeered it as a haven or refuge in which to protect themselves while awaiting the arrival of a properly authorized Allied commander, hoping that a surrender would ensue under the international rules of war, and they would not be left to the mercy of the avenging partisans. There was no fight left in any of the Jerries. They knew the jig was up and were reluctant to fire their weapons for any reason short of self-defense. Their "fortress" was so strangely silent and lacking in drama that we tired of the spectacle and drove on. We asked our partisan guides if they could take us into the heart of the city, and to our overwhelming surprise one of the beaming characters asked, rather nonchalantly, if we cared to see the bodies of Mussolini, Clara Petacci (his faithful mistress of many years), and the rest of his entourage. The

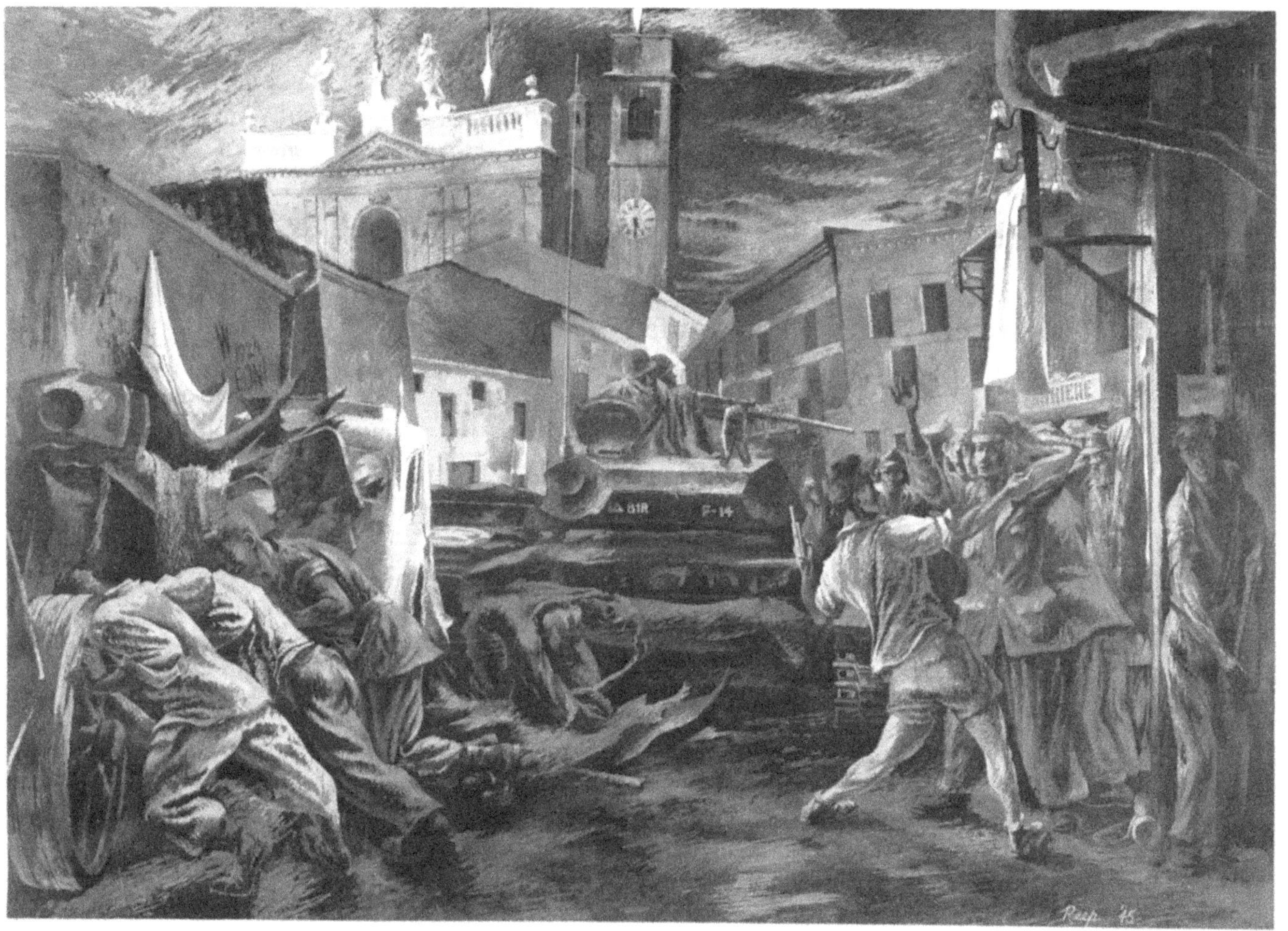

An Italian Town Surrenders

1945. Gouache. 22½ x 30½ in.

During the last days of the campaign, German garrisons were without supply and were surrounded by the partisans who operated through most of northern Italy. It was estimated that over 200,000 partisans assisted the Allied forces. Small groups of American soldiers would accept the surrender of large German forces, unwilling—terrified—to turn themselves over to the partisans. The wreckage of Jerry guns and equipment was everywhere, mostly destroyed by the retreating enemy, but for the most part northern Italy was spared the chaos and ruin known to the rest of the peninsula.

This painting was created from dozens of careful sketches made during the hectic moments of entering the town of Leno. It depicts our men, aided by partisans, rounding up German soldiers and clearing the streets. Our tanks, draped with large, fluorescent orange banners to identify them to our aircraft, lend a spectacular note of contrast to the omnipresent olive greens, somber earth colors, and stark white flags of surrender.

whole lot had been executed a bit north at Lago di Como and their bodies hauled back to Milan to be displayed as a victory symbol. The partisans had captured the bunch while they were attempting to flee to Germany and killed them posthaste, for fear that they might fall under the protection of more sympathetic persons—namely, Americans. At the moment they were hanging by their feet, head down, from a steel girder in front of an Esso gasoline station. It sounded incredible—what luck! We hastened to witness the macabre affair.

Triumphantly entering the massive square in the central city, we saw the bodies of Mussolini and his party being cut down from the black girder. The corpses were laid out neatly in a long line, parallel to one another but with enough space between to allow long queues of the inquisitive as well as those who had deeply hated the Fascists to pass by and scrutinize their erstwhile leaders at close range. Some spectators spit on, kicked, and otherwise roughed up the bodies in anger and resentment. Ladies, especially disapproving the illicit relationship of Il Duce and the beauteous Clara, gave vent to their emotions by removing their shoes and pummeling the frozen faces with the high heels. It was a savage sight to behold.

Within the hour the bodies were removed to a dark, barren room being used as a temporary morgue. Savo and I followed the vehicles there and immediately upon arrival were inundated by animated accounts of the heinous crimes of the Fascists. We viewed the bodies once more, this time quietly, carefully, and with none of the boisterous crowd to contend with. Mussolini was a shriveled man. Whereas his barrel chest and jutting chin made him appear formidable in the newsreels at the movie houses (the only source of pictorial news *in motion* at the time), he was truly very small in stature. Without exaggeration, his arms, now skin and bone, were not much larger in diameter than the handle of a tennis racquet. Conversely, Clara Petacci's pulchritude remained clearly evident. Her complexion was lovely and smooth; her firm body, slightly on the *zaftig* side, had been immaculately attired before being subjected to the brutal indignities. Now her dress was partially torn away and jerked up to her waist, revealing delicate, expensive black lace underpants and brassiere, a garter belt, and sheer silk stockings. Although bruised, swollen, and tragically disheveled, her beauty was of such magnitude that it was difficult to believe that she lay there lifeless.

The partisans guarding their infamous captives, some of whom may have been in on the kill at Lago di Como, milled about proudly in the stirring atmosphere. The day was winding down, and in that crowded, windowless room it was growing quite dark, making photography difficult without the benefit of a camera flash. Nevertheless, I took as many photos as possible in rapid fire, and to my delight the clearest of the lot were those of Benito and Clara. There was no time for sketching.

From the morgue we were led to the San Vittore prison and given a grand tour. This is where the political enemies of the Fascist state had been incarcerated, and the partisans were eager to expose the devices of torture and the locations where inhumane acts had been perpetrated upon their compatriots throughout the long struggle for liberation. According to the Italian Ministry of Foreign Affairs, well over 60,000 Italians had been killed, all of them members of permanent partisan organizations. Thousands more were wounded in acts of reprisal; hundreds were burned alive or hanged, and 33 groups of people had been massacred.

We were shown cases of ink in many colors and told that persons they knew had been forced to drink the vile stuff, later to be taunted when their urine ran blue, green, and red. Savo and I would never comprehend all they tried so desperately to convey, given their excited state and the language barrier, but we believed what we understood and saw enough to confirm the worst. In the partisans' animated, emotional accounts, the pervasive ambiance of sadness, and their wet eyes spoke in more trenchant terms than mere words.

After reading Herman Wouk's carefully researched *War and Remembrance,* I am reminded that very few persons listened to the "rantings" of the Jews when they attempted to expose the atrocities taking place at Dachau, Auschwitz, and other Nazi concentration camps. The information stemming from the heroic Jewish underground was so ghastly and unbelievable that it was shrugged off as mere propaganda. The truth, as we all know today, is that it was even worse. The Nazis knew precisely what they were up to all the while, but the gassing and torturing were kept so confidential that relatively few Germans, either soldiers or civilians, knew much about the mass slaughter.

After departing from the prison, we went directly to the main fire station in Milan, there to spend the night in safety. The various units that serviced the metropolis—water, power, and other utilities personnel, plus police and firemen—had holed up behind the protective walls enclosing large workyards typical of most European cities. Savo and I reveled with the firemen, who were cheering wildly and celebrating the great turn of events. We took numerous photos of one and all, embracing and gesticulating vigorously. At this point we learned that we were the only Americans in Milan save for one wild-haired Associated or United Press reporter, whom we never saw.

I spent the night with the firemen, who had further secured the yard by posting guards around the clock, since it was too early to know what events would unfold in the coming hours. But Savo, who I innocently believed would sleep at the firehouse, too, had made other plans. Again I had underestimated his ability to master a language when the conversation centered on either booze or women, and in short order I found myself chauffeuring him to the apartment of a young lady whom he had never seen yet cleverly arranged to meet. Although we were alone in an eerie solitude of emptied streets, there was some activity in a shop or two along the route. In celebration of Savo's good fortune, I pulled up at a bakery and purchased several artfully sculptured cakes for him to give to his mysterious Milanese beauty. By sending along a gift to the girlfriend of my beloved sergeant, I was participating in his rendezvous. It was the next best thing to giving a gift to my wife, whom I yearned for every evening after work, when my thoughts turned homeward. And this was not the first time I played out my romantic notions through one of Sergeant Radulovic's trysts.

I handed Savo the bag of pretty pastry and took him to the woman's apartment, returning as quickly as possible to the firehouse compound. The streets were inexplicably quiet—I had thought celebrations would be in full swing—and there was a remote possibility that some fanatical Fascist sniper was lurking about to take a potshot at anything that moved, especially an American soldier. I drove faster.

The next morning, bright and early, I retraced the route to fetch Savo and get on with our mission. When I inquired as to whether the expensive cakes had made a big hit, I was shocked by his reply that they were stale and virtually tasteless. It seems that they had been prepared for display purposes, using the chaff of dark wheat and no sugar; civilians knew better than to purchase them. When Savo handed the bag back to me, I took a bite of one and promptly spit it out—it was indeed dreadful. It was Savo's good fortune that he had jammed his pockets full of cans of C-ration cookie-biscuits the night before, from force of habit, and his paramour had devoured them with gusto. Spartan as they may have been, they contained white flour and sugar, ingredients she had not tasted for some time.

On 2 May 1945, half a million German soldiers surrendered to the Allied forces, and the fighting in Italy drew to a close. If, as some military experts claimed, the Wehrmacht had retreated to the Alps in order to consolidate their front, reduce its breadth, and solidify positions, they did so at an awful expense. We returned to our unit headquarters, now situated at the lovely Palazzo Martinengo Caesaresco on the shores of Lago di Garda in northern Italy, there to complete unfinished work while keeping an anxious eye on the remaining fronts in Europe and in the Far East.

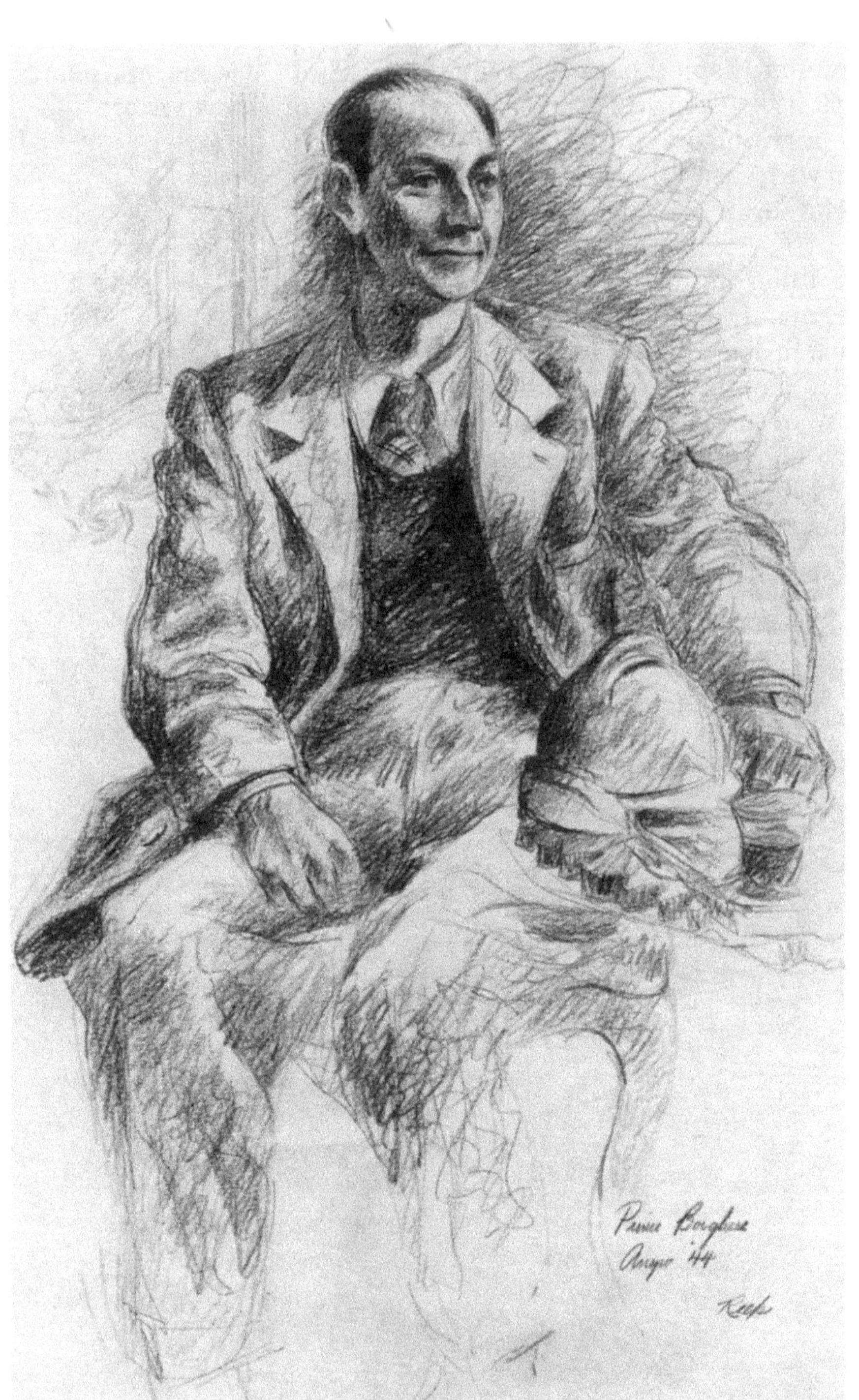

Prince Borghese

1944. Pencil drawing. 8 x 13 in.

The prince allowed the Fifth Army Historical Section to live in his palace on the shores of Lago di Garda in northern Italy after the cessation of hostilities. A charming, intelligent man, the prince seemed unshaken by the tumultuous events of the time—but then, what good would it have done him to react otherwise?

CHAPTER THIRTEEN

Peace at Last

Whenever I journeyed to the front, it proved impossible to foresee what lay ahead or estimate the time I would be gone from the Historical Section. When finally I would head for "home," the entire Fifth Army headquarters was likely to have moved, pulling the artists and historians along and then assigning them to some other remote, peripheral area. I would have to make numerous inquiries in order to discover where my personal belongings had been taken and where I would bunk. Most of the time the artists and historians lived and worked in tents, but there were periods when luck was with us, and we were able to secure some abandoned structure that no other soul wanted. In Florence we worked and slept in an elaborate tobacco factory, which turned out to be a pleasant and convenient accommodation, for it was located near the heart of a magnificent city brimming with unrivaled architectural jewels (Florentine architecture is among my favorites throughout history), a stone's throw from the ancient and fabled Pontevecchio.

Once peace arrived, the brass, in recognition of the rough conditions most soldiers had endured, magnanimously granted everyone the best housing available, and the Historical Section drew a winner. Nothing would compare to the comfort and elegance of the Palazzo Martinengo Caesaresco, the paradise I returned to after our hectic adventures in Milan. This magnificent old palace, a spacious summer home in which Prince Borghese resided, sat on the shore of Lago di Garda in northern Italy, in clear view of the Dolomite Mountains that form the base of the mighty Alps. The prince was a charming, sophisticated, and highly educated man who had temporarily repaired to a remote corner of the vast structure, keeping out of sight most of the time yet seemingly pleased to be among Americans. I had several protracted conversations with him and learned that apart from his life of luxury, he oversaw the agricultural interests of the Borghese family, much like the southern plantation owner of yore who relied upon his sharecroppers. Unfortunately, I came away with the distinct impression that this impressive man of royal birth would have been equally gracious (and probably had been) to a Nazi.

After over two years of bedrolls and sleeping bags, army cots and foxholes, insects, worms, dirt, and shellfire, I thought for sure that I was in heaven. We slept in comfortable beds and enjoyed maid service; there was a bathroom with a tub, hot and cold running water, real chairs in which to relax; we ate three hot meals regularly in a clean mess hall. The officers were provided with a bottle of bourbon each week, as well as cigars and cigarettes. Since I could never inhale without going into a coughing spasm, I developed a taste for those good cigars, of a quality I couldn't afford after returning home. In the highest of army traditions, I'd swap each pack of my cigarettes for two cigars and thus built up a fairly good stockpile. We acknowledged that the brass was once again rewarding us for having helped win the war.

In the long cool evenings the officers of the section gathered at the far end of our massive room directly in front of the large doors that framed a panoramic view of the picturesque lake. All the other officers were historians both in civilian life and in service, hence I found the conversations edifying as we sat drinking bourbon and puffing away on those aromatic cigars, visually feasting on that incomparable mountain vista. The only regrettable part of those tranquil evenings was not having the other artists and enlisted men with us; I would have liked Radulovic and Siporin to participate in our lively conversations. But the army frowned heavily upon what was dubbed fraternization of officers and enlisted men.

We'd chat about our work, about going home to our families and friends, about where we would live. We conjectured whether or not our future would be radically changed by our sobering military experiences. We pondered our reception at home: would our families and friends welcome us back into the old routines? Had they changed too? Most of us had been rudely shaken from our civilian roles, and army life was bound to drastically alter many lifestyles and professions. Though we weren't aware of it at the time, the popular GI educational bill would provide opportunities in higher education heretofore unknown in America and in all of history.

At one point during our evening discussions, I became quite conscious of the fact that I was doing more than my fair share of the talking, and that my topic was always the same—art. When finally I wised up to the ploy, I subtly but insistently turned the discussions to history, a subject I had virtually neglected in my youth. All of the others were Ph.Ds in history and knew their subject well, and I learned much from those exciting, informative sessions. In truth, I felt privileged to sit with that select group of scholars.

Each day the men worked diligently on the final history of the Italian campaign, centering on the role of the American Fifth Army. A cadre of men, mainly officers, developed the written history with the support of two enlisted men, Sidney T. Mathews and Robert W. Komer, who were ultimately promoted to the rank of second lieutenant, thanks to their brilliant contributions. Komer would one day become United States ambassador to Turkey and a powerful figure in Washington politics. A smaller group of enlisted men worked on the maps and other technical illustrations; they had been competent commercial artists in civilian life. The fine artists, or painters, completed more complex works, some of which would be used as illustrative matter for the three final bound volumes of history. The *History of the Fifth Army* constituted nine volumes in all and would ultimately take its place as a noteworthy, complete, and very attractive record of the protracted campaign in Italy. At that time, three volumes had already been printed on Italian presses, and three more were being readied for publication. The final three, containing the work of the combat artists, were later published in the United States.

In addition to working on my paintings, my added responsibilities lay in the overall design and hand-lettering necessary for the covers and frontispieces, and while I had not entered the art world as a professional in civilian life, my studies in art school had been so demanding that I was able to do the work. Freelancing while attending school had given me experience in executing painstaking, handcrafted lettering (a vanishing art), and I found the work on the histories quite relaxing—almost therapeutic—as I worked at a desk with no danger present. It was a far cry from

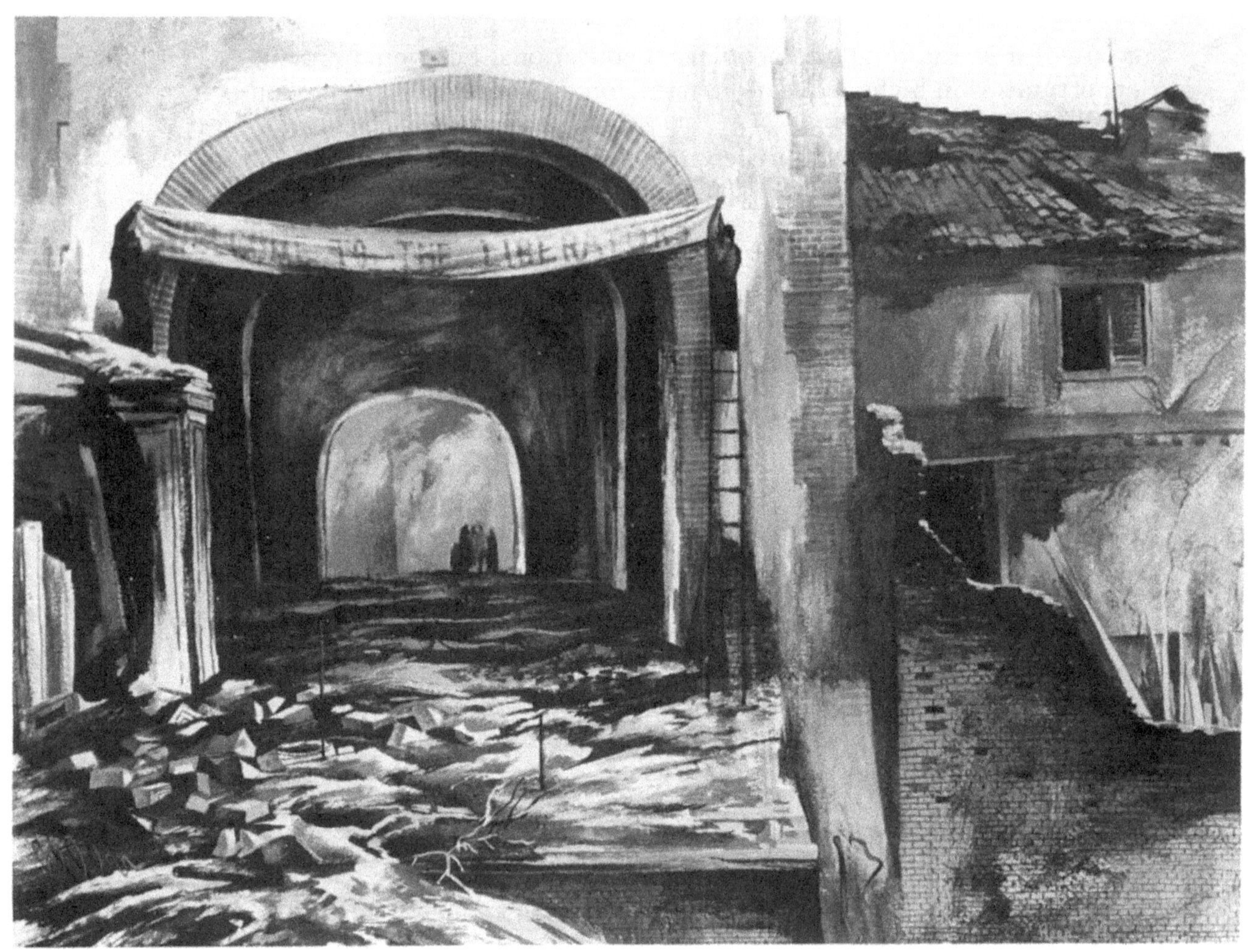

Welcome to the Liberators
1946. Gouache. 20 x 26 in.
Collection of Reuben Uretsky

In the little town of Ponte Buggianese, two men work at hanging a banner welcoming the Allies as liberators. The white flag in the upper right corner indicates that the town has capitulated. The bridge serving as the main entrance to the town, vital to its economy, has long since fallen victim to the bombs of opposing forces as well as German demolition. (This was where I unwittingly passed through the German lines to get my dog to an Italian veterinarian.)

Begun in Italy after the fighting had ceased, this work was stored away for completion as part of my postwar Guggenheim Fellowship project. By that time, numerous philosophical overtones began to dominate my paintings, usually involving the question, "What does war really accomplish?"

what I had been doing for two years on the battlefield, among distractions of every conceivable kind. I recall having to adjust to the tranquillity at the outset.

The artists produced stirring work. Some ideas that had burned in their minds during the conflict had been impossible to do justice to while constantly scrambling about and working in crudely erected tents, but under the welcome conditions afforded by the palace, the paintings poured forth. A positive framework for production is of prime importance for creative persons in any field, and the overall effort by the Historical Section proved exceptional. There is no finer written and pictorial documentation of a major conflict in American history.

The grounds of the Palazzo Martinengo Caesaresco were spacious and provided ample recreational activities for all. After working hours we were able to swim at a splendid private beach complete with small concrete jetties for boating, or we could play croquet, tennis, softball, and other games on courts scattered about the densely wooded property. The men cleared an area in the woods for a volleyball court, and at day's end on two or three afternoons a week, we looked forward to some highly competitive games between the enlisted men and officers. It mattered little that some were fine athletes and others downright uncoordinated, we were all in a happy frame of mind and eagerly looked forward to the contests—although the rivalry may have been tainted with the envy or sub rosa scorn for the brass that most enlisted men routinely and understandably develop.

Concurrent with the late afternoon swimming and volleyball that dominated our free time, a couple of teenage Italian girls found their way into our lives in impressive manner. They had been hitchiking along the road in front of the palazzo on a hot, humid afternoon and simply couldn't resist the invitation to join the men in a refreshing swim at their exclusive beach. Not too surprisingly, they were soon rewarding their hosts with sexual favors, and it took weeks for the officers in charge to make the discovery and put an end to the sport. The enlisted men had artfully concealed a tent in the woods for the girls and kept them fully supplied with food and drink. In all fairness, it had to have been some time since they had eaten good wholesome meals with any degree of regularity. The girls apparently consumed a good deal of GI beer as well; at least that was my impression. It took quite a bit of imbibing to achieve that rosy glow, given its 3.2 percentage of alcohol, but they succeeded.

I had two separate confrontations with the enterprising signorini. One was a rather attractive and chubby little freckle-faced redhead who wore a perpetual smile. Once when I chased an errant volleyball deep into the adjoining woods, I came upon our little darling stark naked, obviously inebriated, and sitting atop a GI in a similar state of euphoria. She was vainly trying to make love with him and perspiring heavily in the hot sunshine. The soldier looked blindly upward into the sky, his watery eyes mirroring countless tiny orbs of the brilliant sun. He was totally out of it, unaware of the unfolding drama or anything else, for that matter. As I fetched the volleyball, the young lady looked over at me, smiling but intent upon her mission, and exclaimed, "Buon giorno." I was so startled by this nonchalant salutation that I replied with some embarrassment, "Scusi, signorina" (pardon me), and hastily departed. The soldier remained motionless, his eyes blank. But the girl was a consummate craftsman at her trade, for never once during our brief exchange of courtesies did she falter or lose her timing.

The other adventure occurred when both girls joined our late afternoon swimming party one lovely day. One wore a skirt and no blouse; the other cavorted about in her birthday suit. All of us, officers and enlisted men, swam as close to them as we dared, some men bolder than others. I hadn't seen a real live woman in the buff for over two years, apart from Savo's lady friend in Bari and the brief encounter in the woods, and to say the least, I was extremely excited.

In the center of Lago di Garda stood a lavish estate on a very beautiful island that we referred to as "Truscott Isle": our intrepid leader, General Lucian K. Truscott, resided there. Through the efficient network of communications all GIs rely upon, we were privy to a number of lurid tales about the place, true or false. For example, members of the Red Cross and Women's Army Corps were strangely attracted to the island and were purported to be invited or assigned there regularly, many times on extremely urgent business. Of course, I have no solid proof of this, yet nothing could conceal our view of the motorboats making their daily rounds to the island and back, carrying necessary provisions, supplies, and feminine cargo.

As we swam with the girls on that eventful afternoon, the motorboat from Truscott Isle came into view. We could see that it would pass just a few hundred feet from where we were splashing and laughing. The driver of the boat sat solemnly at rigid attention with two soldier-sailors standing erect at the stern, and as a consequence the vessel plied a true, unerring course. Even the passengers appeared terribly reserved, and the small craft sliced gracefully through the blue water leaving an elegant white wake as straight as a ruled line. As the boat came abeam of our group of swimmers, the cute little redhead, now topless and clad in only a short black skirt, impetuously leaped up onto the concrete jetty. Facing the boat with feet widely spread, she lifted her skirt high over her head and aimed a rousing bump and grind directly at the craft. I shall never forget the result as long as I live. The operator of the motorboat, who must have taken the full brunt of the girl's routine, lost complete control of his composure as well as the original course. The boat swerved crazily back and forth, its passengers tossed about and trying to maintain their balance—indeed, fighting to stay on board.

Not long after this wondrous event, the two Italian girls mysteriously disappeared, almost as magically as they had arrived.

Rosa was one of the maids who tended to our rooms at the palace. With my poor Italian and her inability to fathom a single word of English—or so she led us all to believe—we did most of our conversing by means of elaborate gesturing and inventive facial expressions. She was rather pretty, had a plumpish hourglass figure with ample bosom, and was extremely shy, but we became good friends.

One evening after dinner I came across Rosa while strolling through the palace gardens. We struck up an elaborate conversation laced with laughter, teasing, and theatrical gesticulation that would have made a veteran actor envious. She was probably only flirting, and I'd come this far through the war without fooling around with another woman and wasn't about to blemish that record at this juncture. But I couldn't resist the temptation to pry out of her why she seemed to care for me. As I think back upon the incident, I suppose that I was undoubtedly desperate to hear a kind word of flattery from a member of the opposite sex. Her delightful response did not disappoint me either, for it was one I shall never forget.

"Oh capitano, voi forza—voi giovane." Rosa had simplified her Italian to fit my miserable attempts at conversation, and I didn't have to consult my pocket dictionary to understand: you are strong, you are young. In no youthful romantic escapades had a young lady confessed anything remotely resembling that candid, pragmatic rejoinder offered in such casual, matter-of-fact terms.

I left Rosa and the garden to head for our grand room overlooking Lago di Garda where the officers gathered in the evenings to test wits and discuss myriad worldly problems. Walking slowly and smiling to myself, I wondered if that dear peasant girl knew how welcome were her words to a lonely, love-starved soldier.

The men in the Historical Section (lovingly referred to as the Hysterical Section) came from all walks of life from throughout the United States. In addition to the artists and writers, for example, there was a dirt farmer from Vermont whom I will refer to as George, although that wasn't his real name. George was of medium height, built like a Mack truck, and strong as a bull. I envisioned him working on his farm from early morn until dark without becoming exhausted in the least. He was now assigned to us as a chauffeur for the unit, taking full charge and care of our sole jeep—my very own *Patsy II,* which was no longer of use to me once the fighting had ceased.

George was inordinately quiet; I can't honestly recall ever having a full conversation with the man. He would tend to the jeep, run errands from time to time, and perform other odd jobs. He was always extremely accommodating while causing little commotion—with one exception. The major problem with George was that he didn't believe in bathing or even washing his clothing. For all I know, perhaps he was a bachelor and lived alone in civilian life.

I didn't see him often when he first joined the section because of my constant forays to the front lines and the paper work awaiting me when I did return briefly. In other words, George and I never worked side by side. Those who did work closely with George, or even in the near vicinity, were profoundly aware of his presence, for they didn't have to see him in order to know that he was in the general area. His person or clothing or both simply reeked to high heaven. As a consequence, the desperate men visited our commanding officer. With grim resolution Colonel Starr ordered two men to chaperone George to the shower unit and see to it that he washed himself properly. He had been sent many times before, only to feign taking a shower and return as smelly as before. This time there could be no escape.

George took his shower obediently, dutifully, and without protest; men under strict orders saw to that. Yet when he returned to the Historical Section, the unfortunate odor returned with him. Serious discussions ensued as to whether this might be a medical problem; there are poor souls who suffer such an embarrassing affliction. Then it was discovered that while George had showered, he hadn't bothered to bring along fresh clothing. He had simply donned the same odorous uniform. For the good of all, and that included the beleaguered George, he was ordered back to the showers to scrub again and follow with clean attire, from socks and underclothes to the whole damn army uniform.

It was on 2 May 1945 that the German armies in Italy and part of Austria had surrendered, completely and unconditionally. Knowing full well that victory in all of Europe was imminent—it was only a matter of time—our thoughts turned ecstatically to going home. On May 9, *Stars and Stripes*, the sole newspaper we had read for two long years, proclaimed in giant headlines, "It's All Over Over Here," and beneath the banner: "Victory in Europe is ours. After more than five and a half years of the bitterest and bloodiest fighting that this continent has ever known, the armed might of Germany, The Wehrmacht and the Nazi Party has been defeated—finally and utterly."

Yet the war in the Pacific was still being waged. Not until some four months later did the long-anticipated news arrive. In three enormous words that virtually covered the front page of *Stars and Stripes*, we were greeted with "PEACE AT LAST," and in smaller type, "Peace has returned to the war weary world." We devoured every detail. Japan had capitulated, and joyousness permeated with relief instantly spread through the ranks of the Allied armies. At long last we were able to think ahead, to plan our future. To be sure, there was work to be completed, but it would prove to be little more than routine. It was all over; we knew that we were on our way home—euphoria reigned.

To my complete surprise, I was promoted to the rank of captain and simultaneously awarded the Bronze Star for "efforts beyond the assignment of my duties." I was in a state of unrivaled happiness, though the honors amounted to mere icing on the cake; returning home to my wife, family, and friends was uppermost in my thoughts.

The first tangible move toward that goal was bound up in what was laboriously entitled the *Officers' Adjusted Service Rating Form*. In my army life two things had nagged at me, and both seemed a dreadful waste of time. One was the incessant marching and drilling that dominated basic training; the other was the relentless bombardment of complex forms requiring immediate attention, duplicatory research, and precise answers. I estimated that every soldier filled out ten million forms a year—or so it seemed. Now, the majority of men were searching for the last and best form of all, the coveted Honorable Discharge papers. But the initial priority was to get back to America; then we could concentrate on the most expedient path to personal freedom.

With conversations abounding over how to accomplish these goals and wild rumors a dime a dozen, no one could be quite certain as to who qualified for shipment home or which system would prevail. As the days wore on, everyone became more and more confused. Scuttlebutt in the services is so rampant that to rely upon it is to ride an emotional rollercoaster.

The first indication of a bonafide rating system finally appeared in our army newspaper and set us all to computing our status. I still own a copy of that particular issue of *Stars and Stripes,* for in applying the newly proclaimed standards I found I was eligible for immediate shipment home by *one little point*; 85 were required, and, according to my meticulous worksheet, I had 86! I excitedly lettered in heavy red crayon above the headlines: "I have eighty-six," and capped it with a huge exclamation point. The dream would soon become a reality.

On the afternoon of 15 September 1945, Lieutenant Colonel Chester G. Starr, our commanding officer, called me into his office. "Do you want to go home, Ed?" Chester was soft-spoken and immensely enjoyed underplaying everything. He looked like the only kid in the crowd with an all-day sucker, one who had just savored a giant lick. The scenario and the question seemed unreal. All my energy had been spent in hoping and in nourishing the dream; now, with the reality of returning home staring back at me, I refused to believe it. But, "Start packing," Chester added, "we leave in the morning."

The colonel and I were being sent to Washington to work in the Pentagon; our assignment was to complete the remaining three volumes of the Fifth Army history and see them published. We would be transferred to the Department of Military Intelligence and find housing in the city, if available. Upon completing the history, we were to be honorably discharged and free to return to our homes. To complete the rosy picture, a sizable amount of severance pay had accrued while we were overseas, and it would be forthcoming at the time of discharge. I joyfully cabled my wife to hop a train and join me in Washington as soon as possible, adding that I would undoubtedly beat her there and unequivocally proclaiming that we would spend the rest of our lives together.

To suggest that I was bordering on the manic may have been a gross understatement. Subsequently, we spent a belated honeymoon in the nation's capital, dreamily contemplating our future. Yet when Pat and I confronted one another after the prolonged, agonizing separation, the scene must have been awkward to behold. She was merely an attractive young lady—the angel wings I had visually attached to her shoulders were missing. She, on the other hand (as she admitted to me some time later), welcomed home a scrawny character in strange combat dress, complete with clunky paratrooper boots, who bore slight resemblance to the striking Adonis she thought she had married. It took several days for the reconciliation to become a riproaring success.

Chester and I worked in the Pentagon daily, carefully overseeing the work being done by the Government Printing Office. I made it a point to check on the disposition of the paintings and drawings that the artists had been shipping home to the Department of Military History and found that they were being cared for in a very professional manner. Knowing that this would please my colleagues, I wrote to inform them of the good news, adding that they were all destined to become extremely famous. My discharge loomed larger as civilian life came into focus, but one small matter had to be attended to, and it bears recounting.

In the zones of combat I had been so engrossed with my work that I found little time for other considerations. The battlefield had erased the early days of training, where sergeants and corporals and officers of all ranks ordered us about with pomposity; that feeling of being low man on the totem pole, nothing, a second-class citizen, had long since vanished from my thinking. At the front most of us knew who we were and what our responsibilies entailed; hence, it was a simple matter to determine who was or wasn't carrying his load. On the field of battle it would have been suicide to function in any other way; the indefinable sense of mutual respect was that important. Not even General Truscott with his fantasy island in the middle of Lago di Garda, or Mark Clark and his vexing vanity, or any of the army brass now aroused envy within me, for I realized that they shouldered mountainous responsibilities and earned every penny they were paid. In this healthy frame of mind, I headed for the Pentagon and the office of a chicken colonel in charge of reserve enlistments, determined to become a part of the army reserve. I had been urged to do so because it would prove a simple way to amass a pile of money (through an ultimate pension) without having to do very much in return. The appointment had been made well in advance, and I arrived punctually.

As I sat outside the colonel's office, an uneasy sensation welled up inside me. I was kept waiting for some time, although I could see that there was no one with the colonel, nor did he appear to be terribly busy. Not even the renowned General Ike had made me cool my heels this long. I tried to be patient, giving the colonel the benefit of the doubt, thinking that perhaps he was trying to solve some critical problem. At last I was invited into his office.

The colonel asked me brusquely if I wanted to join the reserve; it was a simple, direct question bathed in stiff formality and military to the letter. Without waiting for an answer, he went on to point out the number of advantages inherent in doing so, adding that since I was a captain, I could expect to be promoted to the rank of major, especially if I volunteered for the army of occupation in Austria. He made it all sound so enticing, so easy.

I was trying to concentrate on the colonel's words but instead became transfixed by his mouth. It was tightly drawn and puckered in, creating a deep, horizontal crease as rigid as a ruled line scored into fresh clay. His whole countenance seemed set, grim, and musclebound; the only relief lay in his handsome, steely-gray eyes. He appeared tough, yet I had the sensation that he'd been working on that expression for years, like a ham actor, and hadn't quite perfected it. The images of the other chicken colonels who had sat before me like gods on that reviewing panel years earlier at Fort Ord flashed through my mind—those men who forced me to behave like a pure idiot while being subjected to a ridiculous charade designed to test my emotional stability.

I arose from my chair, stood erect, and interrupted the colonel as he spoke. With fresh courage I bluntly said, "Colonel, sir, I don't wish to be in the army reserve." I saluted, wheeled, and left.

Epilogue

While I was stationed at the Pentagon awaiting notification of my formal discharge from the military, Pat and I had the opportunity to visit with army friends just back from overseas and recently reunited with their spouses. We also explored the wonders of our nation's capital, the impressive memorials in particular, and visited Congress in session. We shared slide-viewing with others and pored over the pictures I had brought back from Italy and North Africa.

It is customary for Americans returning from vacations in exotic lands to bring home photographic documentation of their journeys, understandably centering on the subjects whose beauty, color, shape, intricacy, architecture, or embellishment—or even macabre, baroque or downright bawdy humor—particularly struck them. In my travels up and down the Italian peninsula, I too searched for those things, with an emphasis on the great art of the past and the incomparable lessons of the present. For a young artist, especially one so inexperienced in art history, it was simply a stroke of good luck to have been stationed in Italy during the war. Rome is a virtual outdoor museum; equally and singularly attractive to me are Florence, Venice, and Milan. Etruscan, medieval, and Renaissance art abounds, bringing history to one's consciousness in rare and intoxicating manner.

In many ways I am grateful that the prevailing circumstances of war precluded the possibility of arranging routine sightseeing junkets to digest this cultural feast. The method I employed in visiting historic sites was in truth no method at all. For example, I first saw the Leaning Tower of Pisa with German army observers standing on the top tier, staring right back and down at me. After advancing across the Arno

River, I revisited the lovely, graceful tower for leisurely exploration of every detail. One could hardly compare my adventures to those of the typical tourist, but though I may have lost some of the anecdotal folklore that the guides thrive upon, the spontaneous, irregular pattern of my travels worked out for the best in nearly all instances. I had the run of castles and cathedrals, museums and galleries, and many sites quite difficult to gain access to in peacetime. My audience with the Pope and subsequent tour of the Vatican were unhurried—I lingered in the incomparable Sistine Chapel as long as I wished.

It is true that many great treasures had been stored away or boarded and bricked for protection, and a few places were off limits, but many of the important historical edifices and monuments stood in open air and were always available for easy viewing. It would have proved too costly and in some instances impossible to protect everything of consequence. Fortunately, cathedrals, Roman ruins such as the Coliseum, the Leaning Tower, and the like were predesignated as historical monuments and mutually spared by the opposing armies. There was more than enough to see. I lived in awe of the artistic achievements stemming from ancient Italian cultures.

One experience, which I must chronicle, was so vivid and moving that it has endured within me to this day. It occurred in Siena, a modest city situated in the rolling hills some 60 miles south of Florence. Siena is well known for two things: a handsome, spectacularly striped cathedral and (perhaps more popularly) an annual horse race known as the "Palio delle Contrade," which is staged in the Piazza del Campo, or large public square.

Within the cathedral stands the Piccolomini Library, distinguished by the famous frescoes of Pinturicchio, depicting scenes surrounding the life of Pope Pius III: celebrations, rites, and processionals involving various leaders of the church and state of that era. Using a precious little picture book as a guide, I busied myself in identifying the personages appearing in the panels on the walls. After about an hour of careful scrutiny, my eyes tiring, I went to the window and peered down into the large square below.

There was something very familiar yet enigmatic about the piazza that I was casually surveying, and then it dawned on me that I was gazing at the identical square depicted in the Pinturicchio frescoes. Moments before I had been looking upward at a flat, decorated surface; now I was staring down at a live, animated scene in three-dimensional reality. All proportions and relationships were similar; the structures forming the parameters of the town square were identical; even the tactile feel or ambiance created by ancient building materials made the two images strikingly alike. Nothing had changed but the cast of characters. On the wall to my left paraded notables of one sort or another, richly bejeweled and extravagantly attired in thirteenth-century dress; outside in the piazza roamed Italian peasants, farmers, businessmen, nuns, priests, and American soldiers in olive drab. Painted on the floor of the square was an enormous white circle enclosing a bright red cross, placed there to identify the cathedral and surrounding area as a bona fide historical monument and to admonish pilots not to bomb or strafe this sacred place.

A consciousness of history welled up in me with such magnitude that even in faded remembrance words cannot adequately describe the sensation. Never before had a book or a film or even an inspired professor been able to portray with so acute an awareness of time and circumstance the link between then and now.

Despite the inspirational nature of the memorials to our past presidents in Washington, D.C., and the pride one feels in being an American, Pat and I were anxious to return home. So when the honorable discharge finally arrived, we left for New Jersey, there to join in a reunion with my aunt and uncle and my mother and father, who had flown in from California.

The shock waves resulting from my abrupt return to civilian life surfaced endlessly, particularly with regard to expenses, for no longer was I able to rely upon the army for food, travel, and lodging. At every turn there were prices to be paid. As trivial as it may seem, putting a nickel in a pay phone and merely handling coins again became exciting new adventures. Perhaps the best way to shed light upon my financial confusion is to relate my experience with cigars. I had grown quite fond of those quality cigars the army doled out at the front, and since my uncle was rarely without a stogie, I set out to purchase some for him. To my dismay, the price of a box was so exorbitant that I was forced to abandon the idea and come to terms with a new economic reality.

We bought an old Pontiac, the only car available that we could afford, and headed for California, home, and a new start in life. My Aunt Bella loaded us down with all sorts of goodies to tide us over on the long cross-country drive, and it was well that she did so, as we were forced to make the hard-boiled eggs, soda crackers, and salami last nearly the entire journey. We limped into California after suffering two separate motor breakdowns; the lone nickel we had left was reserved for a phone call to alert the family that we had arrived.

Our immediate concern was housing. Returning soldiers and their families had rented or purchased everything available, and our meager savings left us little choice. We temporarily moved in with my parents, which left me without space in which to paint. I had been awarded a Guggenheim Fellowship for creative painting, based upon my work in Italy, and was eager to get rolling on the project, but the annual stipend of $3,000 would not see us through the year, so Pat would have to seek employment. One by one our dreams were getting battered around the edges. In Italy I had grown accustomed to painting in the fields, in tents and warehouses, and in dugouts, all under primitive conditions as well as an unsettled atmosphere. Yet here I was without even the semblance of a studio workspace.

At last a small apartment became available through the Los Angeles Municipal Housing Authority, part of a mammoth complex some 20 miles from the heart of the city and adjacent to the seaside community of San Pedro. One had to qualify for the place by being virtually impoverished, so we had immaculate credentials. We leased the apartment readily, as tiny as it was and distant from our friends and family, and moved in our few belongings with unrivaled enthusiasm. We were alone at last. Pat found a job as a beautician, while I painted each day in the living room, which served as my studio. We owned a portable record player, which I had sent home just prior to leaving for North Africa, but only a single album—Prokofiev's *Alexander Nevski Suite,* which I played over and over again. To this day the melodic refrains remain fresh in my memory.

When I started painting again, there arose an unexpected aesthetic hurdle of such major proportions that I became deeply discouraged. To my dismay, I found that I hadn't developed the degree of sophistication necessary to attain the goals laid out so painstakingly and ambitiously in my Guggenheim proposal. I wasn't bitter, but I wanted to expose the brass and their regal lifestyles, picture inequities between enlisted men and officers, and touch upon what I perceived to be the ease with which some profited from war. In short, I had bitten off more than I could chew. I had been confident to a fault and found it vexing to conceal my utter shame and embarrassment. I turned to those subjects I understood, things I had seen or been a part of, and vowed to paint them in manner and spirit within my level of ability. At least I could pursue this path until better prepared for loftier goals.

My initial efforts were dominated by lonely, disillusioned soldiers whose constant companion was death. Accelerating, I expanded my oeuvre to include lighthearted scenes of troops frolicking or civilian life in ravaged Italian communities. The ambiance of death that I sought took form in a rather puerile use of the human skeleton, always nearby and even astride one lone soldier, the results obvious and scholastic. Dissatisfied, I painted myself—in army uniform but wearing a dunce cap—toasting death, which now appeared in the form of an indistinct, shrouded skeleton. This time, something was left to the viewer's imagination, and that minute touch of subtlety helped immensely. There were still overtones of the melodramatic, perhaps even the corny, but at least I was at work with paint on canvas and not simply theorizing over ambitious ideas beyond reach.

It soon became evident that death had been my companion for so long that I had conditioned myself to ignore its presence; now, in coming face to face with reality, I was attempting to do something about it. In truth, I was belatedly beginning to get good and scared. I relived all my close calls at the front, becoming aware of my own foolishness and the futility of it all. Second-guessing prevailed to complicate the matter further. What was becoming disturbingly clear was that I had grown weary of the whole mess. Combat, suffering, loneliness, and fear—extensions of the battlefield experience—were beginning to sicken me, especially when posed against the wonder and excitement of civilian life. Others were busily engaged in *living* and enjoying the fruits of life, and there was I, cooped up in a tiny room, extending the madness of war.

After about six months of struggling with this growing concern, I asked the Guggenheim Foundation if I might be released from my original proposal, citing the reasons for the request. The unhesitating reply

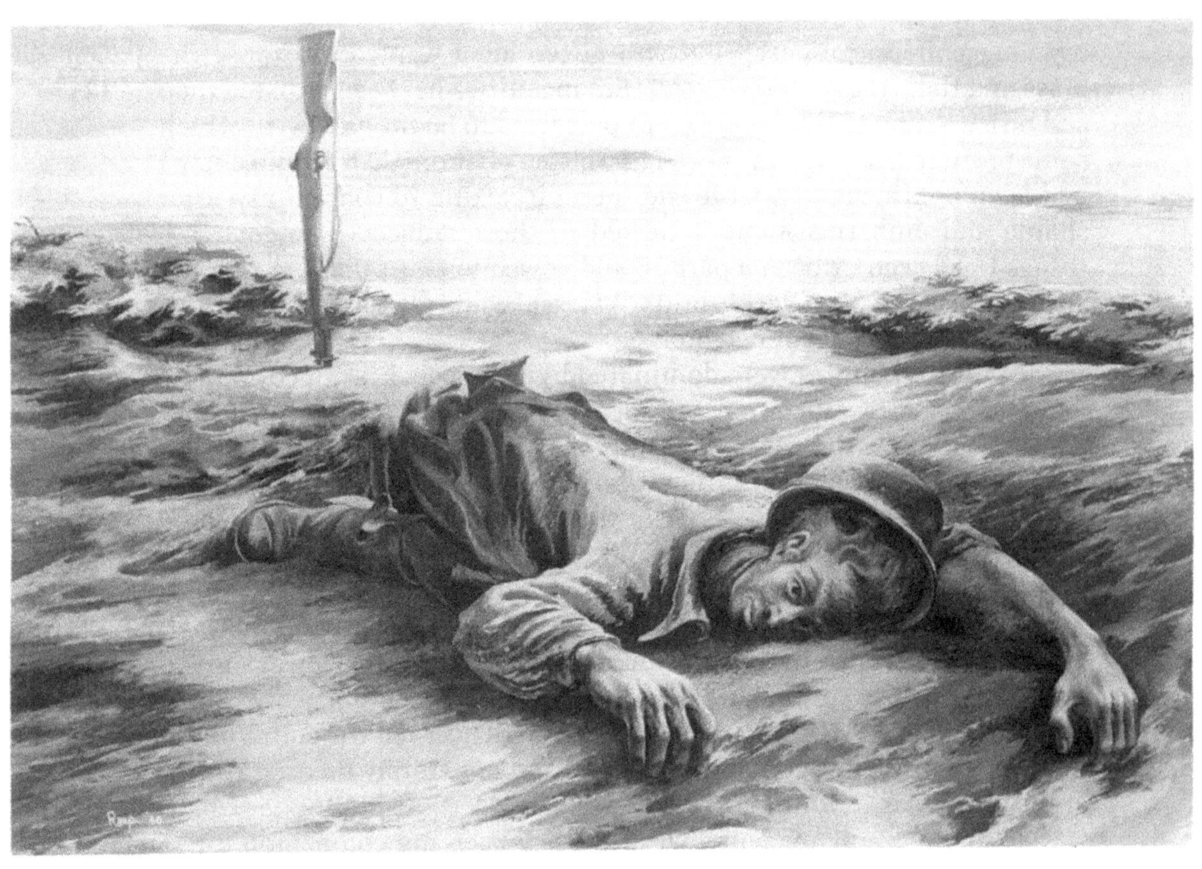

Dead Soldier
1946. Gouache. 20 x 30 in.
Collection of William H. Lamson

Somewhere during the fighting, another soldier and I discovered this dead American soldier, seemingly smiling. He was at peace and, apart from his distorted, crumpled lower body, there was no evidence of injury. My friend, a combat veteran, pointed out that he had been blown up into the air and this is how he landed; then he noted how the soldier's beard had kept growing after he died. We stuck his rifle into the ground to aid the graves registration unit in locating the body. This eidetic image burned in my memory for years, especially in the first years after the war, and I found myself helpless not to set it down. It was this sort of perpetual involvement with sadness that made me turn from anything pertaining to war—books, motion pictures, or paintings.

was for me to pursue any direction I wished; the funds would still be forthcoming. The foundation people never once checked on what I was doing; having determined that a recipient merited the award, they placed full trust in his or her integrity.

No one else can imagine the relief I felt when given permission to dispense with my unnatural preoccupation with warfare; the last of the shackles were removed and buried. I sought out instead the landscape and other subjects where tranquillity and beauty abounded—fully aware that nothing of real consequence was coming from my easel—and the prescription worked. I steadily regained my composure as a painter and, more important, as a human creature. Within two months I was able to return doggedly to the theme of the original Guggenheim proposal.

Conditions in the housing project were not exactly geared to the quiet life. We had been warned of this, but given our desperate desire to be alone, we had chosen to ignore the admonitions. It turned out that the previous tenants were thieves, and when the police called upon us in their search for the culprits, they combed our apartment and uncovered dozens of automobile tires and wheels cached under my studio floor, hidden there by way of an access hold in an adjacent closet. We intrepidly vowed not to let the incident spoil our blissful state. Then our immediate neighbor's son inaugurated a physical fitness program that involved bouncing a basketball incessantly against the wall separating our apartments. The constant thumping startled me at first; when I determined where it came from, I paid a visit to the head of the household next door, who turned out to be a tall, scrawny uncooperative bloke clad in filthy pants and undershirt. This character had one good eye, which wildly focused on me as if I were his mortal enemy, and only after I threatened to summon the police did he consent to have his son arrange for his basketball practice elsewhere.

What finally forced our departure from that sordid place arrived in the form of an unbelievable tragedy: a young mother burned to death in the apartment opposite ours. Being in my studio at work on a painting when the fire broke out, I ran to her aid but was unable to rescue her in time. The details are too gruesome to describe, but nothing in the war had shocked me to a greater degree. There still wasn't any other housing available, and my wife was pregnant. Reluctantly, we went back to live with my parents again.

My sister's home nearby had a spacious three-car garage, and she generously allowed me to convert one-third of it into a studio. There I completed the paintings for the Guggenheim, on cold days moving into her kitchen while she and her husband were away at work. Astonishingly, some of my best work was executed with my canvas propped up on a kitchen table.

There were other unforeseen hurdles to surmount, however. Each day during the war we had rooted for the Russians like the local football team, pinpointing on a huge map their progress in hurling back the Nazis. They were our stout comrades-in-arms; their valiant stand against the German invasion of their homeland, while geographically remote from those of us on the Italian front, had a positive effect upon our morale and subsequent victory. Now, at home and at peace, I was asked to consider the Russians as avowed enemies. Perhaps the politicians and superpatriots who never went to war or experienced conditions on the battlefield could easily make that about-face, but I found it impossible to do so. Those few decrepit Germans I had captured seemed little more than innocent victims of their depraved leaders, and probably could have done little about their plight even if they had so desired. I knew that their leaders were ruthless, as were the Fascists. And what about the Japanese who pulled the sneak attack at Pearl Harbor? I was beginning to assess all military and political bigwigs. Historical accounts of the Nazi game plan reveal how guarded from the public were their crimes and atrocities, and we had just erased that hierarchy or enemy—what sense did it make to substitute another in its place? Could the Russians have changed that rapidly? Or could we, hypocritically, coexist with them in war but not in peace?

I found that the best thing I could do was to concentrate upon making a protest against war itself—all wars—and I exhibited my work wherever and whenever possible. The painting based upon the events in Bologna and the shrine erected to commemorate the fall of the Fascists did more to establish my early career than any other single statement. It took first prize in an open competition sponsored by the American Contemporary Gallery in Hollywood, and with the award came an opportunity for my first solo show in America. From that exposure, I was invited to show the same painting in the Whitney Annual of Contemporary Art at the prestigious Whitney Museum in New York in 1946. One painting plus one good stroke of fortune helped immeasurably to launch my postwar career as a painter.

It was impossible to shake the war from my life, try as I might. I was invited to show in one exhibition after another, often with specific requests for paintings of the war, and innocently found myself in hot water. Not only are charitable groups constantly asking artists to donate their works, but other organizations enlist artists—sometimes clandestinely—to aid their causes. Since I had produced a number of works openly protesting war, I was invited to what I thought was an antiwar exhibition. Little did I know that the true purpose of the show was to assist the "Hollywood Ten," a group of screenwriters and actors who were being harassed by the infamous Senator Joseph McCarthy. It was the day of the red herring, and anyone in disagreement with the honorable Red-baiter was most certainly a Communist. The hapless "ten" whom Joe had singled out were accused of being members of the Communist Party, and quite possibly had been during the Great Depression when so many intellectuals were searching for social reform; how *un-American* they were was another question. I surely didn't know. But McCarthy, ambitious and filled with hatred, was determined to make them pay for that foul deed, and he and his colleagues went after them all, tooth and nail. And because I showed a painting in an exhibition that supported their cause, I received a social call at my home from the FBI.

When the two federal agents arrived, they scared the devil out of me. As I would learn later, it was traditional for one agent to play the role of Mr. Nice Guy while the other did the baiting. I'd become exasperated with the "heavy", just as they planned, and then the good guy would assuage my hurt feelings. In my frustration at this rude inquisition in my very own home, I politely excused myself to phone my Uncle Charley, an attorney who had once been a high-ranking Los Angeles deputy sheriff. He ordered me (in no uncertain terms) to get back in the living room and tell those stalwart characters "to get the hell out of my house." My uncle was furious, for he knew my background and he knew the law. To this day I wouldn't know how or where to join the damn Communist Party even if I wanted to, and I had just fought in a war to help free the world of Nazis. Yet here were two self-righteous men (who probably rode out the conflict

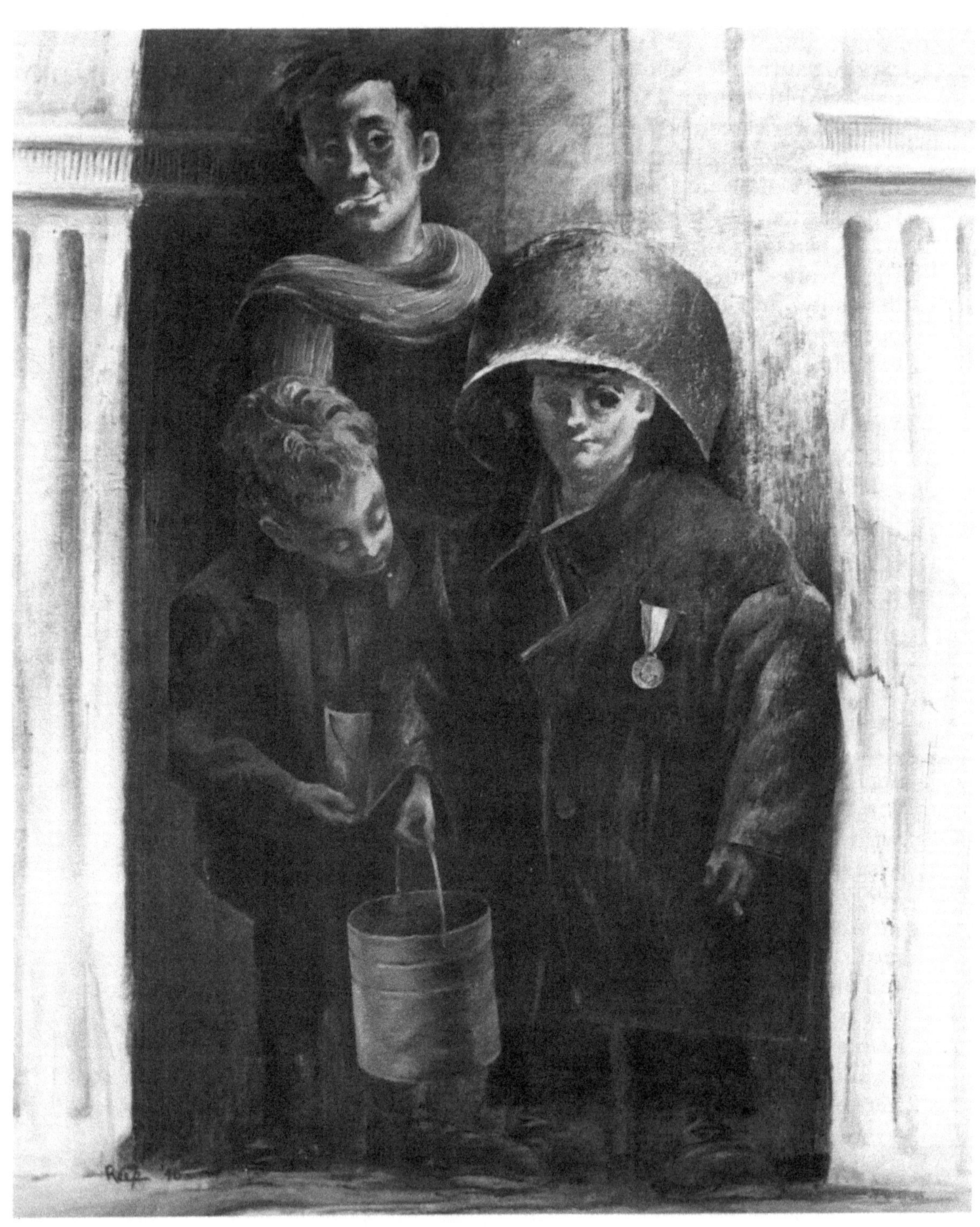

The Garbage Collectors

1946. Oil on canvas. 24 x 36 in.
Collection of B. Eisenberg

Whenever soldiers ate in the field, children, old ladies, and nuns gathered about with empty containers, waiting to raid the garbage cans. There were times (and most GIs shared the experience) when eating before these hungry persons was next to impossible, and we'd dump our plates of food directly into their pails. These three hungry *ragazzi* stand in the recess of a doorway waiting for food scraps. One wears an army helmet liner, a man's coat cut off short at the sleeves and sporting a Franklin D. Roosevelt Victory Medal, and a pair of outsize GI boots. Two boys are smoking cigarette butts found on the ground, while a third peers hopefully into a bucket.

on the home front) making my life miserable. I returned to the living room and repeated my uncle's words. To my astonishment and utter delight, the agents arose and left.

They had alleged that I was supplying military secrets to Japan through an enemy agent, a renowned physicist on the faculty of the California Institute of Technology. I had never been on the Cal Tech campus and had never even heard of the eminent doctor who was purported to be spying for the Japanese. Some birdbrain, another witch-hunter with a red herring stuck in his skull, had undoubtedly made a list of the artists exhibiting at the Hollywood Ten show and trumped up a neat little cock-and- bull story in an attempt to embarrass or defame each exhibitor. It was a preposterous and transparent scheme, amounting to a total waste of government time and money.

Over the years my recollections of the war grew dimmer and dimmer. Rarely alluding to my military experiences except perhaps in jest, refusing to read accounts or novels centering on war, and never attending films filled with the carnage of battle helped considerably; finally, the conflict seemed so distant that it turned strangely fictional, and I began to think of my adventures as if they had been experienced by others. Only after I arrived in North Carolina in 1970, there to join the faculty at East Carolina University fully 25 years after the second great war to end all wars, were my army exploits revived. The university brimmed with retired military personnel from World War II, all of them on pensions; with salary levels low, the school was eager to secure their services. At the same time, the ex-military were handsomely augmenting their retirement income, so it became a perfect marriage. Talk of the war abounded, from the maintenance men to the chancellor. Worse yet, numerous books, many redundant and inconsequential, had been pouring from the opportunistic commercial publishing houses, and much of my work was being used as illustrative matter (including James Jones's *World War II* and Roy Livengood's *Thunder in the Apennines*). Mercifully, I had become immune to discussions of the war, able to join in dispassionately when invited. Only while at work on these memoirs have I felt an occasional tremor and more often an overwhelming sadness.

Prior to my arrival in North Carolina, while John F. Kennedy was president, there was great interest in the construction of a war museum in Washington, D.C., where all of the paintings from American wars, from the classic *Washington Crossing the Delaware* to the present works, would be housed. A separate wing would include such memorabilia as Herman Goering's diamond studded crop and other prizes of war. An innovative young president, Kennedy was interested in numerous programs involving art and culture. He had summoned August Heckscher to the White House, and Heckscher was soon aptly referred to as Kennedy's "Cultural Prime Minister." He was a man highly qualified for the post. *Life* magazine devoted several pages to this phenomenon, a first in America, discussing in detail his duties and plans for the future. How fortunate for me: August and I had become close friends on the Liberty ship that took me to North Africa and had exchanged notes on a couple of occasions after the war. He became the director of the Twentieth Century Fund in New York and ultimately succeeded the noted Robert Moses as New York's parks commissioner. August was of wealthy parentage, well educated, and courageous. His war assignment had been with the Office of Strategic Services (OSS); he was one of those trained to parachute behind enemy lines in order to carry out clandestine missions.

At the outset of the Kennedy regime I had been contacted by various officials in Washington who were searching out the former war artists in their efforts to acquire material for the proposed museum. I had no idea that my old friend Heckscher was quite possibly working behind the scenes on the project, for I had already forwarded my personal observations relative to the museum and had forgotten about the matter. Then my wife and I received an invitation to attend a posh reception in honor of the California complement of war artists. It was held on April 28, 1962, at the Hollyhock House in Barnsdall Park, a magnificent structure designed by none other than Frank Lloyd Wright, and our host would be the Honorable Paul B. Fay, Jr., undersecretary of the navy. Pat and I were quite excited at the prospect of meeting these distinguished people and seeing the war artists once again.

It was Paul Fay's intention to interest the war artists in doing some painting for the government under the auspices of the United States Navy: we would be flown to remote American military bases throughout the world for the purpose of creating our impressions of the activities taking place there. Perhaps the elaborate new museum under consideration would one day benefit from the program.

When Mr. Fay invited me to participate in the program (at this juncture I'd consumed a cocktail or two), I asked politely whether he could outline the terms of the offer. His reply was that the artists would be furnished with materials, lodging, and transportation plus a token per diem for meals. I informed Mr. Fay that many of the artists would have to go into debt in order to accept such an assignment. I myself was employed as a teacher at the Chouinard Art Institute in Los Angeles and had a wife and family to support; if I were to take a leave of absence from school, it would be without pay. Would the government cover my salary? Or were we being prevailed upon to make sacrifices because artists are suckers and notoriously poor businessmen?

This minor item had never crossed Mr. Fay's mind. As a classmate of John Kennedy's at Groton and clearly a member of the upper crust, he must have naively assumed that artists would deem it an honor to contribute their time and energy to such a noble cause—money was not the question. But Mr. Fay had underestimated me; I made it plain that he could count me out, at least under the proposed conditions. If, on the other hand, he could arrange for a substantial stipend that would cover my loss of income, I would reconsider his proposal. The booze was fortifying and I got down to the nitty-gritty: "With all due respect, Mr. Fay, your salary goes on the year round, day and night. You fly to Los Angeles via government transport and are met by military personnel who are waiting to take you wherever you wish; you're provided with a full entourage to do your bidding, and you have a handsome expense account—all at taxpayers' expense. To me, this just isn't equitable. Under this ill-considered plan only those artists who are independently wealthy can afford to participate." And since there are few wealthy artists, I added, those with money might not prove to be the best available.

Now that my spleen had been vented I braced for a scathing reply. But Mr. Fay's rejoinder took me by surprise: "Reep," he said, "you're the only artist I've interviewed who has had the guts to speak to me in all candor. I not only respect you for this and believe that what you say has validity, but you have awakened me to concerns that, quite frankly, have never crossed my mind." Then, handing me his personal card, he asked if I would write down everything I had noted and send it on to his Washington office. When he returned from the junket, he would attempt to do something about the inequities I had suggested.

Within a week I had carefully framed a three-page letter. Mr. Fay replied at length, citing the problems he faced at his end; then he must have turned the matter over to August Heckscher. The following, dated 22 June 1964, was written on Twentieth Century Fund stationery.

> Dear Ed:
>
> It is somewhat appalling to come across a letter of yours which I had put aside to answer personally, and which for that very reason was neglected in the turmoil of the Washington office. I remember so well our wartime crossing, and I was delighted to have the picture recalling those far-off days.
>
> We did not neglect the substance of your letter; I was working along the lines of your communication of May 1962 to the Secretary of the Navy. I had hoped that when I left the post this type of initiative would be carried forward. Unfortunately, the President's death and the general changes that came about caused rather a change of focus.
>
> So what I really want to do now is send you my best wishes and remembrances.
>
> Cordially,
> August

President Kennedy had been assassinated, and Johnson had taken over; I was never to hear from Fay or Heckscher again and not a word further from any Washington office about the proposed war museum.

In the early 1970s, while artist-in-residence at East Carolina University, I received a call from the Office of Military History in Washington, asking whether I would consider undertaking a painting assignment overseas, either to cover the Vietnam War or to document the tenth anniversary of the Berlin Wall. After discussing the offer at length, I agreed to go to Berlin if the terms were acceptable, explaining that I'd had my fill of actual combat in World War II and that I would enjoy going to Berlin simply to visit the heart of the German nation. It would be enlightening to learn exactly what made the Germans tick—something I had never been able to fathom. They asked whether I knew of another artist who was qualified for the Vietnam assignment, and I later recommended a colleague of mine in the printmaking area at East Carolina, a courageous man and excellent artist named Donald Sexauer. He was subsequently accepted and produced a distinguished portfolio of prints.

My wife and I were flown to Berlin in first-class accommodations, and I was accorded a G-15 rating, which—unbeknownst to me at the time—is the rank of a brigadier general. We were billeted in a lavish apartment, complete with a stock of every imaginable liquor. So this was how the brass lived! We loved it.

We had two apartments during our three-week stay in Berlin, both spacious and luxuriously furnished; the second was in Templehof Airport, purported to be the largest building in the world and designed by Albert Speer, Adolf Hitler's genius architect and confidant. One could easily imagine the place filled with the top echelon of Nazi warlords at the height of their glory. A Mercedes-Benz, complete with German chauffeur, was at our disposal night and day; I was provided with all necessary materials and more, and was paid a handsome per diem. Echoes of my admonition to Secretary Fay raced through my mind; this was the way an artist ought to be treated—like any other VIP.

In return, I worked every single day that we spent in West Berlin—including weekends—and produced several watercolors, a half-dozen large and relatively complex pen-and-ink drawings, and countless small notes and sketches. I also shot a dozen rolls of film. All of this would provide detailed information when I returned to the States to commence work on two final oil paintings.

One of the canvases dealt with a bold slogan that had been applied to the wall by West Berliners. It read "Die Mauer Muss Fallen" (the wall must fall), and the motto, or vow, was crudely painted below a bugle signaling a call for freedom. The portion of the wall selected for the graffito brutally cut through a beloved church of historical significance, virtually absorbing the structure and preventing Berliners who had worshiped here for generations from entering. A classic marble sculpture of Jesus Christ remained mounted on the facade of the church to agonize and bait the devout, while bolted above the Christ figure was a sinister-looking light, positioned to illuminate the area at night and prevent East Germans from escaping to the West. Placing the light precisely above the image of Christ seemed the epitome of cruelty.

The second large canvas depicted the Berlin Wall in all its tragic, inhumane consequences—at least that was my intention. In the Secteur Français (there are four sectors: British, French, American, and German) I stood atop a viewing ramp to sketch the ugly sight before me. This portion of the wall consisted of a street's original shop buildings; only

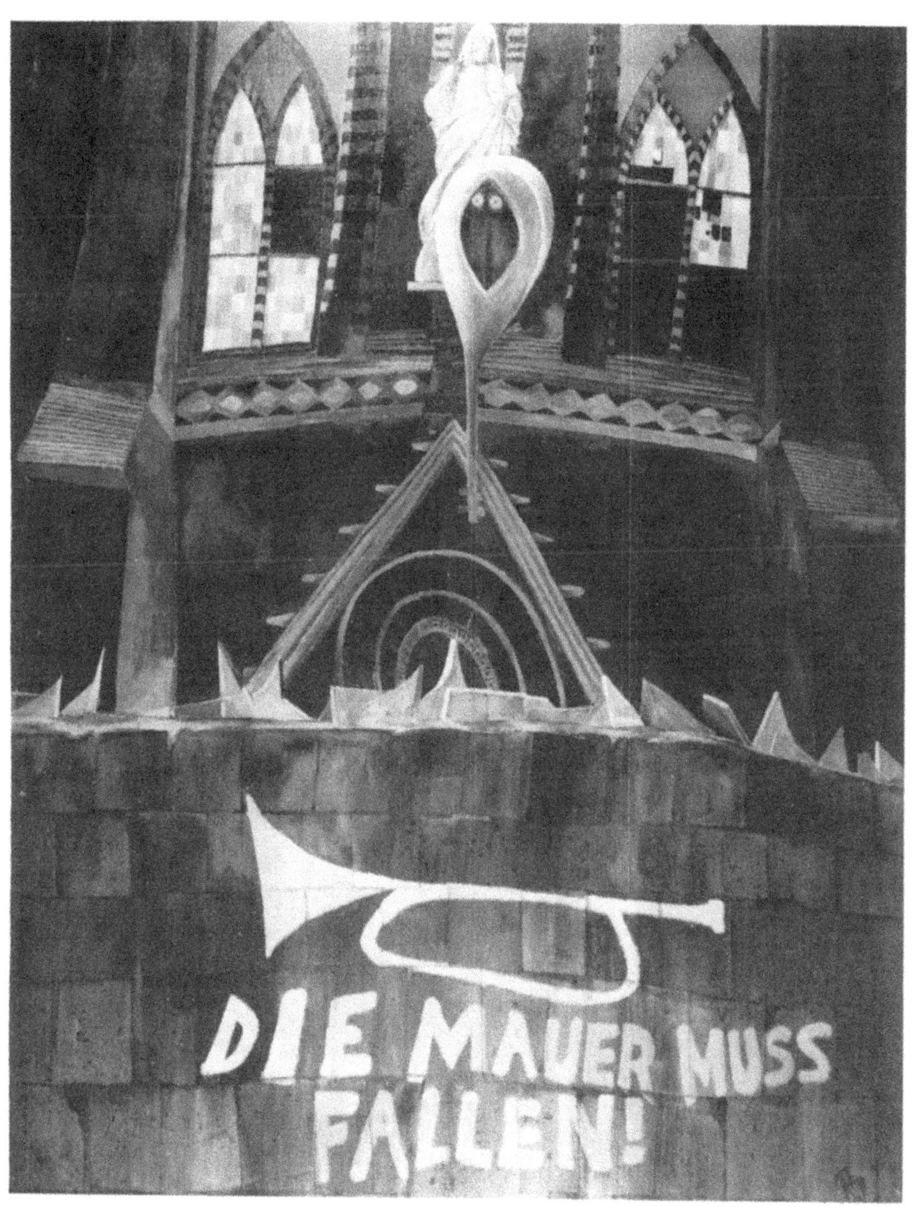

Die Mauer Muss Fallen

1972. Oil on canvas. 48 x 60 in.

A church entrance is cruelly blocked from devout West Berliners. The Russians, their land devastated and their casualties massive because of the German invasion of their homeland, vindictively showed little mercy in establishing the Berlin Wall.

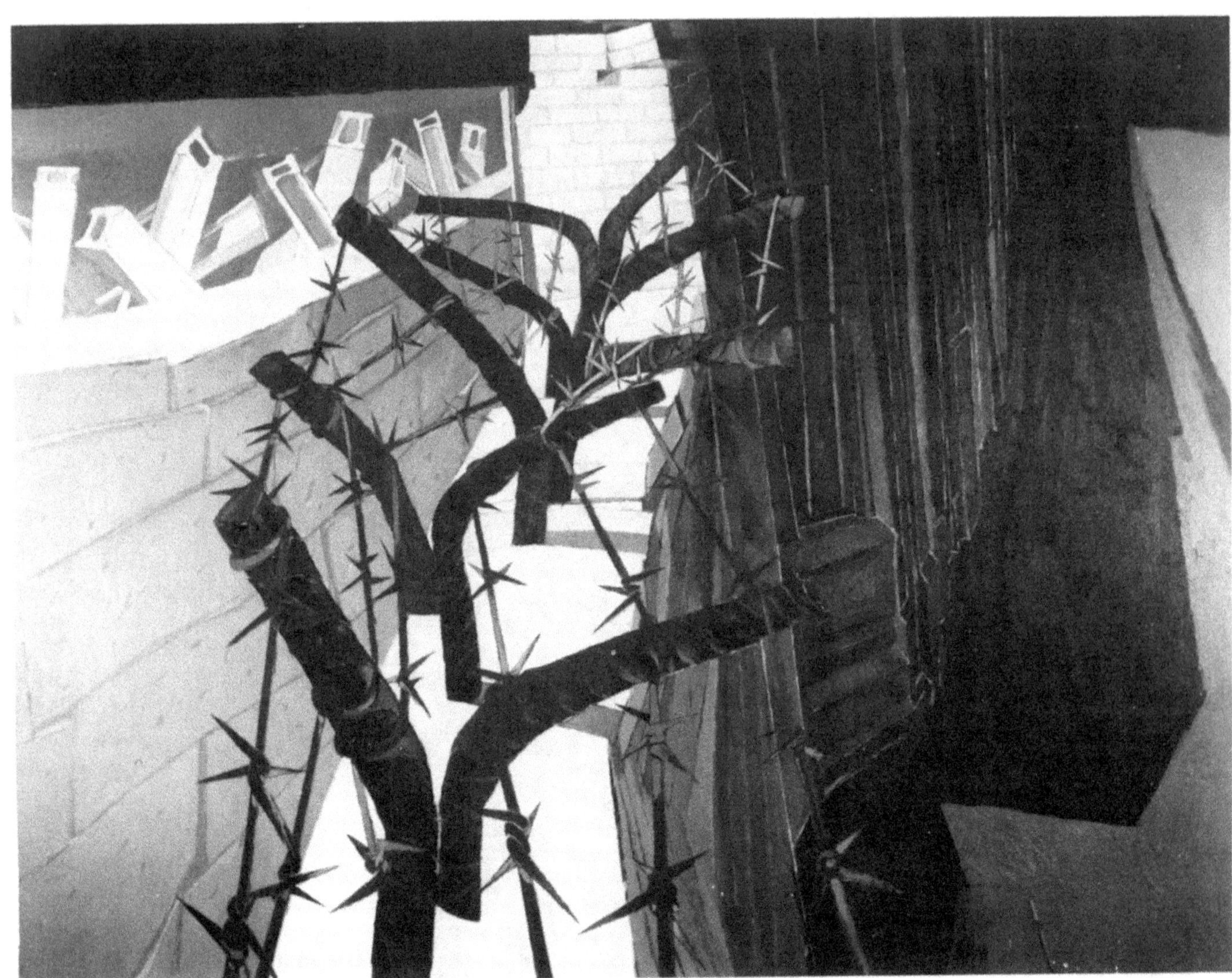

Idiot's Garden

1972. Oil on canvas. 48 x 60 in.

Political ramifications aside, one cannot help pondering the uncivilized state of humankind in general when viewing such a macabre "garden." To me, the Berlin Wall stands as a stout testimonial to man's idiocy, as well as an exercise in futility and waste.

their facades remained, and the windows and doors were plugged with massive concrete blocks. Where there were gaps between the buildings, concrete block walls had been erected, on top of which thick bars of twisted iron jutted upward at frenzied angles, supporting heavy barbed wire—placed there, of course, to discourage anyone from scaling the wall. I have never seen such barbed wire anywhere else. The spikes were easily a half-inch in diameter and three inches in length; anyone caught on them could be fatally impaled.

And this was only the *last* impediment one had to contend with if contemplating escape, for behind the first wall rose another of concrete blocks and about eight feet high, and behind that a monstrous-looking affair made of heavy steel girders painted a ghostly white, deeply cemented into the earth to form an impenetrable antivehicle trap quite similar to the tank traps employed during the war. Not shown in my painting was a large clearing back of the wall on the East German side, brightly illuminated at night and punctuated at intervals with tall guard towers housing both Russian soldiers and East Berlin police armed with machine guns.

I used the subject verbatim; it would have been impossible to invent anything more despicable. The walls are couched against a black bar of color symbolizing death, and a blood-red sky glowers above. The title of the painting describes my sentiments: *Idiot's Garden—The Berlin Wall.* At that point in my career I had ceased to give a damn about the reaction of my sponsors or whoever was responsible for my being there, for it was far more important to be able to express simultaneously my hatred for war and the shame I felt for my fellow inhabitants of the earth. The barbarous wall stood as mute testimony that man's inhumanity to man was still alive and well.

The two Berlin Wall paintings may one day prove to be more significant as antiwar statements than the bulk of my work done during the actual conflict. The latter was primarily documentary; now, as a far more mature artist, I could get to the point without undue embellishment or pictorial garbage. Maybe these two images will be the last from my easel to deal with war. I hope and pray that will be the case, and that wars will one day cease to exist.

In March 1978, I was invited to lecture at the University of Michigan at Ann Arbor as a guest of the Department of History. The subject of the minicourse was the role of the war artist, and the panel included the famed Bill Mauldin, possibly the greatest of the war cartoonists. Some of the artists discussed war art through the ages and offered illuminating, philosophical viewpoints, while I confined myself to a concise description of my adventures and concluded with a number of personal observations. It was my intention then, as now, to present a true portrait of an artist in combat. The ranks of those artists who served during World War II are thinning, and much remains to be gleaned from their work. The audience, mainly future historians, seemed eager to hear what we had to offer, battling a wicked snowstorm in order to attend the series. That was the last time I voiced my impressions publicly.

What role do artists in war enact? What contributions have they made? Has the effort been wasted, or is such documentation necessary? Will it be understood or simply ignored? Under utopian conditions there would be no wars and hence no need for answers to these questions, but until that glorious day, artists remain indispensable in their struggle to record human sacrifice and suffering. Who other than the artist and poet can play such a vital role in humanity's quest for dignity, for they alone reveal what others fail or refuse to see. If educators and clergymen could clear up their own fuzzy thinking by putting aside special interests, perhaps they could significantly assist this effort. There are few enough statesmen in our current society, so inundated with petty politicians, greedy businessmen, and myopic bigots often posing as superpatriots. In their search for truth alone, the artists' exposition of things not visible to the average person remains unique, attesting to the nobility of common people who more often than not are unwillingly engaged in conflicts stemming from the obduracy or misconduct of their leaders.

The artist bequeaths a document of the uselessness, the anguish, and the savagery of war in the hope that future generations may avoid the pitfalls. Not even a camera records what the artist is able to perceive, for it is mechanical and bloodless and cannot detect right from wrong.

The war artist reveals that all wars are similar; the war artist's work relentlessly drums that message home. Through centuries of conflict, one constant persists, standing alone and above all others. Human lives are shortened, families are left homeless, children are orphaned, women and men are widowed, and young warriors go all too early to their graves so that old men can win their senseless arguments.

Index

www.ingramcontent.com/pod-product-compliance
Lightning Source LLC
LaVergne TN
LVHW080324060826
844660LV00030B/1269